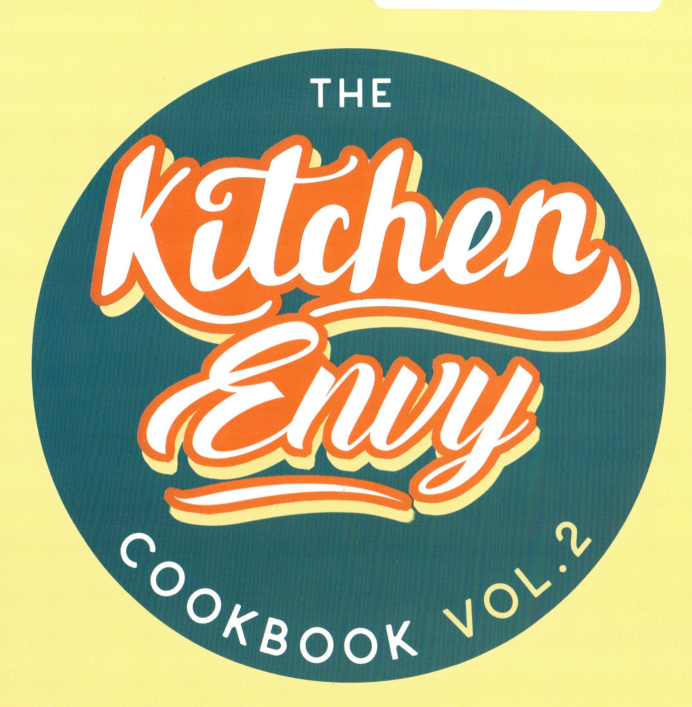

EASY SOULFUL RECIPES,
DRINKS & DESSERTS FROM
ALL AROUND THE WORLD

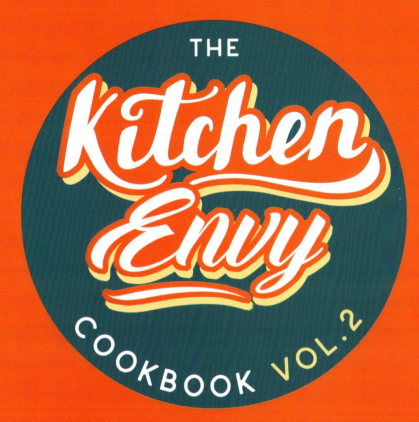

SUPREME KUISINES &
MANY MORE TINGZ

JAI NICE

Copyright © 2022 by Kitchen Envy

All rights reserved. No part of this book may be used or reproduced in any manner whatsoever without written permission except in the case of brief quotations embodied in critical articles and reviews.

The recipes within this book were created for the ingredients and techniques indicated. Individual results may vary due to inconsistencies in elements such as ingredients, cooking temperatures, typos, errors, omissions, or individual cooking ability. The author and publisher of this book are not responsible for any allergies or adverse reactions that you may have to the recipes in this book, whether the recipe has been expressly followed or modified.

LCCN: 2022917447
ISBN-13: 979-8-218-07308-4 (Paperback Edition)
ISBN-13: 979-8-218-08061-7 (Hardcover Limited Edition)

Author: Jai Nice

Book Design: The Book Designers

CONTENTS

INTRO x

KITCHEN ESSENTIALS xii

BRUNCHIN' 1

ISLAND TINGZ 30

MEAT BY THE SEA 62

COOKIN' UP A BIRD 94

KRAV'N CARBS 118

YOU'RE JUST A SIDE 150

SIMPLY SNACKIN' 180

HOLIDAY ESSENTIALS 214

AIR FRYER ESSENTIALS 242

MOMS-ON-THE-GO 272

VEGAN VIBES 296

NO WAIST BUT TASTE 332

GETTIN' SUM'N SWEET 376

DRINKS AND SMOOTHIES 418

SIP AFTER DARK 464

INDEX 489

DEDICATION

Dear Granny,

First, I want to say thank you. Thank you for stepping up, taking me in, and raising me since I was 2 years old. I don't know where I'd be today if it weren't for you. You literally taught me everything I know. How to always keep God first. How to cook, clean, and take care of the household. And especially how to work hard as I watched you work two jobs to take care of us. You are the reason I'm the woman I am today, and I'll forever remember everything you taught me. I owe it all to you.

You fought a long, hard battle and I know that you left because you needed to. As much as we wanted you here with us, God needed you more. To be absent from the body means you are present with the Lord and now that your task on earth is complete, we have gained an angel.

Please keep us strong while we are feeling weak and sad. We all miss you and love you dearly. This is not goodbye, it's see you later. Until we meet again. Love you forever, Jessie ♥

TRIBUTE TO KIN CORDELL

This book is dedicated to one of my dearest friends, my brother and fashion photographer of 7+ years, Cordell. I can't imagine how I would've gotten the first book completed without you swooping into my rescue. Somehow, we got through putting together this 2nd one without you here. I felt your spirit with me every day and continue to. To one of my biggest supporters, motivators, honest taste-testers and an all-around pure-hearted teddy bear – you are loved and missed!

INTRO

Welcome to The KitchenEnvy Cookbook: Volume 2! My name is Jai Nice, but in the kitchen, they call me Jai. I am a fashion designer, hardworking mother and passionate home chef who has built a life for myself using my creative talents to help others.

Everybody wants to know where it all began, and truthfully, my cooking journey isn't much different from most young black girls growing up in America – it started in my grandmother's kitchen. Yes, I was in love with food long before I had the idea for my fashion line, KlosetEnvy. I grew up in a household that was a mixture of African-American and Caribbean cultures, and that upbringing not only influenced my love for cooking but also my understanding of creating fusion meals like my Jerk Chicken Stir Fry.

My daughter, Snooks, gets to witness first-hand how learning from different cultures helps me see the world and food differently - she's even the reason I started my cooking page, @cookinwithjai on Instagram. She's been my unofficial videographer, video editor, creative director and sous chef - assisting me with bringing to life the meals I come up with in my head. And she taste-tests everything! I'm grateful I get a chance to share the kitchen with my daughter in the same way I shared the kitchen with my grandmother so many years ago. I can't quite describe the bond that is formed by learning from an elder in the kitchen, but if you know you know! And if you didn't have the opportunity for this type of bond growing up, I hope this cookbook opens your kitchen to beautiful new memories with the people you love.

I was motivated to write another cookbook by my passion for learning new dishes and cooking techniques. Many of the meals included here came from me trying out random things in my kitchen! I had so much fun playing around with spices, textures, sauces, and cuts of meat. I can't wait for you to see what I've created. From Mongolian Beef & Broccoli, Oreo Cheesecake Cookies, and Strawberries & Cream Pancakes, to more traditional Caribbean dishes like my Jerk Marinade and Brown Stew Fish, or my personal favorites: the Crab Garlic Bread and Salmon Flatbread Pizza - my knowledge of food has expanded so much since my first book.

I made it a point to include a tasty little something for everyone! This book has meals for large family events like the Garlic & Herb Turkey and Cornbread Dressing from the Holiday Essentials chapter, flavorful meals for vegans and vegetarians like the BBQ Oyster Mushroom Sliders and Chili Marinated Tofu Plate found in the Vegan Vibes portion, and even busy moms who need quick homemade meals after a long day will love the Garlic Bread Pizza and Air Fryer Cornish Hens in the Moms-On-The-Go and Air Fryer Essentials sections. You'll also love my refreshing after-dinner drink recipes like La Vida Es Un Brisa from the Sip After Dark chapter.

I'm not going to pretend that all of these new skills came to me easily because that would be a lie! The Strawberries and Cream Pancakes took me several tries to get the strawberry flavor just right. When it came to the baking section, Gettin' Sum'n Sweet, I was honestly about ready to throw in the towel! This section took the most time and was the most challenging for me to complete. Honestly, it took almost a third of the total time to complete all 220+ recipes in the cookbook! To be clear, I do not consider myself a baker - I am a cook, but I made sure to create sweets that were simple and delicious. It's the perfect chapter for non-bakers and those who love sweet treats but need the instructions to be very straightforward.

    I put in a lot of hard work creating this cookbook. I assembled a team, tested all the recipes, personally made sure every picture came out perfectly, then read and re-read the instructions to ensure that they are crystal clear and easy for you to follow. This book was a labor of love, but a labor, nonetheless. My hope is that you appreciate the effort I put into creating this cookbook for you, and that I meet and exceed your expectations. Truthfully, I'm both nervous and excited about the feedback I'm going to get, but I'm definitely most excited to see what you create in your own kitchens. It brings me joy to share my meals with loved ones, and to share my meals with you. Enjoy!

> **MY PLEASURE COMES FROM GIVING. I LOVE TO COOK FOR OTHERS AND SEE THE SATISFACTION ON THEIR FACES WHEN THEY TAKE A BITE OF MY FOOD.**

KITCHEN ESSENTIALS

I'm so excited for you to dive in and get cooking! To make you experience even more enjoyable, I've drawn up a brand-new list of key items you'll need in order to produce the recipes that I've laid out in this book. I know first-hand that creating a meal can feel like putting the pieces of a puzzle together, and you can't get it right if you don't have all the pieces!

For your convenience, I've also included utensil and cookware lists in each recipe so you don't have to return to this page every time you get the urge to cook. However, here, you can find every ingredient, utensil, and piece of cookware in one convenient place.

I listed a few essential tools from my KitchenEnvy cookware collection as well, which can all be found at www.thekitchenenvy.com.

Cleaning and Sanitation

- Water + White Vinegar
- Use a mixture of water and vinegar to wash off your meats, especially chicken and seafood.
- A little vinegar goes a long way, so you can use ¼ cup of vinegar for every 2 cups of water.

The Must-Haves

- All-Purpose Flour
- Brown Sugar
- Cornstarch
- Eggs
- Olive Oil
- Unsalted Butter
- Vegetable Oil
- White Sugar

Seasonings

- Beef Bouillon Cubes/Powder
- Bell Peppers
- Black Pepper
- Blackened Seasoning
- Cajun Seasoning
- Chicken Bouillon Cubes/Powder
- Chicken Stock
- Chili Powder
- Chipotle Powder
- Cilantro
- Crushed Red Pepper
- Dried Oregano
- Fresh Rosemary
- Fresh Thyme
- Garlic Chili Paste
- Garlic Paste
- Garlic Powder
- Garlic Salt
- Ginger Paste
- Green Onions

Kitchen Essentials | **xiii**

- Hoisin Sauce
- Hot Chili Crisp
- Minced Garlic
- Mrs. Dash Seasoning, Original
- Old Bay Seasoning
- Onion Powder
- Paprika
- Parsley
- Pollo Seasoning
- Scotch Bonnet
- Seasoned Salt
- Sesame Oil
- Soy Sauce
- Sriracha Sauce
- Tomato Bouillon Cubes/Powder
- White Onions

Essential Cookware

- Baking Sheet
- Cookie Sheet
- Casserole Dish
- Cast Iron Pan
- Cupcake Liners
- Deep Fryer
- Frying Pan
- Griddle
- KitchenEnvy Air Fryer
- KitchenEnvy Breakfast Pan
- KitchenEnvy Over-The-Sink Strainer
- KitchenEnvy Wok
- Mixing Bowls
- Muffin Pan
- Saucepan
- Sauté Pan
- Stockpot

Necessary Utensils

- Aluminum Foil
- Blender
- Can Opener
- Cheese Grater
- Food Processor
- Hand Mixer
- KitchenEnvy Chef's Knife
- KitchenEnvy Measuring Cups
- KitchenEnvy Measuring Spoons
- KitchenEnvy Meat Cleaver
- KitchenEnvy Paring Knife
- KitchenEnvy Peeler
- KitchenEnvy Silicone Utensils
- KitchenEnvy Spatulas
- KitchenEnvy Tongs
- KitchenEnvy Whisk
- Ladle
- Parchment Paper
- Potato Masher
- Silicone Molds
- Thermometer

CINNAMON ROLL PANCAKES 2

STRAWBERRIES & CREAM PANCAKES 5

PANCAKE FRUIT TACOS 6

BREAKFAST BOMBS 9

MINI OMELETS 10

LOADED BREAKFAST POTATOES 13

FRENCH TOAST BITES 14

FRENCH TOAST ROLLS 17

BANANA FOSTER STUFFED FRENCH TOAST 18

PIN WHEELS 21

MINI WAFFLE CINNAMON ROLL SANDWICHES 22

BREAKFAST QUESADILLAS 25

SOUTHERN FRIED CHICKEN & BISCUITS 26

BREAKFAST HOT POCKETS 29

CINNAMON ROLL PANCAKES

- 2 cups Flour
- 3 teaspoons Baking Powder
- 2 teaspoons Baking Soda
- 1/8 teaspoon Salt
- 5 tablespoons Sugar
- 5 tablespoons Melted Unsalted Butter
- 2 teaspoons Vanilla Extract
- 3 cups Buttermilk
- 3 Eggs

CINNAMON MIXTURE

- 1 cup Brown Sugar (dark or light)
- 1/4 cup White Sugar
- 1 tablespoon Cinnamon
- 1/2 teaspoon Nutmeg
- 1 teaspoon Vanilla extract
- 1/2 cup Melted Unsalted Butter

ICING

- 1 cup Powdered Sugar
- 1/2 cup Heavy Whipping Cream

UTENSILS/COOKWARE NEEDED:

- 3 Mixing Bowls
- Whisk
- Small Rubber Spatula
- Ziplock or Piping Bag
- KitchenEnvy Breakfast Pan or Griddle
- Spatula

TOTAL TIME: 40 MINS
SERVES: 6

STEP 1. Combine the flour, baking powder, baking soda, salt, and sugar in a mixing bowl. Mix all the dry ingredients together.

STEP 2. Make a well in the middle of the dry ingredients then add the butter, vanilla, buttermilk, eggs to the mixing bowl. Whisk the ingredients together to create the pancake batter.

STEP 3. FOR THE CINNAMON MIXTURE: Place all the ingredients listed for the cinnamon mixture into a mixing bowl and, using a small spatula, mix well. Put the mixture in a Ziplock or piping bag (if you're using a Ziplock bag, put the mixture in the bag then squeeze the air out of the bag and cut one corner, creating a makeshift piping bag).

STEP 4. FOR THE ICING: Place the powdered sugar and heavy cream in a mixing bowl and combine using a small rubber spatula, set aside.

STEP 5. Coat the griddle or pan with non-stick cooking spray then place over medium-low heat (if you want the pancake edges crispier, add 2 teaspoons of vegetable oil to the griddle or skillet). Pour on the batter a half cup at a time, then starting from the center of the pancake batter, pipe the cinnamon mixture onto the pancake batter in a spiral shape.

STEP 6. When bubbles cover the surface of the pancake, it is ready to flip. DO NOT flip until the batter has set in (bubbled). Flip the pancake with a spatula. The top side of the pancake should be golden brown, and the edges should have a slight crisp. Continue cooking on the other side for 2-4 mins. Repeat until all the pancake batter is used.

STEP 7. Use a fork to drizzle the icing onto the finished pancakes and serve hot.

BRUNCHIN'

STRAWBERRY & CREAM PANCAKES

STEP 1. Combine the flour, Nesquik powder, baking powder, baking soda, salt, and sugar in a mixing bowl. Mix all the dry ingredients together.

STEP 2. Make a well in the middle of the dry ingredients then add the butter, vanilla, buttermilk, and eggs to the mixing bowl. Whisk the ingredients together to create the pancake batter.

STEP 3. FOR THE COMPOTE: Cut the strawberries into small chunks. Preheat a saucepan over medium heat, then add the strawberries and sugar. Cook until strawberries are soft, then mash them with a fork until the chunks are even smaller. Let the compote cool then add ¾ of the compote to the pancake batter.

STEP 4. Coat the griddle or pan with non-stick cooking spray then place over medium-low heat. Pour on the batter a half cup at a time.

STEP 5. When bubbles cover the surface of the pancake, it is ready to flip. DO NOT flip until the batter has set in (bubbled). Flip the pancake with a spatula. The top side of the pancake should be golden brown, and the edges should have a slight crisp. Continue cooking on the other side for 2-4 mins. Repeat until all the pancake batter is used.

STEP 6. FOR THE ICING: Place all the ingredients listed for the cream cheese icing into a mixing bowl and combine using a small rubber spatula, then drizzle the icing over the finished pancakes.

STEP 7. Garnish the pancakes with the rest of the strawberry compote and serve hot.

- 2 ⅔ cups Flour
- ⅓ cup Strawberry Nesquik Powder
- 3 ½ teaspoons Baking Powder
- 2 teaspoons Baking Soda
- ⅛ teaspoon Salt
- 5 tablespoons Sugar
- 5 tablespoons Melted Unsalted Butter
- 3 teaspoons Vanilla Extract
- 3 cups Buttermilk
- 3 Eggs

STRAWBERRY COMPOTE

- 10-12 Strawberries
- ½ cup Sugar

CREAM CHEESE ICING

- 4 oz Cream Cheese, Softened
- ½ cup Powdered Sugar
- ¼ cup Heavy Whipping Cream

UTENSILS/COOKWARE NEEDED:

- 2 Mixing Bowls
- Whisk
- Saucepan
- KitchenEnvy Breakfast Pan or Griddle
- Spatula
- Small Rubber Spatula

TOTAL TIME: 40 MINS
SERVES: 6

PANCAKE FRUIT TACOS

- 2 cups Flour
- 3 teaspoons Baking Powder
- 2 teaspoons Baking Soda
- ⅛ teaspoon Salt
- 5 tablespoons Sugar
- 5 tablespoons Melted Unsalted Butter
- 2 teaspoons Vanilla Extract
- 3 cups Buttermilk
- 3 Eggs
- Assorted Fruit of Your Choice, Diced
- Whipped Cream, As Desired

CREAM CHEESE SPREAD

- 4 oz Cream Cheese, Softened
- 1 teaspoon Vanilla Extract
- ½ cup Powdered Sugar
- ⅛ cup Heavy Whipping Cream

UTENSILS/COOKWARE NEEDED:

- 2 Mixing Bowls
- Whisk
- KitchenEnvy Breakfast Pan or Griddle
- Spatula
- Small Rubber Spatula

TOTAL TIME: 20 MINS
SERVES: 6

STEP 1. Combine the flour, baking powder, baking soda, salt, and sugar in a mixing bowl. Mix all the dry ingredients together.

STEP 2. Make a well in the middle of the dry ingredients then add the butter, vanilla, buttermilk, eggs to the mixing bowl. Whisk the ingredients together to create the pancake batter.

STEP 3. Coat the griddle or skillet with non-stick cooking spray then place over medium-low heat. Pour in the batter a half cup at a time.

STEP 4. When bubbles cover the surface of the pancake, it is ready to flip. DO NOT flip until the batter has set in (bubbled). Flip the pancake with a spatula. The top side of the pancake should be golden brown. Continue cooking on the other side for 2-4 mins. Repeat until all the pancake batter is used and make sure to let the pancakes cool for at least 5 mins before assembling the tacos.

STEP 5. FOR THE SPREAD: Place all the ingredients listed for the cream cheese spread into a mixing bowl and combine using a small rubber spatula.

STEP 6. FOR ASSEMBLY: Spread the cream cheese mixture onto the pancakes and fold the pancakes in half slightly to form the shape of a taco. Slice your favorite fruit and place it inside the pancakes, making the fruit the filling to your tacos! Top with whipped cream and serve with a side of syrup.

BRUNCHIN'

BREAKFAST BOMBS

STEP 1. Preheat the oven to 350 degrees.

STEP 2. Use a rolling pin to roll out the biscuits one by one (if you don't have a rolling pin, you can stretch the biscuits with your hands until they're flat).

STEP 3. Dice the bacon and sausage into bite-sized pieces, then warm a pan to medium heat and add a little vegetable oil. Place bacon and sausage into the pan and cook until crispy. Remove the meat from the pan and drain on paper towels, then set aside.

STEP 4. In the same pan, fry the potatoes until they're cooked all the way through and crispy. Remove them from the pan and set aside.

STEP 5. In a bowl, whisk together the eggs and milk then season with black pepper. In the same pan the bacon, sausage and potatoes were cooked in, add a little oil and cook the eggs until they're fluffy. Remove the eggs from the pan and set aside.

STEP 6. FOR THE HONEY BUTTER: Warm a saucepan over medium-low heat and melt the butter and honey together, then remove from heat and set aside.

STEP 7. FOR ASSEMBLY: On the flattened biscuits, add 1 tablespoon of each cooked ingredient (eggs, hashbrowns, bacon, sausage) plus 1 tablespoon of shredded cheese. Fold the biscuit dough around the ingredients like a taco, then pinch the open ends to the center until it forms a ball. Make sure to pinch the sides tightly so the ingredients don't come out while the bombs are cooking!

STEP 8. Spray a casserole dish with non-stick cooking spray and place the breakfast bombs in the dish, then brush the tops of the bombs with the honey butter. Place in the oven and bake for 5-10 mins, or until the biscuit dough is golden-brown.

STEP 9. Remove the breakfast bombs from the oven and brush the tops with more honey butter, serve hot.

- 1 roll of Large Biscuits
- ½ cup Bacon, Diced (Turkey or Pork)
- ½ cup Sausage Patties, Diced (Turkey or Ham)
- 2 teaspoons Vegetable Oil
- ½ cup Frozen Hashbrowns or Potatoes O'Brien
- 3 Large Eggs
- 1 tablespoon Milk
- A dash of Black Pepper
- Shredded Cheese of Your Choice
- Non-stick Cooking Spray

HONEY BUTTER

- 2 tablespoons Honey
- 1 tablespoon Unsalted Butter

UTENSILS/COOKWARE NEEDED:

- Rolling Pin (optional)
- KitchenEnvy Breakfast Pan
- Small Rubber Spatula
- Mixing Bowl
- Whisk
- Saucepan
- Casserole Dish

TOTAL TIME: 40 MINS
SERVES: 6

NOTE: If you're vegetarian or vegan, substitute the meats and eggs in the filling for the veggies and egg substitute of your choice!

MINI OMELETS

- Non-stick Cooking Spray
- 2 cups of Potatoes (hashbrowns, tater tots, etc)
- ¼ Green Bell Peppers, Small Diced
- ¼ Red Bell Pepper, Small Diced
- ½ Onion, Small Diced
- 6 Cherry Tomatoes, Small Diced
- 6 Eggs
- ⅛ cup Milk
- ¼ teaspoon Garlic Powder
- ¼ teaspoon Onion Powder
- ¼ teaspoon Black Pepper
- Shredded Cheese (optional)

UTENSILS/COOKWARE NEEDED:

- Muffin Pan
- Mixing Bowl
- Whisk

TOTAL TIME: 25 MINS
SERVES: 6

STEP 1. Preheat the oven to 350 degrees.

STEP 2. Coat a muffin pan with non-stick cooking spray, then place 2 tablespoons of the potatoes at the bottom of each section in the muffin pan.

STEP 3. Next, add a layer of the veggies (peppers, onions, tomatoes) on top of the potatoes.

STEP 4. Crack the eggs into a mixing bowl, then whisk lightly with the milk and seasonings. Pour ⅛ cup of egg into each section in the muffin pan. If you're adding shredded cheese, sprinkle the desired amount on top of the eggs.

STEP 5. Place the pan in the oven and bake for 10 mins or until the eggs are cooked through. Remove the mini omelets from the pan and serve hot.

BRUNCHIN'

LOADED BREAKFAST POTATOES

STEP 1. Warm a pan over medium heat then add 1 teaspoon of oil and sauté the onions and bell peppers. Add the potatoes to the pan and season them with the onion powder, garlic powder, black pepper and Cajun seasoning. Stir and cook the potatoes until they're cooked through and crispy. Remove them from the pan and set aside on a serving plate.

STEP 2. In the same pan the potatoes were cooked in, drizzle in the remaining vegetable oil then crack the egg into the pan. Break the yolk and season to taste, then flip the egg and cook the yolk.

STEP 3. Place the fried egg on top of the loaded potatoes and serve!

- 2 teaspoons Vegetable Oil
- 1 Onion, Small Diced
- 2 Bell Peppers, Small Diced
- 3-6 Large Potatoes, Small Diced
- 1 teaspoon Onion Powder
- 1 teaspoon Garlic Powder
- 1 teaspoon Black Pepper
- ½ teaspoon Cajun Seasoning
- 1 Egg

UTENSILS/COOKWARE NEEDED:

- KitchenEnvy Breakfast Pan or Griddle
- Spatula

TOTAL TIME: 35 MINS

SERVES: 4

> WHENEVER SOMEONE ASKS WHAT MY PASSION IS, I SAY FASHION IS MY FIRST LOVE, BUT COOKING IS WHERE MY HEART IS.

BRUNCHIN'

FRENCH TOAST BITES

- 1 pack Hot Dog Buns
- 3 Eggs
- ½ cup Milk
- ¼ teaspoon Vanilla Extract
- ¼ teaspoon Cinnamon
- ⅛ teaspoon Nutmeg
- 2 ½ tablespoons Sugar

CARAMEL SAUCE (OPTIONAL)

- 1 cup Brown Sugar
- ⅓ cup White Sugar
- 5 tablespoons Unsalted Butter
- ⅛ Heavy Whipping Cream

CINNAMON SUGAR

- ½ cup White Sugar
- ¼ cup Cinnamon

UTENSILS/COOKWARE NEEDED:

- 3 Mixing Bowls
- Whisk
- KitchenEnvy Breakfast Pan or Griddle
- Spatula
- Saucepan

TOTAL TIME: 30 MINS
SERVES: 4

STEP 1. Slice the hot dog buns into 3rds then set aside.

STEP 2. Crack the eggs into a mixing bowl, then pour in the milk and vanilla extract. Lightly beat the egg mixture then add cinnamon, nutmeg and sugar. Continue mixing until all the ingredients are combined.

STEP 3. Dip the sliced hot dog buns into the egg mixture and allow the excess egg to drip off. Add butter to the pan and toast the buns over medium heat for 2-3 mins on each side, or until golden-brown and crispy. Remove from the pan and set aside. Repeat until all the French toast bites are cooked.

STEP 4. FOR THE SAUCE (OPTIONAL): Warm a saucepan over medium-low heat, then add all the ingredients listed for the caramel sauce. Whisk and bring to a simmer, then once the caramel starts to bubble, reduce the heat to low and stir occasionally.

STEP 5. Mix together the cinnamon sugar and toss the French toast bites in the mixture. Plate and serve hot with a side of caramel sauce.

BRUNCHIN'

FRENCH TOAST ROLLS

STEP 1. Cook sausage links in a pan over medium heat until they're golden-brown, then remove them from the pan and set aside.

STEP 2. Cut off the crusts of the bread, then flatten each slice with a rolling pin.

STEP 3. Crack the eggs into a mixing bowl, then pour in the milk and vanilla extract. Lightly beat the egg mixture then add cinnamon, nutmeg and sugar. Continue mixing until all the ingredients are combined.

STEP 4. Place a sausage link at the center of each piece of flattened bread and roll the bread around the sausage. Dip the rolls into the egg mixture and allow the excess egg to drip off. Add butter to the pan and toast the rolls over medium heat for 2-3 mins on each side, or until golden-brown and crispy. Serve hot with a side of syrup.

- 1 pack of Sausage links (turkey or pork)
- Loaf of Bread
- 3 Eggs
- ½ cup Milk
- ¼ teaspoon Vanilla Extract
- ¼ teaspoon Cinnamon
- ⅛ teaspoon Nutmeg
- 2 ½ tablespoons Sugar

UTENSILS NEEDED:

- KitchenEnvy Breakfast Pan or A Griddle
- Rolling Pin
- Mixing Bowl
- Whisk
- Sauté Pan

TOTAL TIME: 30 MINS
SERVES: 4

BANANAS FOSTER STUFFED FRENCH TOAST

- Loaf of Brioche
- 3 Eggs
- ½ cup Milk
- ¼ teaspoon Vanilla Extract
- ¼ teaspoon Cinnamon
- ⅛ teaspoon Nutmeg
- 2 ½ tablespoons Sugar

FILLING

- 4 oz Cream Cheese, Softened
- ½ cup Instant Banana Pudding Mix
- 1 teaspoon Vanilla Extract
- ⅓ cup Heavy Whipping Cream

CARAMELIZED BANANAS

- 1 Banana
- 1 cup Brown Sugar
- ⅓ cup White Sugar
- 5 tablespoons Unsalted Butter
- ⅛ Heavy Whipping Cream

UTENSILS/COOKWARE NEEDED:

- 3 Mixing Bowls
- Whisk
- Small Rubber Spatula
- KitchenEnvy Breakfast Pan or Griddle
- Spatula
- Sauté Pan

TOTAL TIME: 40 MINS
SERVES: 6

STEP 1. Slice the brioche loaf, set aside.

STEP 2. Crack the eggs into a mixing bowl, then pour in the milk and vanilla extract. Lightly beat the egg mixture then add cinnamon, nutmeg and sugar. Continue mixing until all the ingredients are combined.

STEP 3. FOR THE FILLING: Place all the ingredients listed for the filling into a mixing bowl and combine using a small rubber spatula.

STEP 4. Spread a generous amount of the mixture onto 2 slices of brioche. Sandwich the 2 slices together with the cream cheese sides facing each other.

STEP 5. Dip the sandwiched slices of brioche into the egg mixture and allow the excess egg to drip off. Add butter to the pan and toast the brioche over medium heat for 2-3 mins on each side, or until golden-brown and crispy. Remove from the pan and set to the side.

STEP 6. FOR THE SAUCE: Slice banana into about 1-inch-thick slices and set aside.

STEP 7. In a small pan, add all the ingredients for the caramelized bananas EXCEPT the banana slices. Once the caramel starts to bubble, add the banana slices and cook for no more than 3 mins (if they cook any longer than that, the bananas will be too soft and start to get mushy). Make sure all the banana slices are coated in the caramel.

STEP 8. Slice the French toast in half diagonally and plate, then top with the cream cheese icing and caramelized bananas. Serve hot.

BRUNCHIN'

PIN WHEELS

STEP 1. Preheat oven to 350 degrees.

STEP 2. Combine the eggs and milk in a mixing bowl, then add the seasonings (black pepper, onion powder, garlic powder). Mix well.

STEP 3. Coat the baking sheet with non-stick cooking spray then pour the eggs onto it. Bake the eggs for 12-15 mins. Remove the eggs from the oven and let cool at least 5 mins.

STEP 4. FOR ASSEMBLY: Roll out the crescent rolls and separate them, then pinch 2 together at a time so they make one flat layer (should form squares vs. triangles). Cut the egg to fit the size of the crescents. Add 1 layer of egg, 1 layer of cheese and 1 layer of deli meat, then roll tightly. Slice the rolls into thirds, (the slices should form pin wheels!)

STEP 5. Coat a Pyrex dish with non-stick cooking spray, then line the pinwheels side by side in the dish. Bake for 20 mins or until the crescent dough is golden-brown and the cheese has melted.

STEP 6. Remove the pinwheels from the oven and serve hot.

- 8 Eggs
- ¼ cup Milk
- 1 teaspoon Black Pepper
- 1 teaspoon Onion Powder
- 1 teaspoon Garlic Powder
- Non-stick Cooking Spray
- 1-8 oz containers Crescent Rolls
- Sliced Cheese of Your Choice
- Deli Meat of Your Choice

UTENSILS/COOKWARE NEEDED:

- Mixing bowl
- Whisk
- Baking Sheet
- Rolling Pin
- Small Pyrex Dish

TOTAL TIME: 45 MINS
SERVES: 6

MINI WAFFLE CINNAMON ROLL SANDWICH

- 6 slices Bacon, Cut in Half (Turkey or Pork)
- 6 Sausage Patties, Cut in Half (Turkey or Pork)
- 1 roll Ready-Made Cinnamon Roll Dough
- 2 Eggs
- ½ teaspoon Black Pepper
- ½ teaspoon Garlic Powder
- ½ teaspoon Onion Powder
- 1 Potato, Shredded
- ½ cup Shredded Cheese (optional)

UTENSILS/COOKWARE NEEDED:

- Mini Waffle Maker
- KitchenEnvy Breakfast Pan
- 2 Mixing Bowls
- Spatula

TOTAL TIME: 30 MINS
SERVES: 4

STEP 1. Preheat mini waffle maker.

STEP 2. Warm a pan over medium heat and cook the bacon and sausage until crispy, then drain on paper towels and set aside.

STEP 3. Separate the cinnamon roll dough and flatten each circle with your hands, then place the cinnamon roll dough in the waffle maker and flatten more. Cook the dough until golden-brown, then remove from the waffle maker and set aside.

STEP 4. Crack the egg into a mixing bowl and beat lightly, then season with black pepper, garlic powder, and onion powder. Mix the eggs with the shredded potatoes and pour the mixture onto the waffle maker. Cook until golden brown and crispy, then remove from the waffle maker and set aside. (If using cheese, sprinkle the desired amount onto the finished potatoes then cook an additional 2 mins to allow the cheese to melt).

STEP 5. FOR ASSEMBLY: Place one cinnamon roll waffle on a plate as the bottom bun to your sandwich, then place the potato/egg waffle on top of the cinnamon roll, and the bacon and sausage on top of the potato/egg then use another cinnamon roll waffle as the top bun. Serve hot.

BRUNCHIN'

BREAKFAST QUESADILLAS

STEP 1. Warm a sauté pan over medium heat then add a little oil. Sauté the spinach and season with salt and pepper. Once the spinach has wilted down, remove from the pan and set aside.

STEP 2. Scramble the eggs with the milk then, in the same pan the spinach was cooked in, add oil and cook the eggs. Once the eggs are done, remove them from the pan and set aside.

STEP 3. In the same pan the spinach and eggs were cooked in, add more oil and fry the hashbrowns until the potatoes are crispy and cooked through.

STEP 4. FOR ASSEMBLY: Lay out a flour tortilla and add the eggs, spinach, cheese and tomatoes. Top with another flour tortilla.

STEP 5. In the same pan the spinach, eggs and hashbrowns were cooked in, add a little oil and cook the quesadilla 2 mins on one side then flip it and cook the other side until the cheese is melted.

STEP 6. Cut the quesadilla into 4 pieces, plate and serve with salsa on the side.

- 3 teaspoons Vegetable Oil
- 1 cup Spinach, Wilted
- ¼ teaspoon Salt
- ¼ teaspoon Black Pepper
- 2 Eggs
- 3 tablespoons Milk
- 1 cup Shredded Hashbrowns
- Flour Tortillas
- ½ cup Shredded Cheese
- ¼ cup Cherry Tomatoes, sliced
- Salsa (optional)

UTENSILS/COOKWARE NEEDED:

- Sauté Pan
- Mixing Bowl
- Whisk
- Spatula

TOTAL TIME: 20 MINS
SERVES: 4

SOUTHERN FRIED CHICKEN & BISCUITS

- Oil for Frying
- 2 Chicken Breasts
- ½ teaspoon Black Pepper
- ½ teaspoon Italian Seasoning
- ½ teaspoon Mrs. Dash Seasoning
- ½ teaspoon Garlic Powder
- ½ teaspoon Onion Powder
- 2 Eggs
- 1 roll Large Buttermilk Biscuits

FLOUR MIXTURE

- 4 cups Flour
- 1 teaspoon Black Pepper
- 1 teaspoon Onion Powder
- 1 teaspoon Cajun Seasoning

GRAVY

- 1 ½ tablespoons Unsalted Butter
- 3 cups Heavy Whipping Cream
- 2 ½ cups Half & Half Milk
- Flour (1 teaspoon at a time)
- ½ teaspoon Black Pepper
- ½ tablespoon Garlic Salt
- ½ teaspoon Seasoned Salt
- ½ tablespoon Parsley, Chopped

UTENSILS/COOKWARE NEEDED:

- Meat Mallet or Rolling Pin
- 2 Mixing Bowls
- Frying Pan or Deep Fryer
- Saucepan
- Whisk

TOTAL TIME: 40 MINS
SERVES: 6

STEP 1. Preheat frying oil to 350 degrees.

STEP 2. Clean the chicken breasts using vinegar and water, then use a meat mallet or rolling pin to flatten them out (should be the same thickness as chicken parm). Season both sides of the chicken with black pepper, Italian seasoning, Mrs. Dash, garlic powder and onion powder.

STEP 3. In one dish, crack the eggs and lightly beat them. In another dish, mix the ingredients FOR THE FLOUR MIXTURE.

STEP 4. Dip the chicken in the egg mixture then the flour, then egg again and the flour mixture one more time. Submerge the chicken in the hot oil and fry for 5-8 mins. (If using a frying pan, make sure to flip the chicken breasts over halfway through!) Remove the chicken from the oil and drain on a wire rack or paper towels. Set aside.

STEP 5. Bake the biscuits as directed on the container, then set aside once they're done.

STEP 6. FOR THE GRAVY: Warm the butter in a saucepan over medium heat, then pour in heavy whipping cream and half & half. Whisk while gradually adding the flour until the mixture thickens into a gravy. While stirring the gravy, season it with black pepper, garlic salt, seasoned salt and parsley. Simmer for 3-5 mins, stirring occasionally. Remove from heat and set aside.

STEP 7. FOR ASSEMBLY: Place a biscuit on a plate and top with a piece of chicken, then pour gravy over the top and serve.

BRUNCHIN'

BREAKFAST HOT POCKETS

STEP 1. Preheat the oven to 400 degrees.

STEP 2. Cut each sheet of puff pastry into thirds and brush with melted butter, then add 1 teaspoon of cooked bacon, 1 teaspoon of scrambled eggs, 1 teaspoon of shredded cheese and 1 teaspoon of shredded potatoes to half the pastry. Fold the other half of the puff pastry over the ingredients and use a fork to seal the sides. Make sure to leave enough room so the filling doesn't come out while the pastries are baking! Repeat until all the puff pastry and filling is used.

STEP 3. Cut 3 slits into the tops of the pastries, then mix the egg wash and brush it onto the tops.

STEP 4. Place the pastries on a parchment-lined baking sheet and bake 5-8 mins, or until they are golden-brown. Remove the hot pockets from the oven and serve hot.

- 1 pack Puff Pastry
- ¼ cup Unsalted Butter, Melted
- 6 slices Bacon, Cooked and Chopped
- 3 Eggs, Scrambled and Cooked
- ½ cup Shredded Cheese of Your Choice
- ½ cup Shredded Potatoes, Cooked
- 1 Egg + 1 tablespoon Water (Egg Wash)

UTENSILS/COOKWARE NEEDED:

- Parchment Paper
- Baking Sheet
- Pastry brush

TOTAL TIME:

SERVES: 3

NOTE: This dish is a great way to reuse your breakfast leftovers!

OXTAIL STEW 32

OXTAILS 35

ITAL (PUMPKIN STEW) 36

JERK MARINADE 39

MANGO JERK WINGS 40

HONEY GARLIC JERK LAMB CHOPS 43

PINEAPPLE JERK SHRIMP BOWL 44

FESTIVAL 47

FRIED DUMPLING 48

ACKEE AND SALT FISH 51

BROWN STEW FISH 52

CURRY CHICKEN 55

BROWN STEW CHICKEN 56

JAMAICAN CABBAGE 59

RICE AND PEAS 60

OXTAIL STEW

- 3 lbs Oxtails
- 1 Green Bell Pepper, Medium Diced
- ¼ cup Green Onions, Chopped
- ½ White Onion, Sliced
- 3 cloves Garlic, Chopped
- 3 sprigs Fresh Thyme
- 1 Scotch Bonnet, De-Seeded
- ½ tablespoon Seasoned Salt
- 1/6 teaspoon Cayenne Pepper
- ½ tablespoon Oxtail Seasoning
- ½ tablespoon Onion Powder
- 1 teaspoon Black Pepper
- 1 tablespoon Worcestershire Sauce
- 1 tablespoon Soy Sauce
- 1 tablespoon Browning Sauce
- 5 tablespoons Olive Oil
- 6 cups Boiling Water
- 1 lb bag Red Kidney Beans, Light or Dark
- 1 can Coconut Milk
- ¼ White Onion, Chopped
- 4-6 Whole Garlic Cloves
- 2 Beef Bouillon Cubes or 2 tablespoons of Beef Bouillon Powder
- 1 teaspoon Black Pepper
- ½ teaspoon Garlic Salt
- 1 teaspoon Onion Powder
- 1 teaspoon Garlic Powder
- 1 teaspoon Seasoned Salt
- ⅛ cup Pimento Seeds/Allspice Berries
- 1 cup Beef Stock
- ⅓ cup Ketchup
- 2 tablespoons Unsalted Butter

STEP 1. Wash the oxtails using vinegar and water, then place them in a large mixing bowl. Add the bell pepper, green onion, white onion, garlic, thyme, scotch bonnet, seasoned salt, cayenne, oxtail seasoning, onion powder and black pepper. Next, pour in the Worcestershire, soy and browning sauces. Using clean hands, toss the mixture to combine the ingredients thoroughly.

STEP 2. Warm the olive oil in a large pot or Dutch oven over medium-high heat. Remove only the oxtails from the mixing bowl and place them in the pot, set the vegetables aside. Brown the oxtails on each side for 5-8 mins depending on the thickness (thicker oxtails will need to be cooked longer).

STEP 3. Gently pour in the boiling water until the oxtails are halfway covered, then lower the heat to medium-low and cover the pot. Cook for 30-45 mins, checking the oxtails every 30 mins and adding more water to make sure the oxtails remain halfway covered. The water should start to thicken into a gravy, so make sure not to add too much water. The gravy should not be thin like soup, this is key to the process!

STEP 4. Once the oxtails are halfway cooked (after the 30-45 mins), add in the kidney beans, coconut milk, onions, garlic cloves, beef bouillon, spices, pimento seeds, beef stock and the vegetables that were set aside. Cover the pot and simmer for another 1-2 hrs, checking the pot every 30 mins to make sure the oxtails and beans stay covered in the gravy. Cook until the oxtails and beans are fork tender, and the gravy thickens to your preference.

STEP 5. FOR THE SPINNERS: Pour the flour and garlic salt into a bowl, then gradually add the water until the dough begins to form. If the dough is too sticky, add more flour. Break off a piece and roll into the shape of something that looks like short fingers. When there's 45 mins left for the stew to cook, drop the dumplings into the pot. If the liquid in the stew is getting too low, add another ½ cup of beef stock. Continue cooking then in the last 5 minutes, add the ketchup and butter into the pot and stir.

SPINNERS/DUMPLINGS:
- 3 cups Flour
- ½ tablespoon Garlic Salt
- 1 cup Water

UTENSILS/COOKWARE NEEDED:
- Mixing Bowls
- Large Pot or Dutch Oven
- Long-Handled Spoon

TOTAL TIME: 3-4 HRS
SERVES: 8-10

STEP 6. Allow the stew to cool for at least 10 mins before plating, serve with jasmine rice (see pg. 176).

NOTE: Grace's is a Jamaican brand and will give the dish an authentic flavor, but any browning sauce will work!

ISLAND TINGZ

OXTAILS

STEP 1. Wash the oxtails with vinegar and water, then place them into a large mixing bowl.

STEP 2. Add the bell pepper, green onion, white onion, garlic, thyme, scotch bonnet, pimentos, seasoned salt, cayenne pepper, oxtail seasoning, onion powder and black pepper. Next pour in the Worcestershire, soy and browning sauce. Using clean hands, toss the mixture to combine the ingredients thoroughly.

STEP 3. Warm the olive oil in a large pot or Dutch oven over medium-high heat. Remove only the oxtails from the mixing bowl then place them in the pot. Set the vegetables aside. Brown the oxtails on each side for 5-8 mins depending on the thickness (thicker oxtails will need to be cooked longer).

STEP 4. Gently pour in the boiling water until the oxtails are halfway covered, then lower the heat to medium-low and cover the pot. Cook for 30-45 mins, checking the oxtails every 30 mins and adding more water to make sure the oxtails remain halfway covered. The water should start to thicken into a gravy, so make sure not to add too much water. The gravy should not be thin like soup, this is key to the process.

STEP 5. After the oxtails have cooked halfway or for 1 ½-2 hrs, add the beef bouillon cube. Toss in the vegetables that were set aside and stir everything together, then add the butter beans and ketchup. Cover the pot and cook for another hour, simmering until the oxtails are fork tender and the gravy has thickened.

STEP 6. Plate and serve with rice and peas (pg. 60).

- 3 lbs Oxtails
- 1 Green Bell Pepper, Medium Diced
- ¼ cup Green Onions, Chopped
- ½ White Onion, Sliced
- 3 cloves Garlic, Chopped
- 3 sprigs Fresh Thyme
- 1 Scotch Bonnet, De-Seeded
- ⅛ cup Pimento Seeds/ Allspice Berries
- ½ tablespoon Seasoned Salt
- 1/6 teaspoon Cayenne Pepper
- ½ tablespoon Oxtail Seasoning
- ½ tablespoon Onion Powder
- 1 teaspoon Black Pepper
- 1 tablespoon Worcestershire Sauce
- 1 tablespoon Soy Sauce
- 1 tablespoon Browning Sauce
- 5 tablespoons Olive Oil
- 1-2 cups Boiling Water
- 1 Beef Bouillon Cube
- 1 can Butter Beans (No Lima Beans)
- 1 tablespoon Ketchup

UTENSILS/COOKWARE NEEDED:

- Mixing Bowls
- Large Pot or Dutch Oven
- Long-Handled Spoon

TOTAL TIME: 2-3 HRS

SERVES: 8-10

NOTE: Grace's is a Jamaican brand and will give the dish an authentic flavor, but any brand of browning sauce will work!

ISLAND TINGZ

ITAL (PUMPKIN STEW)

- 1 tablespoon Olive Oil
- 1 tablespoon Garlic, Chopped
- ½ White Onion, Sliced
- 4 sprigs Thyme
- 1 Scotch Bonnet, De-Seeded & Minced
- 1 ½ cans coconut milk or coconut paste
- 1 bag Red Kidney Beans, Light or Dark
- 6 cups Boiling Water
- 1 teaspoon Garlic Salt
- 1 tablespoon Garlic Powder
- 1 tablespoon Onion Powder
- 1 tablespoon Seasoned Salt
- 1 tablespoon Black Pepper
- 2 tablespoons Unsalted Butter
- 2-3 Vegetable Bouillon Cubes
- 3 Carrots
- 4-6 Potatoes
- 1 Butternut Squash
- Boiling Water or Vegetable Stock
- 1 tablespoon Seasoned Salt
- 1 tablespoon Italian Seasoning
- 1 tablespoon Onion Powder
- 1 tablespoon Garlic Powder
- 1 tablespoon Black Pepper
- ½ teaspoon Garlic Salt
- ½ teaspoon Cayenne Pepper

SPINNERS/DUMPLINGS:

- 3 cups Flour
- ½ tablespoon Garlic Salt
- 1 cup Water

UTENSILS/COOKWARE NEEDED:

- Mixing bowl
- Large Pot
- Long-Handled Spoon

STEP 1. Warm a large pot over medium heat, drizzle in the olive oil and cook the garlic, onions, thyme and scotch bonnet. Sauté for 3-5 mins then add the coconut milk, kidney beans and water. Season with the garlic salt, garlic powder, onion powder, seasoned salt, black pepper, butter and 1 veggie bouillon cube. Lower the heat to low, cover the pot and let it cook for 45 mins.

STEP 2. Peel and large dice the carrots, potatoes and butternut squash, making sure to scoop the seeds out of the squash before dicing. Add all the veggies to the pot with the beans, then pour in enough boiling water or vegetable stock to cover the veggies. Cover the pot and continue simmering for 2 hours.

STEP 3. FOR THE SPINNERS: Pour the flour and ½ tablespoon of garlic salt in a bowl, then gradually add the water until the dough begins to form. If the dough is too sticky, add more flour. Break off a piece and roll into the shape of short fingers. After the stew has cooked for 2 hours, drop the dumplings in then add the remaining stew seasonings and bouillon cubes. Stir and cook for another 30 mins.

STEP 4. Allow the stew to cool for at least 10 mins before plating, serve with jasmine rice (see pg. 176).

NOTE: This is a great vegetarian/vegan stew commonly eaten by Rastamen but can be enjoyed by anyone who likes hearty soups!

TOTAL TIME: 3 HRS
SERVES: 6

ISLAND TINGZ

JERK MARINADE

STEP 1. Use gloves to remove the seeds and slice the scotch bonnets, if you like really spicy jerk sauce, you can leave the seeds in. Throw the scotch bonnets into a blender, then add in the garlic cloves, green onions, white onion, thyme, pimento seeds or black peppercorns, brown sugar, ginger, cinnamon, nutmeg, garlic salt, black pepper, browning sauce, lemon juice, olive oil and water.

STEP 2. Blend until the sauce is smooth.

- 4 Scotch Bonnet Peppers
- 6-8 Garlic Cloves
- 4 Green Onions, Cut in Half
- ½ White Onion, Sliced
- 6-8 sprigs Fresh Thyme, Stem Removed
- ⅛ cup Pimento Seeds or Black Peppercorns
- ¾ cup Brown Sugar
- 1 ½ tablespoons Fresh Ginger, Sliced
- 1 tablespoon Cinnamon
- 1 tablespoon Nutmeg
- ½ teaspoon Garlic Salt
- 1 tablespoon Black Pepper
- ½ tablespoon Browning Sauce
- ½ tablespoon Lemon Juice
- 1 tablespoon Olive Oil
- ¼ cup Water

UTENSILS/COOKWARE NEEDED:
- Blender
- Small Rubber Spatula

SERVES: 6
TOTAL TIME: 10 MINS

NOTE: if placed in a mason jar and refrigerated, this sauce can last for 2-3 months.

MANGO JERK WINGS

- 2 lbs Chicken Party Wings
- Non-stick Cooking Spray

JERK MARINADE:
- 4 Scotch Bonnet Peppers
- 6-8 Garlic Cloves
- 4 Green Onions, Cut in Half
- ½ White Onion, Sliced
- 6-8 sprigs Fresh Thyme, Stem Removed
- ⅛ cup Pimento Seeds or Black Peppercorns
- ¾ cup Brown Sugar
- 1 ½ tablespoons Fresh Ginger, Sliced
- 1 tablespoon Cinnamon
- 1 tablespoon Nutmeg
- ½ teaspoon Garlic Salt
- 1 tablespoon Black Pepper
- ½ tablespoon Browning Sauce
- ½ tablespoon Lemon Juice
- 1 tablespoon Olive Oil
- ¼ cup Water

MANGO SAUCE:

1 Large Mango, Diced
3 Whole Garlic Cloves
½ cup White Onions, Sliced
¼ cup Brown Sugar
¼ teaspoon Cayenne Pepper
⅛ cup Water
½ cup Ketchup
Unsalted Butter
⅛ cup Worcestershire Sauce

UTENSILS/COOKWARE NEEDED:

Blender
Mixing Bowls
Baking Sheet
Parchment Paper or Aluminum Foil
Saucepan
Small Rubber Spatula

STEP 1. Preheat the oven to 400 degrees.

STEP 2. FOR JERK MARINADE: Use gloves to remove the seeds and slice the scotch bonnets, if you like really spicy jerk sauce, you can leave the seeds in. Throw the scotch bonnets into a blender, then add in the garlic cloves, green onions, white onion, thyme, pimento seeds or black peppercorns, brown sugar, ginger, cinnamon, nutmeg, garlic salt, black pepper, browning sauce, lemon juice, olive oil and water. Blend until the sauce is smooth. Set aside.

STEP 3. Wash the chicken wings using vinegar and water then pat dry. Put the chicken in a large mixing bowl and pour on enough jerk sauce to coat all the wings. Marinate for at least 30 mins. Line a baking sheet with foil or parchment paper, then spray it with non-stick cooking spray and lay the chicken in a single layer on the pan. Bake the wings for 30-45 mins, flipping them over halfway through.

STEP 4. FOR THE MANGO SAUCE: Warm a saucepan over low heat. In a blender, add in the diced mango, garlic cloves, white onions, brown sugar, cayenne, and water. Blend until smooth then pour the mixture into a saucepan and add the ketchup, butter and Worcestershire sauce. Mix well and simmer for 5-10 mins. If the sauce gets too thick, thin it out with water, 1 tablespoon at a time. The sauce should be thin enough to toss the cooked wings in.

STEP 5. Broil the wings in the oven for 3-5 mins or until the wings are crispy. Remove them from the oven, then place them in a mixing bowl and toss them in the mango sauce. Plate and serve hot.

TOTAL TIME: 1 ½ HRS
SERVES: 6

ISLAND TINGZ

HONEY GARLIC JERK LAMB CHOPS

STEP 1. FOR JERK MARINADE: Use gloves to remove the seeds and slice the scotch bonnets, if you like really spicy jerk sauce, you can leave the seeds in. Throw the scotch bonnets into a blender, then add in the garlic cloves, green onions, white onion, thyme, pimento seeds or black peppercorns, brown sugar, ginger, cinnamon, nutmeg, garlic salt, black pepper, browning sauce, lemon juice, olive oil and water. Blend until the sauce is smooth then pour the marinade into a mixing bowl and set aside.

STEP 2. Wash the rack of lamb using vinegar and water and pat dry. Cut the rack between each bone until you get individual lamb chops. Place the lamb chops into the bowl with the jerk marinade and mix until all the lamb chops are coated in the jerk sauce. Marinate for at least 30 mins.

STEP 3. Warm a large pan over medium heat, drizzle in the olive oil and sear the lamb chops with the garlic cloves, rosemary and thyme. Cook the lamb for 2-3 mins on each side or until the chops are golden-brown. Repeat until all the lamb chops are cooked, then remove them from the pan and set aside.

STEP 4. FOR THE HONEY GARLIC SAUCE: Clean the pan the lamb chops were seared in then add all the ingredients listed for the honey garlic sauce. Whisk together and simmer for 3-5 mins, then place the lamb chops back in the pan and toss them in the honey sauce.

STEP 5. Remove the chops from the pan, plate and serve hot.

NOTE: If␣your're not a fan of lamb, you can substitute the lamb chops with your favorite protein (chicken thighs, pork chops, turkey legs, etc.)

- 1 Rack of Lamb
- 2 tablespoons Olive Oil
- 3 Whole Garlic Cloves
- 2 sprigs Fresh Rosemary
- 4-5 sprigs Fresh Thyme

JERK MARINADE:
- 4 Scotch Bonnet Peppers
- 6-8 Garlic Cloves
- 4 Green Onions, Cut in Half
- ½ White Onion, Sliced
- 6-8 sprigs Fresh Thyme, Stem Removed
- ⅛ cup Pimento Seeds or Black Peppercorns
- ¾ cup Brown Sugar
- 1 ½ tablespoons Fresh Ginger, Sliced
- 1 tablespoon Cinnamon
- 1 tablespoon Nutmeg
- ½ teaspoon Garlic Salt
- 1 tablespoon Black Pepper
- ½ tablespoon Browning Sauce
- ½ tablespoon Lemon Juice
- 1 tablespoon Olive Oil
- ¼ cup Water

HONEY GARLIC SAUCE:
- ¼ cup Honey
- 1 tablespoon Minced Garlic
- ⅛ cup Soy Sauce
- 3 tablespoons Unsalted Butter
- ¼ teaspoon Paprika

UTENSILS/COOKWARE NEEDED:
- Blender
- Mixing Bowl
- Tongs
- Large Pan
- Whisk

TOTAL TIME: 1 HR
SERVES: 6

PINEAPPLE JERK SHRIMP BOWL

- 8-12 Large Shrimp, Peeled and Deveined
- 2 tablespoons Unsalted Butter
- ½ tablespoon Garlic, Chopped
- ½ tablespoon Parsley, Chopped
- Cooked Jasmine Rice (see pg. 176)

JERK MARINADE:

- 4 Scotch Bonnet Peppers
- 6-8 Garlic Cloves
- 4 Green Onions, Cut in Half
- ½ White Onion, Sliced
- 6-8 sprigs Fresh Thyme, Stem Removed
- ⅛ cup Pimento Seeds or Black Peppercorns
- ¾ cup Brown Sugar
- 1 ½ tablespoons Fresh Ginger, Sliced
- 1 tablespoon Cinnamon
- 1 tablespoon Nutmeg
- ½ teaspoon Garlic Salt
- 1 tablespoon Black Pepper
- ½ tablespoon Browning Sauce
- ½ tablespoon Lemon Juice
- 1 tablespoon Olive Oil
- ¼ cup Water

UTENSILS/COOKWARE NEEDED:

- Blender
- Mixing Bowls
- Medium Sized Pan

TOTAL TIME: 45 MINS
SERVES: 4

STEP 1. Slice the pineapple in half lengthwise (being careful not to slice all the way through) then slice the inside 4 times lengthwise and 5 times across, creating small chunks. Scoop out the chunks of pineapple and place them in a bowl. Keep the hollowed-out pineapple halves for plating and set them aside.

STEP 2. FOR THE JERK MARINADE: Use gloves to remove the seeds and slice the scotch bonnets, if you like really spicy jerk sauce, you can leave the seeds in. Throw the scotch bonnets into a blender, then add in the garlic cloves, green onions, white onion, thyme, pimento seeds or black peppercorns, brown sugar, ginger, cinnamon, nutmeg, garlic salt, black pepper, browning sauce, lemon juice, olive oil and water. Blend until the sauce is smooth then pour the marinade into a mixing bowl and set aside.

STEP 3. Wash the shrimp using vinegar and water then pat dry. Pour the shrimp into the bowl with the jerk marinade and mix until the shrimp is completed coated in the jerk sauce. Marinate at least 30 mins.

STEP 4. Warm a medium sized pan over medium-high heat then add the butter, garlic and parsley. Sauté 1-2 mins then add the shrimp. Sear the shrimp for 3-5 mins then add the pineapple chunks and cook for another 2 mins.

STEP 5. Place the pineapple halves on a plate or platter and fill them halfway with the cooked jasmine rice, then the rest of the way with the cooked shrimp and pineapple mixture. Serve hot.

ISLAND TINGZ

FESTIVAL

STEP 1. Preheat frying oil to 350 degrees.

STEP 2. Sift the dry ingredients over a large mixing bowl, then mix in the butter with your hands until it's melted into the flour. It should take 5-8 mins to get the butter mixed in.

STEP 3. Pour in the vanilla extract then gradually add the buttermilk to the mixture, ¼ cup at a time, mixing with your hands until the dough forms. If the dough is too sticky, add more flour. Cover the bowl with plastic wrap and set it aside for 20 mins.

STEP 4. Roll some dough in your palm to create a thick finger shape then drop them into the frying oil using a large spoon. Cook until the festival are golden-brown and remove them from the oil. Drain on paper towels or a wire rack, then plate and serve hot.

- Oil for Frying
- 4 cups Flour
- 2 ½ cups Cornmeal
- 1 tablespoon Baking Powder
- 1 ½ cups Sugar
- 1 teaspoon Salt
- 1 cup Cubed Unsalted Butter
- 2 tablespoons Vanilla Extract
- 1 ½ cups Buttermilk

UTENSILS/COOKWARE NEEDED:

- Large Frying Pan or Deep Fryer
- Sifter
- Mixing Bowl
- Large Spoon

TOTAL TIME: 40 MINS
SERVES: 6

NOTE: Festival are great as a side for any of the dishes in this chapter, from oxtails to brown stew chicken!

ISLAND TINGZ

FRIED DUMPLING

- Oil for Frying
- 4 cups Flour
- 1 tablespoon Baking Powder
- 4 tablespoons Sugar
- 1 teaspoon Salt
- 1 cup Cubed Unsalted Butter
- 1 ¼ cups Water

UTENSILS/COOKWARE NEEDED:

- Large Frying Fan or Deep Fryer
- Sifter
- Mixing Bowl
- Large Spoon

TOTAL TIME: 40 MINS

SERVES: 6

STEP 1. Preheat frying oil to 350 degrees.

STEP 2. Sift the dry ingredients over a large mixing bowl, then mix in the butter with your hands until it's melted into the flour. It should take 5-8 mins to get the butter mixed in.

STEP 3. Gradually add the water to the mixture, ¼ cup at a time, mixing with your hands until the dough forms. If the dough is too sticky, add more flour. Cover the bowl with plastic wrap and set to the side for 20 mins.

STEP 4. Use your hands to form the dough into balls and drop them into the frying oil using a large spoon, cook until the dumplings are golden-brown. Remove them from the oil and drain on paper towels or a wire rack, then plate and serve hot.

I LOVE COOKING FOR THE SAME REASON THAT I LOVE FASHION — THE THRILL OF CREATING SOMETHING NEW.

ISLAND TINGZ

ACKEE AND SALT FISH

STEP 1. Boil the salt fish for 10-15 mins to remove the salt. Drain the salt fish then flake the fish apart, being careful to remove any bones that may still be in the fish. Place the flaked fish into a mixing bowl and set aside.

STEP 2. Strain the ackee then pour it into boiling water for 5 mins. Drain the ackee and set aside.

STEP 3. Warm a medium sized pan with over medium heat then drizzle in olive oil and sauté the thyme, green onions, tomato, white onion, garlic and scotch bonnet for 10-12 mins. Add the flaked saltfish and drained ackee, then season with the garlic powder, onion powder and black pepper. Cook for another 5-8 mins, making sure not to stir the mixture too much because the ackee will break apart.

STEP 4. Plate and serve hot.

- 1-2 pieces Salt Fish
- 2 tins of Ackee
- 1 teaspoon Olive Oil
- 4 sprigs Fresh Thyme
- 1 cup Green Onions, Chopped
- 1 Tomato, Sliced
- 1 Whole White Onion, Sliced
- ¼ cup Garlic, Chopped
- 1 Scotch Bonnet, De-Seeded and Minced
- ½ tablespoon Garlic Powder
- ½ tablespoon Onion Powder
- ½ tablespoon Black Pepper

UTENSILS/COOKWARE NEEDED:

- 2 Medium Pots
- Mixing Bowls
- Strainer
- Small Rubber Spatula

TOTAL TIME: 35 MINS
SERVES: 6

ISLAND TINGZ

BROWN STEW FISH

- Oil for Frying
- 2 Whole Snapper Fish or Fish of Your Choice, Scaled and Gutted
- 1 teaspoon Fish Seasoning
- 1 teaspoon Old Bay
- 1 teaspoon Black Pepper

SAUCE:

- 2 tablespoons Olive Oil
- 3-4 sprigs Fresh Thyme
- 1 Yellow or Orange Bell Pepper, Sliced
- 4 Green Onions, Chopped
- 1 White Onion, Sliced 4-5
- 1 Tomato, Sliced
- 1 Scotch Bonnet, De-Seeded and Minced Whole Garlic Cloves, Chopped
- 1 cup Ketchup
- 3 tablespoons Unsalted Butter
- 1 Tomato Bouillon Cube
- ½ teaspoon Black Pepper
- 2 cups Water

UTENSILS/COOKWARE NEEDED:

- Large Frying Pan
- Large Pan
- Spatula

TOTAL TIME: 30 MINS
SERVES: 6

STEP 1. Preheat frying oil to 375 degrees.

STEP 2. Cut the fish down the front of the belly to ensure the fish is fully open, then slice the fish along the backbone. Cut the fish in half horizontally then slice slits into the skin of the fish so seasonings get beneath the skin. Make sure to flip the fish over and cut slits on the other side. Wash the fish using vinegar and lime juice then pat dry. Season with fish seasoning, Old Bay, and black pepper on both sides and inside the belly.

STEP 3. Lay the seasoned pieces of fish into the hot oil slowly, making sure not to splash the grease. Cook the fish for 4-6 mins on each side or until the skin is crispy. Drain the fried fish on a wire rack or paper towels and set aside.

STEP 4. FOR THE SAUCE: In a large pan, warm olive oil over medium heat then sauté the fresh thyme, bell peppers, green onions, white onion, tomato, scotch bonnet and chopped garlic. Cover and cook for 10-15 mins, stirring occasionally. Uncover and add the ketchup, browning sauce, butter, garlic salt, onion powder, tomato bouillon, black pepper and water. Cover the pan and simmer for 5-8 more mins.

STEP 5. Add the fish to the pan with the sauce and let it cook another 10 mins. Make sure the fish doesn't break apart in the pan.

STEP 6. Plate and serve with jasmine rice (see pg. 176).

ISLAND TINGZ

CURRY CHICKEN

STEP 1. Begin by removing all the skin from the chicken. Chop off the bottom ends of the drumsticks with the meat cleaver and discard the trimmings. Wash the chicken using vinegar and water then pat dry. Place the chicken in a mixing bowl then season with the poultry seasoning, black pepper, garlic salt, garlic powder, bell peppers, scotch bonnet, then add the green onions, garlic and thyme. Mix thoroughly to completely coat the chicken.

STEP 2. In a large pot or Dutch oven, warm the olive oil over medium heat then burn (toast) the curry powder in the pan.

STEP 3. Remove only the chicken from the mixing bowl and place it into the pot with the toasted curry. Cook the chicken for 3-4 mins on each side for a nice golden-brown sear (increase the cook time for thicker chicken).

STEP 4. After browning the chicken, remove it from the pot and set it aside. Leave the drippings in the pot and add in the veggies that were set aside. Pour in the water then the pimento seeds to create a gravy.

STEP 5. Place the chicken back into the pot with the bouillon cube and simmer for 25 mins, or until the gravy thickens and the chicken is tender. Check the chicken to make sure it is cooked through and there is no more pink.

STEP 6. Plate the curry chicken and sauce over jasmine rice (see pg. 176).

- 4-6 Chicken Drumsticks or Any Cut of Chicken
- 2 tablespoons Poultry Seasoning
- 1 teaspoon Black Pepper
- 1 tablespoon Garlic Salt
- 1 teaspoon Garlic Powder
- ½ Green Bell Pepper, Medium Diced
- ½ Red Bell Pepper, Medium Diced
- 1 Scotch Bonnet, De-Seeded and Minced
- 1 Green Onion, Chopped
- 1 tablespoon Garlic, Minced
- 3 sprigs Fresh Thyme
- 3 tablespoons Olive Oil
- 1 tablespoon Curry Powder
- 1 ½ cups Water
- 1 tablespoon Pimento Seeds/Allspice Berries
- 1 Chicken Bouillon Cube

UTENSILS/COOKWARE NEEDED:

- Meat Cleaver or Large Knife
- Mixing Bowl
- Large Pot or Dutch Oven
- Large Spoon

TOTAL TIME: 45 MINS

SERVES: 6

NOTE: Curry powder will stain, so be cautious when handling this ingredient. It can also upset the stomach, so you must toast it first. In the islands, we say "burn the spice!"

BROWN STEW CHICKEN

- 4 lbs Chicken Legs or Thighs
- 1 tablespoons Browning Sauce
- 1 tablespoon All-Purpose Seasoning
- 1 tablespoon Onion Powder
- 1 tablespoon Garlic Salt
- ½ tablespoon Black Pepper
- 1 tablespoon Minced Garlic
- ½ Green Bell Pepper, Medium Diced
- ½ Orange Bell Pepper, Medium Diced
- 2 Carrots, Chopped
- 1 ½ Green Onions, Chopped
- 3 sprigs Fresh Thyme
- 2 tablespoons Olive Oil
- 3 Russet Potatoes, Peeled and Medium Diced
- 1 Chicken Bouillon Cube
- 1 Scotch Bonnet, De-Seeded and Minced
- 1 tablespoon Ketchup
- Boiling Water

UTENSILS/COOKWARE NEEDED:

- Meat Cleaver or Large Knife
- Mixing Bowl
- Large Pot or Dutch Oven
- Large Spoon

TOTAL TIME: 45 MINS
SERVES: 6

STEP 1. Remove the skin from the chicken before you begin. If using chicken legs, chop off the bottom joint of the chicken legs using a meat cleaver. Wash the chicken using vinegar and water, then pat dry and place in a mixing bowl.

STEP 2. Pour the browning sauce onto the chicken along with the all-purpose seasoning, onion powder, garlic salt, black pepper, minced garlic, bell peppers, carrots, green onions and thyme. Stir to make sure the chicken is coated in the mixture.

STEP 3. Warm the olive oil in a large pot or Dutch oven over medium heat. Remove only the chicken from the mixing bowl and place it into the pot, then brown the chicken for 5-7 mins on each side.

STEP 4. Add the potatoes, chicken bouillon cube, scotch bonnet and the veggies that were set aside into the pot. Mix in the ketchup, then fill the pot about halfway with water. Cover and simmer for about 30 mins or until the chicken is cooked through and there is no more pink.

STEP 5. Let cool at least 10 mins, then plate the brown stew chicken and sauce over jasmine rice (see pg. 176).

ISLAND TINGZ

JAMAICAN CABBAGE

STEP 1. Chop the stalk of broccoli into bite-sized pieces then rinse and drain the excess water. Place the broccoli in a mixing bowl and set aside. Repeat the same process for the head of cabbage and set aside in a separate bowl.

STEP 2. Warm a large pan over medium heat, drizzle in the olive oil and sauté the minced garlic for 1-2 mins then add the cabbage and 1 tablespoon of water to the pan. Cover and steam for 5 mins,

STEP 3. Remove the lid and add the broccoli, red onions, carrots, garlic salt, all-purpose seasoning, black pepper and crushed red pepper. Stir, cover and let the cabbage steam for another 3-5 mins.

STEP 4. Uncover the pan, add the other tablespoon of water and steam for 5-8 mins more. Plate and serve hot.

- 1 stalk Fresh Broccoli, Chopped
- 1 head Cabbage, Chopped
- 1 tablespoon Minced Garlic
- 2 tablespoons Water
- ¼ cup Red Onions, Sliced
- 1-10 oz bag Shredded Carrots
- 1 teaspoon Garlic Salt
- 1 tablespoon All-Purpose Seasoning
- 1 teaspoon Black Pepper
- ¼ teaspoon Crushed Red Pepper (optional)

UTENSILS/COOKWARE NEEDED:

- Mixing Bowl
- Large Pan or Pot

TOTAL TIME: 20 MINS

SERVES: 6-8

NOTE: I love serving this dish with curry chicken or oxtails!

ISLAND TINGZ

RICE AND PEAS

- 10 cups Water
- 1lb Red Kidney Beans (peas)
- 3 tablespoons Unsalted Butter
- 1-13 oz can Coconut Milk
- 1 Scotch Bonnet, Whole or De-Seeded and Minced
- 3 sprigs Fresh Thyme
- 1 Chicken, Beef or Vegetable Bouillon Cube (optional)
- ¼ teaspoon All-Purpose Seasoning
- ¼ teaspoon Black Pepper
- ¼ teaspoon Garlic Powder
- ⅛ teaspoon Garlic Salt
- 1 tablespoon Pimento Seeds/Allspice Berries
- 3 cups Jasmine Rice

UTENSILS/COOKWARE NEEDED:

- Large Pot
- Colander
- Plastic Grocery Bag, Cleaned

TOTAL TIME: 1HR
SERVES: 12-14

STEP 1. Soak the beans overnight.

STEP 2. Boil the water in a large pot then pour in the peas and cook for 45-90 mins, or until the peas are semi-soft.

STEP 3. Add the butter, coconut milk, scotch bonnet and thyme to the pot then stir the ingredients together. Season the peas with the bouillon and the remaining seasonings listed then stir. Cover the pot and cook for another 5-8 mins.

STEP 4. Rinse the rice in a large pot or colander then add it to the pot with the peas. Cover the pot with a plastic bag, then place a lid over the bag.

STEP 5. Allow the rice and peas to steam on low heat for roughly 30 mins. Remove the plastic bag and serve immediately.

NOTE: Let the rice and peas steam, do NOT stir once the pot is covered.

The plastic bag is a special trick that makes the perfect rice, I like to use a plastic grocery bag. Cut the bag in half then use the side without dye on it. Wash the bag with soap and water before placing it over the rice.

Rice and Peas is a prominent Jamaican side dish. The dish is Jamaican slang but in American terms, it is merely white rice and kidney beans. It is the perfect side dish for oxtails!

ISLAND TINGZ

Meat
BY THE SEA

LOADED LOBSTER TAIL 64

LOBSTER SPICY NOODLES 67

FULLY LOADED SHRIMP POTATO 68

SHRIMP SCAMPI 71

SHRIMP & BROCCOLI ALFREDO 72

SPICY SHRIMP DUMPLINGS 75

TURKEY CHILI 76

SALMON PHILLY 79

MONGOLIAN BEEF & BROCCOLI 80

LAMB FRIED RICE 83

BACON WRAPPED STUFFED BURGER 84

SURF & TURF 87

RIB TIPS 88

CRAB LEGS 91

LOBSTER ROLLS 92

LOADED LOBSTER TAIL

- 4 Lobster Tails

FILLING

- 3-5 Shrimp, Peeled and Deveined
- ½ cup Canned Crab Meat
- 1/6 cup Mayonnaise
- 1 tablespoon Honey Mustard
- ¼ cup Breadcrumbs
- 1 tablespoon Garlic, Minced
- ½ tablespoon Worcestershire Sauce
- ½ teaspoon Old Bay Seasoning
- ¼ teaspoon Garlic Powder
- ½ teaspoon Black Pepper
- ⅛ teaspoon Paprika
- ½ tablespoon Garlic Paste
- 1 teaspoon Parsley, Chopped
- 1 teaspoon Cilantro, Chopped

SEASONED BUTTER

- 2 tablespoons Melted Unsalted Butter
- 1 teaspoon Parsley, Chopped
- ⅛ teaspoon Paprika
- 1 teaspoon Minced Garlic
- ⅛ teaspoon Cajun Seasoning
- ⅛ teaspoon Garlic Salt
- ¼ teaspoon Lemon Juice

UTENSILS/COOKWARE NEEDED:

- Scissors
- 2 Mixing Bowls
- Baking Dish
- Aluminum Foil

TOTAL TIME: 30 MINS
SERVES: 4

STEP 1. Preheat the oven to 400 degrees.

STEP 2. FOR THE FILLING: Wash the shrimp using vinegar and water, then cut into bite sized pieces and pour into a large mixing bowl. Add in the crab meat along with the remaining ingredients. Mix well until fully combined, then set aside, preferably over ice or in the fridge.

STEP 3. FOR THE BUTTER: In a separate bowl mix together the melted butter, parsley, paprika, minced garlic, Cajun seasoning, garlic salt, and lemon juice. Stuff the tops of the lobster tails with the crab/shrimp filling then brush with the seasoned butter and place on a baking dish. Cover the dish with foil and bake for 15 mins.

STEP 4. Remove the loaded lobster tails from the oven, brush the tops with the remaining seasoned butter, then plate and serve hot.

MEAT BY THE SEA

LOBSTER SPICY NOODLES

STEP 1. Preheat the oven to 400 degrees.

STEP 2. In a bowl mix the melted butter, parsley, paprika, minced garlic, Old Bay, Cajun seasoning, lemon juice and garlic powder. Set aside.

STEP 3. Cut open the lobster tails using scissors then pull the meat out halfway and sit it on top of the shells. Wash the lobster tails using vinegar and water, pat dry. Brush the lobster with the seasoned butter and place on a baking dish, then cook for 10-15 mins. Remove from the oven and set aside.

STEP 4. FOR THE BROTH: In a medium sized pan or pot, melt the butter over medium heat then add minced garlic, parsley, hot sesame oil, hot chili crisp, soy sauce, garlic powder, black pepper and chicken bouillon. Sauté for 2-3 mins then pour in the boiling water. Add the ramen noodles and cook for 3-5 mins, stirring often. DO NOT add the ramen noodle seasoning packet.

STEP 5. Plate the noodles in a bowl with a lobster tail on top, serve hot.

- 4 Lobster Tails
- 2 tablespoons Unsalted Butter, Melted
- 1 teaspoon Parsley, Chopped
- 1/8 teaspoon Paprika
- 1 teaspoon Minced Garlic
- 1/8 teaspoon Cajun Seasoning
- 1/4 teaspoon Lemon Juice
- 1/8 teaspoon Garlic Powder

BROTH

- 2 tablespoons Unsalted Butter
- 1 tablespoon Minced Garlic
- 1/2 tablespoon Parsley, Chopped
- 4 tablespoons Hot Chili Crisp
- 1/8 cup Soy Sauce
- 1/2 teaspoon Garlic Powder
- 1/2 teaspoon Black Pepper
- 2 Chicken Bouillon Cubes
- 4 cups Boiling Water
- 4 packs Ramen Noodles
- 1/2 teaspoon Crushed Red Pepper (optional)

UTENSILS/COOKWARE NEEDED:

- Mixing Bowl
- Scissors
- Pastry Brush
- Baking Dish
- Medium Sized Pot

TOTAL TIME: 35 MINS
SERVES: 4

FULLY LOADED SHRIMP POTATO

- 3 Large Potatoes
- 1 tablespoon olive oil
- 12 Shrimp, Peeled and Deveined
- ½ teaspoon Old Bay Seasoning
- ½ teaspoon Garlic Powder
- ½ teaspoon Black Pepper
- ½ tablespoon Minced Garlic

SAUTÉ SHRIMP

- 2 teaspoons Melted Unsalted Butter
- 1 teaspoon Minced Garlic
- 1 teaspoon Parsley, Chopped

SAUCE

- 2 teaspoons Unsalted Butter
- ¼ cup White Onions, Chopped
- 1 tablespoon Minced Garlic
- 1 cup Heavy Whipping Cream
- ½ tablespoon Old Bay Seasoning
- ½ tablespoon Black Pepper
- 1 cup Shredded Cheddar Cheese

POTATO FILLING

- Insides from the Baked Potatoes
- ⅛ cup Melted Unsalted Butter
- ¼ teaspoon Garlic Salt
- ¼ teaspoon Black Pepper
- 1 teaspoon Dried Chives
- ¼ cup Heavy Whipping Cream
- ¼ cup Sour Cream
- 1 teaspoon Garlic Paste
- ¼ cup Shredded Cheddar Cheese

UTENSILS/COOKWARE NEEDED:

- Aluminum Foil
- 2 Mixing Bowls
- Sauté Pan
- Rubber Spatula
- Casserole Dish or Baking Sheet

TOTAL TIME: 1 HR

SERVES: 6

STEP 1. Preheat the oven to 400 degrees. Wash the potatoes then poke with a fork. Rub them with oil and roll the potatoes loosely in foil. Bake for 30-35 mins or until the potatoes are soft.

STEP 2. Wash the shrimp using vinegar and water, then season them with Old Bay, garlic powder, parsley, black pepper and minced garlic.

STEP 3. FOR THE SAUTÉ SHRIMP: In a sauté pan, melt butter over medium heat then cook the minced garlic for 1-2 mins. Add the shrimp and parsley to the pan and cook for 3-5 mins, making sure not to overcook your shrimp! Remove them from the pan and set aside.

STEP 4. FOR THE SAUCE: In the same pan the shrimp was cooked in, melt the butter then sauté the chopped onions, minced garlic, and parsley for 3 mins. Pour in the heavy cream and simmer, then season with Old Bay and black pepper. Continue simmering, stirring often, then sprinkle in the cheddar cheese, ¼ cup at a time. Stir until the cheese is completely melted and the sauce is smooth, then set aside.

STEP 5. FOR THE FILLING: Remove the potatoes from the oven and let them cool for at least 10 mins, or until they are cool enough for you to hold in your hand. Cut the potatoes in half most of the way down, making sure not to cut them all the way in half. Scoop out most of the insides of the potato, leaving about half an inch of potato still in the skins. Place the insides in a bowl and add all ingredients listed for the potato filling, then mash everything together until smooth.

STEP 6. Put the potato filling back in the skins, and then place them into a casserole dish. Layer by topping with half of the sauce, the cooked shrimp, the remaining sauce then more cheddar cheese. Sprinkle a little parsley for garnish and bake the potatoes for another 10-15 mins or until the cheese is melted and bubbly. Serve hot!

MEAT BY THE SEA

SHRIMP SCAMPI

STEP 1. Preheat the oven to 400 degrees.

STEP 2. Wash the shrimp using vinegar and water, then place in a mixing bowl. Season the shrimp with garlic powder, parsley, and black pepper then set aside, preferably over ice or in the fridge.

STEP 3. FOR THE BAGUETTE: Slice the bread into ½ inch–1-inch pieces then, in a mixing bowl, combine the parsley and melted butter. Brush the mixture onto both sides of the sliced bread then toast in the oven for 5-10 mins, or until the bread is golden brown. Remove from the oven and set aside.

STEP 4. FOR THE SAUCE: In a sauté pan, melt butter over medium heat and cook the chopped garlic, then add the lemon juice, white wine, heavy whipping cream, garlic powder and garlic salt. Bring to a simmer then sprinkle in the cheese and whisk until the cheese is melted. Add in the paprika for color, then place the seasoned shrimp in the pan in one flat layer. Cook the shrimp for 3-5 mins, flipping them over in the sauce halfway through. Make sure not to overcook your shrimp!

STEP 5. Add more cheese over the top of the shrimp and let it melt. Plate and serve with the toasted bread on the side.

- 13-15 Tiger Shrimp, Peeled and Deveined
- ½ teaspoon Garlic Powder
- 1 teaspoon Parsley, Chopped
- ½ teaspoon Black Pepper
- 1 French Baguette

SAUCE:

- 4 tablespoons Melted Unsalted Butter
- ¼ cup Garlic, Chopped
- ½ cup White Cooking Wine or Chicken Stock
- ⅛ cup Heavy Whipping Cream
- ½ teaspoon Garlic Powder
- ¼ cup Shredded Parmesan or Romano Cheese
- ¼ teaspoon Paprika

UTENSILS/COOKWARE NEEDED:

- 2 Mixing Bowls
- Small Rubber Spatula
- Pastry Brush
- Large Pan
- Whisk

TOTAL TIME: 25 MINS

SERVES: 6

MEAT BY THE SEA

SHRIMP & BROCCOLI ALFREDO

- 1 lb Shrimp, Peeled and Deveined
- ½ teaspoon Old Bay Seasoning
- ½ teaspoon Garlic Powder
- ½ teaspoon Black Pepper
- 1 teaspoon Parsley, Chopped
- 4 tablespoons Unsalted Butter
- ½ tablespoon Minced Garlic
- 1 bag Broccoli Florets

ALFREDO SAUCE:

- ⅛ cup Parsley, Chopped
- ⅛ cup Cilantro, Chopped
- 3 cloves Fresh Garlic, Chopped
- 2 cups Heavy Whipping Cream
- 1 cup Shredded Parmesan
- 1 cup Shredded Mozzarella
- 1 cup Shredded Italian-Style Cheese Blend
- 1 teaspoon Old Bay Seasoning
- ½ teaspoon Garlic Powder
- ⅛ teaspoon Black Pepper

PASTA:

- Pinch of Salt
- 1 lb Rigatoni Noodle Pasta
- ¼ teaspoon Garlic Salt
- ½ stick Unsalted Butter

UTENSILS/COOKWARE NEEDED:

- Mixing bowl
- Sauté Pan
- Large Pot
- Whisk
- Rubber Spatula

TOTAL TIME: 1 HR
SERVES: 6

STEP 1. Wash the shrimp using vinegar and water, then place them in a mixing bowl. Season the shrimp with Old Bay, garlic powder, black pepper, and parsley. In a sauté pan, melt butter over medium heat then cook the minced garlic for 1-2 mins. Add the seasoned shrimp to the pan and cook for 3-5 mins, then add in the broccoli and cover. Cook for another 5-10 mins or until the broccoli is cooked through. Remove from the pan and set aside.

STEP 2. FOR THE SAUCE: In the same pan, sauté the parsley, cilantro, and garlic over medium-low heat. Pour in the heavy cream then bring to a slow simmer. Whisk in the parmesan, mozzarella and Italian cheeses, a half cup at a time, until the sauce begins to thicken. Sprinkle in the blackened seasoning, Old Bay, garlic powder and black pepper, stir well. Allow the sauce to continue thickening to a creamy consistency, which should take about 30 mins.

STEP 3. FOR THE PASTA: Boil a pot of water with a pinch of salt and add a tablespoon of olive oil to keep the pasta from sticking. Toss in the Rigatoni noodles and boil for roughly 8 mins, or until the noodles are al dente then drain the pasta water. Add garlic salt and butter to the pasta and toss to combine well.

STEP 4. Add the shrimp and broccoli back into the pan with the alfredo sauce, then toss in the pasta and mix until all the pasta is coated in the sauce. Plate and serve hot.

MEAT BY THE SEA

SPICY SHRIMP DUMPLINGS

STEP 1. Bring a medium pot of water to a boil and line a bamboo steamer basket with parchment paper then place the steamer on top of the pot.

STEP 2. Wash the shrimp using vinegar and water, then mince them or throw them into a food processor and pour the minced shrimp into a mixing bowl. Mince the green onions and carrots or throw them into the food processor, then add them to the bowl with the shrimp. Season the mixture with ginger paste, black pepper and sesame oil and mix well.

STEP 3. FOR THE SAUCE: In a sauté pan, warm the olive oil over medium heat and add the garlic. Pour in the green onions, hot chili crisp, hot sesame oil and soy sauce. Cook together for 5 mins and set aside.

STEP 4. FOR ASSEMBLY: Lay out your dumpling wrappers and have the bowl of water nearby, then add 1 teaspoon of the shrimp mixture to each dumpling wrapper. Circle the wrappers with a bit of the water and fold them in half over the shrimp mixture. Starting in the middle of the dumpling, pinch and fold the sides together. Repeat until all the mixture is used.

STEP 5. Place the dumplings in the bamboo steamer and cook for 5-8 mins, or until the shrimp is cooked through. Repeat until all the dumplings are done, then toss in the sauce and serve hot.

- 5-8 Shrimp, Peeled and Deveined
- 1 cup Green Onions
- 1 cup Shredded Carrots
- 2 teaspoons Minced Garlic
- 1 teaspoon Ginger Paste
- ½ teaspoon Black Pepper
- 1 tablespoon Sesame Oil
- Dumpling Wrappers
- Small Bowl of Water

SAUCE:

- ½ tablespoon Olive Oil
- ½ tablespoon Minced Garlic
- ⅛ cup Green Onions
- 1 tablespoon Hot Chili Crisp
- ⅛ cup Hot Sesame Oil
- ⅛ cup Soy Sauce

UTENSILS/COOKWARE NEEDED:

- Medium Pot
- Bamboo Steamer
- Parchment Paper
- Food Processor
- Sauté Pan
- Small Rubber Spatula

TOTAL TIME: 30 MINS
SERVES: 6

MEAT BY THE SEA

TURKEY CHILI

- 2 tablespoons Olive Oil
- ¼ cup White Onions, Medium Diced
- ⅛ cup Garlic, Chopped
- 1 tablespoon Parsley, Chopped
- 2 lbs Ground Turkey or Beef
- ½ lb Ground Italian Sausage (optional)
- 2 large cans of Tomato Sauce
- ½ cup Canned Diced Tomatoes
- 1 cup Tomato Paste
- 2 cans Tricolored Beans
- 1 can Pinto Beans
- 1 can Red Kidney Chili Beans
- 1-2 Tomato Bouillon Cubes
- ½ tablespoon Garlic Powder
- ¼ teaspoon Garlic Salt
- 1 tablespoon Chili Powder
- ½ tablespoon Cumin
- ½ tablespoon Crushed Red Pepper
- 1 tablespoon Black Pepper
- 1 tablespoon Oregano
- 1 tablespoon Fennel Seeds

GARNISH (OPTIONAL):
- Tortilla strips
- Shredded cheese

UTENSILS/COOKWARE NEEDED:
- Stock pot
- Rubber Spatula or Wooden Spoon

TOTAL TIME: 1 HR
SERVES: 12

STEP 1. Warm a stock pot over medium-low heat. Pour in the olive oil and sauté the onions, garlic and parsley for 3-5 mins. Crumble in the ground turkey and sausage then cook for 10-12 mins, or until the meat is cooked through and there's no more pink. Drain the meat and add it back in the pot.

STEP 2. Pour in the tomato sauce, diced tomatoes and tomato paste then stir. Drain and rinse all beans except for the chili beans, then pour all the beans into the pot and stir. Add the bouillon cubes and all the seasonings listed then simmer for 30-45 mins.

STEP 3. Plate the chili in a bowl, garnish with tortilla strips, cheese and sour cream and serve hot.

MEAT BY THE SEA

SALMON PHILLY

STEP 1. Wash the salmon using vinegar and water and pat dry. Rub the salmon with olive oil then season with the Old Bay, black pepper and onion powder on both sides then set aside in a mixing bowl, preferably over ice or in the fridge.

STEP 2. Slice the mushrooms, bell peppers and red onion then sauté in a large pan over medium heat. Cover the pan and cook for 10-12 mins or until the veggies are soft, stirring occasionally. Once they're done, remove the veggies from the pan and set aside.

STEP 3. In the same pan, melt the butter and add the seasoned salmon to the pan. Sear for 2-3 mins, flipping the filets over halfway through the cook time. Using a spatula, break up the salmon filets and add the veggies back into the pan. Add the Cajun seasoning and continue cooking for 2-3 mins, then place a layer of the sliced cheese overtop and garnish with chopped parsley. Turn the heat down to low and cover the pan to let the cheese melt.

STEP 4. FOR ASSEMBLY: Brush the hoagie rolls with the melted butter and toast for 2-3 mins or until the rolls are brown. If they aren't already split, cut the hoagie rolls in half ¾ of the way through, making sure not to cut them completely in half. Fill the rolls with the Salmon Philly mixture, then plate and serve.

- 4 Salmon Filets, Skins Removed
- 1 tablespoon Olive Oil
- ½ teaspoon Old Bay Seasoning
- ½ teaspoon Black Pepper
- ½ teaspoon Onion Powder
- 1 cup Fresh Mushrooms, Sliced
- 1 Whole Red Bell Pepper, Sliced
- 1 Whole Green Bell Pepper, Sliced
- 2 tablespoons Unsalted Butter
- ½ tablespoon Cajun Seasoning
- Sliced Cheese of Your Choice
- Melted Unsalted Butter

UTENSILS/COOKWARE NEEDED:

- 2 Mixing Bowls
- Large Sauté Pan
- Spatula

TOTAL TIME: 30 MINS

SERVES: 4

NOTE: A great option if you don't eat red meat or chicken but miss the taste of a Philly Cheesesteak!

MEAT BY THE SEA

MONGOLIAN BEEF & BROCCOLI

- Oil for Frying
- 1 lb Thin Sliced Beef
- 2 teaspoons Minced Garlic
- 1 tablespoon Old Bay Seasoning
- 1 tablespoon Black Pepper
- 1 tablespoon Onion Powder
- 4 tablespoons Worcestershire Sauce
- 3 cups Broccoli
- 10-12 Dried Red Chiles

FLOUR MIXTURE

- 2 cups Flour
- ¼ cup Corn Starch
- 1 teaspoon Black Pepper

SAUCE

- ½ cup Hoisin Sauce
- ½ cup Brown Sugar
- 1 tablespoon Oyster Sauce
- 1 tablespoon Ginger Paste
- ½ cup Green Onions
- 2 tablespoons Hot Chili Crisp
- ¼ cup Soy Sauce
- 2 tablespoons Unsalted Butter
- 1 tablespoon Garlic, Chopped
- 1 cup Beef Stock

UTENSILS/COOKWARE NEEDED:

- 2 Mixing Bowls
- Large Frying Pan
- Whisk
- KitchenEnvy Wok
- Spatula

TOTAL TIME: 25 MINS
SERVES: 6

STEP 1. Add frying oil to a large pan then warm over medium-low heat.

STEP 2. In a mixing bowl, season the beef with minced garlic, Old Bay, black pepper, onion powder and Worcestershire sauce. Mix until the beef is coated with all the ingredients, then set aside.

STEP 3. FOR THE FLOUR: Pour the flour, corn starch and black pepper into a baking dish or mixing bowl and mix well. Coat the beef with the flour mixture on both sides and fry until golden. Drain on paper towels or a wire rack and set aside.

STEP 4. FOR THE SAUCE: In a mixing bowl combine hoisin sauce, brown sugar, oyster sauce, ginger paste, green onions, hot chili crisps, and soy sauce.

STEP 5. Heat the wok over medium-high heat and add the butter, chopped garlic, beef stock, the reserved broccoli, fried beef, and the sauce you made. Cover the pan and continue cooking for 5-10 mins, or until the broccoli is cooked through.

STEP 6. Plate and serve with jasmine rice (see pg. 176).

MEAT BY THE SEA

LAMB FRIED RICE

STEP 1. Wash the lamb using vinegar and water and pat dry. Cut the lamb off the bone and dice into small pieces, then place them into a bowl and season with dried thyme, Worcestershire sauce, minced garlic, parsley, Mrs. Dash, garlic salt, black pepper and paprika. Mix well and set aside.

STEP 2. Warm a wok over medium-high heat. Add the olive oil, garlic cloves and fresh rosemary. Toss the lamb into the wok and sear for 8-10 minutes, then remove from the pan and set aside.

STEP 3. FOR THE FRIED RICE: In the same pan the lamb was cooked in, add 1 tablespoon of olive oil, the minced garlic, parsley, cilantro, onions, green beans, peas, carrots and corn. Sauté for 4-5 mins, then remove the vegetables from the wok. Set aside in the same bowl as the lamb.

STEP 4. Clean the wok then place it over medium heat and pour in another tablespoon of olive oil. Crack the eggs into the wok and scramble them until they have cooked through. Remove the eggs from the pan and place them in the same bowl as the lamb and veggies.

STEP 5. Add the last of the olive oil to the wok and warm it over medium-high heat. Place the precooked white rice into the wok then season with Mrs. Dash, black pepper and garlic salt. Pour in the hoisin sauce and soy sauce and stir until the rice is completely coated. Continue stir-frying the rice for 3-4 mins then add in the lamb, veggies and eggs.

STEP 6. Plate in a bowl and serve hot.

- 1 Rack of Lamb
- ⅛ cup Worcestershire Sauce
- 1 teaspoon Minced Garlic
- 1 tablespoon Parsley, Chopped
- 1 teaspoon Mrs. Dash Seasoning
- ½ teaspoon Garlic Salt
- ½ tablespoon Black Pepper
- ½ teaspoon Paprika
- 3 sprigs Fresh Rosemary

FRIED RICE

- 3 tablespoons Olive Oil
- 1 tablespoon Minced Garlic
- 1 tablespoon Parsley, Chopped
- 1 tablespoon Cilantro, Chopped
- ½ cup White Onions, Small Diced
- ¼ cup Green Beans, Fresh or Frozen
- ¼ cup Frozen Peas and Carrots
- ¼ cup Corn, Fresh or Frozen
- 2 Eggs
- 4 cups Cooked White Rice, Chilled 12-24hrs
- ¼ teaspoon Mrs. Dash Seasoning
- 1 tablespoon Black Pepper
- 1 tablespoon Garlic Salt
- 1 tablespoon Hoisin Sauce
- 1 ½ tablespoons Soy Sauce

UTENSILS/COOKWARE NEEDED:

- 2 Mixing Bowls
- KitchenEnvy Wok
- Spatula

TOTAL TIME: 35 MINS
SERVES: 6

BACON WRAPPED STUFFED BURGER

- 1 lb Ground Turkey or Beef
- ¼ cup Chopped Onions
- ½ tablespoon Parsley, Chopped
- 1 tablespoon Minced Garlic
- 1 teaspoon Blackened seasoning
- 1 teaspoon Garlic Powder
- 1 teaspoon Onion Powder
- 1 teaspoon Black Pepper
- 1 teaspoon Paprika
- 1 tablespoon Worcestershire Sauce
- 1 Egg
- ⅔ cup Breadcrumbs
- 1 block Cheddar Cheese, Cubed
- 4-6 slices Bacon, Turkey or Pork

UTENSILS/COOKWARE NEEDED:

- Mixing bowl
- Baking Sheet
- Rubber spatula

TOTAL TIME: 1 HR
SERVES: 4

STEP 1. Preheat the oven to 400 degrees.

STEP 2. Place the ground turkey in a mixing bowl with the chopped onions, parsley, minced garlic, blackened seasoning, garlic powder, onion powder, black pepper, paprika, Worcestershire sauce, the egg and breadcrumbs. Mix well then roll the mixture into balls and flatten them into patties. Place a cube of cheese on every other patty, then place a patty without cheese on top of one that does have cheese. Seal the sides of the patties together to make sure the cheese doesn't come out while the patties cook.

STEP 3. Wrap the strips of bacon around the patties and place the wrapped burger patties on a baking sheet coated with non-stick cooking spray.

STEP 4. Bake for 35-40 mins, then broil for 12 mins or until the bacon is crispy. Plate on burger buns with your favorite toppings and serve!

MEAT BY THE SEA

SURF & TURF

STEP 1. Preheat the oven to 400 degrees. Wash the bunch of broccolini and place in a baking dish, then season with olive oil and garlic salt then put the dish in the oven and roast for 10-15 mins. Remove the broccolini from the oven and set aside.

STEP 2. FOR THE TURF: Wash the steak using vinegar and water and pat dry. Season with the Worcestershire sauce, blackened seasoning, black pepper, Italian seasoning, garlic powder and paprika. Sear on a griddle pan with the butter, garlic, rosemary and thyme for 10-12 mins depending on how thick your steak is. Remove the steak from the pan and let it rest on a plate.

STEP 3. FOR THE SURF: Wash the shrimp using vinegar and water and pat dry, then place the shrimp in a mixing bowl. Season them with minced garlic, blackened seasoning and Mrs. Dash and sear for 3-5 mins on the same griddle pan the steak was cooked on. Remove the shrimp from the griddle and place on the same plate that the steak is resting on.

STEP 4. Add the broccolini to the plate and serve with your favorite steak sauce.

- 1 bunch of Broccolini
- 1 tablespoon Olive Oil
- ½ teaspoon Garlic Salt

TURF

- 1 Steak of Your Choice
- 1 ½ teaspoon Worcestershire Sauce
- ½ teaspoon Blackened Seasoning
- ½ teaspoon Black Pepper
- ½ teaspoon Italian Seasoning
- ½ teaspoon Garlic Powder
- ½ teaspoon Paprika
- 2 tablespoons Unsalted Butter
- 3-4 cloves Garlic
- 2 sprigs Fresh Rosemary
- 2 sprigs Fresh Thyme

SURF

- 6-10 Tiger Shrimp, Peeled and Deveined
- 1 teaspoon Blackened Seasoning
- 1 tablespoon Mrs. Dash Seasoning

UTENSILS/COOKWARE NEEDED:

- Baking Dish
- Griddle
- Mixing bowl
- Spatula or Tongs

TOTAL TIME: 35 MINS
SERVES: 2

MEAT BY THE SEA

RIB TIPS

- 1 pack Rib Tips, Beef or Pork
- ¼ cup Brown Sugar
- 1 tablespoon Paprika
- ½ tablespoon Onion Powder
- ½ tablespoon Garlic Powder
- ½ tablespoon Black Pepper
- ½ tablespoon Lemon Pepper
- 1 tablespoon Chipotle Powder
- ½ tablespoon Blackened Seasoning
- 1 tablespoon Olive Oil
- ¼ - ½ cup BBQ Sauce of Choice

UTENSILS/COOKWARE NEEDED:

- 2 Mixing Bowls
- Large Pan
- Spatula
- Baking Dish
- Aluminum Foil

TOTAL TIME: 2 HRS
SERVES: 6

STEP 1. Preheat the oven to 400 degrees.

STEP 2. Wash the rib tips using vinegar and water and pat dry, then place them in a mixing bowl. Season with the brown sugar, paprika, onion powder, garlic powder, black pepper, lemon pepper, chipotle powder, and blacked seasoning. Massage the seasoning into the rib tips until they are fully coated.

STEP 3. Warm a large pan over medium-high heat and add the olive oil, then pan sear the rib tips for 5-10 mins or until they're nice and brown. Transfer them to a baking dish and cover the dish with foil, then place it in the oven for 45 mins-1 hr. Pull the rib tips from the oven and brush them with your favorite BBQ sauce, then place them back in the oven for 5 mins on broil.

STEP 4. Remove the rib tips from the oven and allow to cool at least 5 mins before serving. Plate and serve with your favorite BBQ sides!

MEAT BY THE SEA

CRAB LEGS

STEP 1. Wash the crab legs thoroughly using vinegar and water, then remove the meat from the shell and try to keep the meat whole.

STEP 2. Heat a sauté pan over medium heat then add the butter, parsley, and minced garlic. Stir in the de-shelled crab leg meat and cook for 5-8 mins. Remove them from the pan and serve hot.

- 4 King Crab Legs
- 4 tablespoons Unsalted Butter
- ⅓ cup Parsley, Chopped
- ¼ cup Minced Garlic

UTENSILS/COOKWARE NEEDED:

- Sauté Pan
- Spatula

TOTAL TIME: 20 MINS
SERVES: 6

MEAT BY THE SEA

LOBSTER ROLLS

- 2-3 Lobster Tails
- 3 tablespoons Unsalted Butter
- 1 tablespoon Garlic Paste
- ½ tablespoon Parsley, Chopped
- ¼ cup Old Bay Seasoning
- ¼ cup Garlic Powder
- ¼ cup Black Pepper
- 3-4 Hoagie Rolls
- ¼ cup Mayonnaise
- 2 tablespoons Dijon Mustard

UTENSILS/COOKWARE NEEDED:

- Mixing bowl
- Sauté Pan
- Spatula

TOTAL TIME: 30 MINS

SERVES: 3

STEP 1. Wash the lobster tails using vinegar and water then cut open the lobster tails using scissors. Pull the meat out and chop the lobster. Place it in a mixing bowl and set aside.

STEP 2. Warm a sauté pan over medium heat and sauté the chopped lobster in the butter, garlic, parsley and seasonings for 2-3 mins. Make sure not to overcook your lobster!

STEP 3. FOR ASSEMBLY: Toast the hoagie rolls in a pan or in the oven then place them on plates. Brush the rolls with mayo and mustard to your liking, then fill the rolls with the cooked lobster and serve!

THE KITCHEN IS A PLACE TO EXPERIENCE HAPPY VIBES, MAKE GREAT MEMORIES AND BOND WITH LOVED ONES.

MEAT BY THE SEA

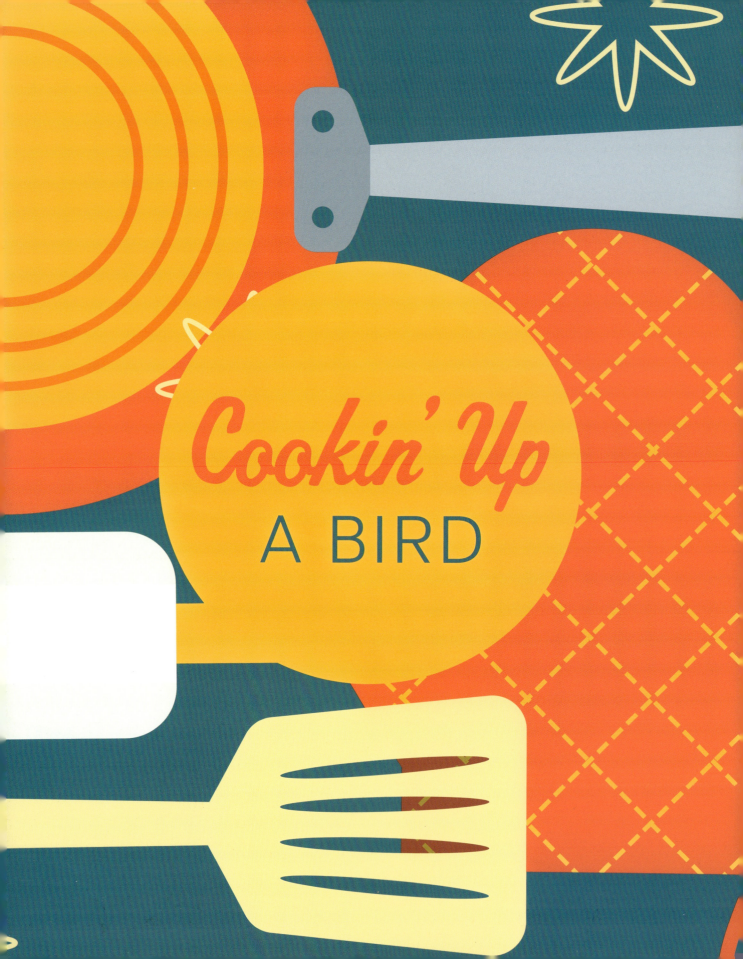

STUFFED CHICKEN BREASTS 96

SWEET CHILI THAI CHICKEN THIGHS 99

TANDOORI CHICKEN SKEWERS 100

ORANGE CHICKEN 103

CAJUN SPICED WHOLE CHICKEN 104

SWEET CHILI CHICKEN STIR FRY 107

CHICKEN & DUMPLINGS 108

WHISKEY GLAZED CHICKEN 111

TURKEY STUFFED MEATBALLS 112

CHICKEN PARM 115

SMOTHERED TURKEY WINGS 116

STUFFED CHICKEN BREASTS

- 1 pack Chicken Breasts
- 1 tablespoon Olive Oil
- 1 teaspoon Garlic Powder
- 1 teaspoon Onion Powder
- 1 teaspoon Italian Seasoning
- 1 teaspoon Pollo Seasoning
- 1 teaspoon Chipotle Powder
- 12-16 Whole Sun-Dried Tomatoes
- 1 ball of Fresh Mozzarella Cheese, Sliced
- 2 cups Frozen Spinach

UTENSILS/COOKWARE NEEDED:

- Mixing Bowl
- Baking Dish
- Aluminum Foil

TOTAL TIME: 40 MINS.
SERVES: 6

NOTE: If you use fresh spinach, sauté with ½ teaspoon olive oil, ½ teaspoon of garlic salt and 1 teaspoon of minced garlic.

STEP 1. Preheat the oven to 400 degrees.

STEP 2. Wash the chicken breasts using vinegar and water, then pat dry and slice a pocket on the side of the chicken to have an opening for the filling. Place the chicken in a bowl, drizzle with olive oil then season with garlic powder, onion powder, Italian seasoning, pollo seasoning and chipotle powder. Make sure the seasonings fully coat the chicken.

STEP 3. Stuff each chicken breast with 4-6 sun-dried tomatoes, 2 slices of cheese and 1 tablespoon of spinach. Place the stuffed chicken breasts in a baking dish, then cover the dish with foil and bake for 20 mins or until the chicken is cooked through and there is no more pink.

STEP 4. Remove the chicken from the oven and let cool at least 5 mins. Slice, plate and serve hot.

COOKIN' UP A BIRD

SWEET CHILI THAI CHICKEN THIGHS

STEP 1. Wash the chicken thighs using vinegar and water, then pat dry.

STEP 2. Place the chicken in a cool cast iron pan and rub with the olive oil, minced garlic then season with paprika, brown sugar, garlic powder, onion powder, and black pepper. Make sure to get the seasonings all over the chicken thighs, front and back, then cover the pan with foil and place it in the oven for 20 mins.

STEP 3. FOR THE SAUCE: Drain and reserve the drippings from the cooked chicken. Pour 2 tablespoons of it into a small mixing bowl with the corn starch to create a slurry. Pour the remaining drippings into a sauce pan then mix in the rest of the ingredients listed for the sauce. Bring the sauce to a simmer and slowly stir in the slurry until it thickens to your liking.

STEP 4. Pour the sauce over the chicken and pop the pan back in the oven for 5 mins on broil.

STEP 5. Plate and serve with jasmine rice (pg. 176).

- 7-8 Chicken Thighs
- 2 tablespoons Olive Oil
- ½ tablespoon Minced Garlic
- ½ teaspoon Paprika
- 2 tablespoons Brown Sugar
- ½ teaspoon Garlic Powder
- ½ teaspoon Onion Powder
- ½ teaspoon Black Pepper

SAUCE:

- Juice from the Cooked Chicken
- ½ tablespoon Cornstarch
- 1 tablespoon Garlic, Chopped
- ½ teaspoon Paprika
- 2 tablespoons Honey
- 1 tablespoon Soy Sauce
- 1 tablespoon Hoisin Sauce
- 2 tablespoons Sriracha Sauce
- 2 tablespoons Unsalted Butter

UTENSILS/COOKWARE NEEDED:

- Cast Iron Pan
- Aluminum Foil
- Mixing Bowl
- Saucepan

TOTAL TIME: 30 MINS
SERVES: 6

TANDOORI CHICKEN SKEWERS

- 1 pack Chicken Breasts
- 1 cup Whole Milk Yogurt
- ½ teaspoon Garlic Paste
- ½ teaspoon Ginger Paste
- 2 teaspoons Olive Oil
- 1 teaspoon Lemon Juice
- ½ tablespoon Coriander
- ¼ teaspoon Garlic Salt
- ½ tablespoon Garam Masala
- ½ tablespoon Cumin
- ½ tablespoon Chili Powder
- ½ tablespoon Turmeric
- ½ tablespoon Paprika

UTENSILS/COOKWARE NEEDED:

- Mixing Bowls
- Skewers
- Baking Sheet
- Parchment Paper
- Aluminum Foil

TOTAL TIME: 1 HR

SERVES: 6

NOTE: If grilling the Tandoori Chicken, be sure to presoak the wooden skewers in water for at least 1 hr before placing the chicken on the baking sheet, this will help prevent the skeweres from burning.

STEP 1. Preheat the oven to 400 degrees.

STEP 2. Wash the chicken breasts using vinegar and water, then cut the chicken into large chunks and place the chunks in a bowl. Add in the yogurt, garlic paste, ginger paste olive oil, lemon juice and all the seasonings listed. Mix well and marinate for at least 30 mins, preferably over ice or in the fridge.

STEP 3. Put the marinated chicken chunks onto skewers, about 4 pieces on each skewer, until you've used all the chicken. Place the skewers on a baking sheet lined with parchment paper, then cover the pan with foil and bake for 15 to 20 minutes. Uncover and bake the skewers for another 5 mins on broil.

STEP 4. Plate and serve with jasmine rice (see pg. 176).

COOKIN' UP A BIRD

ORANGE CHICKEN

STEP 1. Preheat frying oil in a large pan over medium heat.

STEP 2. Wash the chicken thighs using vinegar and water, then pat them dry and dice the chicken into medium-sized chunks. In a mixing bowl, season the chunks with minced garlic, soy sauce, sesame oil, garlic salt, onion powder, black pepper, and coriander then add the egg and corn starch. Mix well and set aside.

STEP 3. FOR THE FLOUR: Whisk together all the ingredients listed for the flour mixture in a bag or bowl, then coat the seasoned chunks of chicken in the flour then fry for 3-5 mins or until the chicken is cooked through (no more pink).

STEP 4. FOR THE SAUCE: Warm a saucepan over medium-low heat and combine everything listed for the sauce EXCEPT the cornstarch. Bring the sauce to a simmer, then pour 2 tablespoons of the sauce into a small bowl and add in the corn starch to create a slurry. Continue to simmer the sauce and slowly stir in the slurry until the sauce thickens to your liking. Toss the fried chunks of chicken into the sauce and mix until the chicken is completely coated in sauce.

STEP 5. Plate and serve with jasmine rice (see pg. 169).

TOTAL TIME: 40 MINS
SEVES: 6

- Oil for Frying
- 1 pack Boneless, Skinless Chicken Thighs
- 1 tablespoon Minced Garlic
- 2 tablespoons Soy Sauce
- 1 teaspoon Sesame Oil
- ⅛ teaspoon Garlic Salt
- ½ teaspoon Onion Powder
- ½ teaspoon Black Pepper
- ½ teaspoon Coriander
- 1 Egg, whisked
- ¼ cup Corn Starch

FLOUR MIXTURE:
- 3 cups Flour
- 1 teaspoon Black Pepper
- 1 teaspoon Garlic Powder
- 1 teaspoon Onion Powder

SAUCE:
- ⅔ cup Orange Juice
- Zest of 1 Orange
- 1 tablespoon Garlic, Chopped
- 1 tablespoon Ginger Paste
- ½ cup Brown Sugar
- 3 tablespoons Soy Sauce
- ½ teaspoon Garlic powder
- ½ tablespoon Garlic Salt
- ½ teaspoon Black Pepper
- 1 tablespoon Crushed Red Pepper
- ½ teaspoon White Vinegar
- ⅓ cup Honey
- ½ teaspoon Sesame Oil
- ½ teaspoon Corn Starch

UTENSILS/COOKWARE NEEDED:
- Large Pan
- 2 Mixing Bowls
- Whisk
- Saucepan
- Spatula

CAJUN SPICED WHOLE CHICKEN

- 1 Whole Chicken
- ¼ cup Olive Oil
- 2 tablespoons Melted Unsalted Butter
- 1 tablespoon Garlic, Chopped
- 1 tablespoon Cilantro, Chopped
- 1 tablespoon Parsley, Chopped
- 1 tablespoon Onion Powder
- 1 tablespoon Garlic Powder
- 1 tablespoon Black Pepper
- 1 tablespoon Paprika
- ½ tablespoon Chipotle Powder
- ½ tablespoon Garlic Salt
- 1 tablespoon Blackened Seasoning
- 1 tablespoon Chicken Bouillon Powder

UTENSILS/COOKWARE NEEDED:

- Mixing Bowl
- Roasting Pan
- Aluminum Foil

TOTAL TIME: 3 HRS
SERVES: 6

STEP 1. Preheat the oven to 400 degrees.

STEP 2. Wash the chicken using vinegar and water, then cut the chicken in half and pat it dry (this is to make sure the seasonings stick to the chicken). Mix together the olive oil, butter, chopped garlic, cilantro, parsley and all the seasoning listed in a bowl then massage the seasoning mix all over the chicken, inside and out and underneath the skin.

STEP 3. Place the chicken in a roasting pan and cover the pan with foil. Roast the chicken for 1 ½-2 hrs depending on the size of the chicken. When there's 15 mins left, uncover the chicken and put the oven on broil to get the skin nice and crispy.

STEP 4. Let the chicken rest at least 15 mins before slicing. Plate and serve with your favorite sides!

COOKIN' UP A BIRD

SWEET CHILI CHICKEN STIR FRY

STEP 1. Wash the chicken thighs using vinegar and water, then dice them into medium chunks and place the chicken in a bowl. Add the minced garlic, ginger paste, garlic powder, onion powder, black pepper, Cajun seasoning and cornstarch then mix well, making sure the chicken is fully coated with the seasonings.

STEP 2. Warm a wok over medium-high heat then drizzle in the oil and sauté the chunks of chicken, diced bell peppers and onions for 10-12 mins.

STEP 3. FOR THE SAUCE: In a mixing bowl, combine all the ingredients listed for the sauce and whisk.

STEP 4. Pour the sauce into the wok with the stir fry and cook for another 5-10 mins, or until the chicken is cooked through.

STEP 5. Plate and serve with jasmine rice (see pg. 176).

- 1 pack Boneless, Skinless Chicken Thighs
- 1 tablespoon Minced Garlic
- ½ tablespoon Ginger Paste
- ½ tablespoon Garlic Powder
- ½ tablespoon Onion Powder
- ½ tablespoon Black Pepper
- ½ tablespoon Cajun Seasoning
- 3 tablespoons Corn Starch
- 1 tablespoon Vegetable Oil
- 1 Red Bell Pepper, Medium Diced
- 1 green Bell Pepper Medium Diced
- 1 yellow Bell Pepper, Medium Diced
- 1 Red Onion, Medium Diced

SAUCE:
- ½ cup Ketchup
- ¼ cup Soy Sauce
- 1 tablespoon Oyster Sauce
- 1 tablespoon Hot Sesame Oil
- 1 tablespoon Hot Chili Crisp
- ½ cup Sweet Chili Sauce
- 1 tablespoon Crushed Red Pepper

UTENSILS/COOKWARE NEEDED:
- Mixing Bowls
- KitchenEnvy Wok
- Whisk

TOTAL TIME: 30 MINS
SERVES: 6

CHICKEN & DUMPLINGS

- 1 pack Chicken Breast
- 1 teaspoon Black Pepper
- 1 teaspoon Garlic Powder
- 1 teaspoon Onion Powder
- 1 teaspoon Mrs. Dash Seasoning
- 1 tablespoon Olive Oil
- 4 Carrots, Medium Diced
- 4 stalks Celery, Medium Diced
- 1 White Onion, Medium Diced
- ½ teaspoon Minced Garlic
- 2 tablespoons Unsalted Butter
- 2 tablespoons Flour
- 4 cups Chicken Stock
- ½ cup Heavy Whipping Cream
- 2 Chicken Bouillon Cubes
- 1 tablespoon Parsley, Chopped
- ½ teaspoon Black Pepper
- ⅛ teaspoon Garlic Salt
- 3 Bay Leaves
- 1 tablespoon Poultry Seasoning
- 2 cups Frozen Peas

DUMPLINGS

- 2 cups Flour
- ½ cup Heavy Cream
- 1 teaspoon Parsley, Chopped
- 1 teaspoon Garlic Salt
- ½ tablespoon Baking Powder
- ½ tablespoon Melted Unsalted Butter

UTENSILS/COOKWARE NEEDED:

- Mixing Bowls
- Large Pot
- Ice Cream Scoop
- Long-Handled Spoon

TOTAL TIME: 2 HRS
SERVES: 6

STEP 1. Wash the chicken breasts using vinegar and water, then dice them into medium chunks and place the chunks in a bowl. Season the chicken with black pepper, garlic powder, onion powder and Mrs. Dash and mix well.

STEP 2. Warm a large pot over medium heat, add the olive oil and sauté the seasoned chunks of chicken for 10-12 mins or until the chicken is cooked through. Remove from the pan and set aside.

STEP 3. In the same pot the chicken was cooked in sauté the carrots, celery, onions and garlic for 5-10 mins. Melt the 2 tablespoons of butter in the pot then stir in the flour to create a roux. Pour the chunks of chicken back into the pan, then add the chicken stock, heavy cream, bouillon cubes, parsley, black pepper, garlic salt, bay leaves and poultry seasoning. Cover the pot and cook for 30-40 mins.

STEP 4. FOR THE DUMPLINGS: In a large mixing bowl combine all the ingredients listed for the dumplings until they form a dough.

STEP 5. Using an ice cream scoop, pop the dumplings into the large pot with the chicken soup and add the frozen peas. Remove the bay leaves from the pot, then simmer for another 25-30 mins.

STEP 6. Plate in a bowl and serve hot.

COOKIN' UP A BIRD

WHISKEY GLAZED CHICKEN

STEP 1. Preheat the oven to 400 degrees and frying oil to 350 degrees.

STEP 2. Wash the chicken thighs using vinegar and water, then pat dry and season with the Mrs. Dash, onion powder, garlic powder, black pepper, paprika and parsley. Make sure to season both sides of the chicken. Set aside.

STEP 3. FOR THE FLOUR MIXTURE: In a large bowl or bag, combine the flour with all the ingredients listed for the flour mixture.

STEP 4. In a separate bowl, mix together the whole egg and egg white. Dip the chicken thighs in the egg mixture then the flour mixture and fry for 10-15 mins or until the chicken is cooked through and extra crispy. Drain the fried chicken on paper towels or a wire rack and set aside. Repeat until all the chicken is fried and if you start to run low on flour or egg, just add more to the mixture you already made.

STEP 5. FOR THE SAUCE: Warm a saucepan over medium heat and add the vegetable oil, then sauté the onions and garlic. Add all the other ingredients listed for the sauce into the pan with the onions and garlic then stir. Reduce the heat to low and allow the sauce to simmer for 5-7 mins, or until it thickens.

STEP 6. Place the chicken thighs into a baking dish then pour the sauce over them. Cover the pan with foil and bake for 10-15 mins.

STEP 7. Remove the chicken from the oven, plate and serve with mashed potatoes or rice.

TOTAL TIME: 2 ½ HRS

SERVES: 6

NOTE: For crispier chicken, repeat the breading process by dipping it into the egg mixture and flour mixture a second time.

- Oil for Frying
- 1 pack Chicken Thighs
- ½ teaspoon Mrs. Dash Seasoning
- ½ teaspoon Onion Powder
- ½ teaspoon Garlic Powder
- ½ teaspoon Black Pepper
- ½ teaspoon Paprika
- ½ teaspoon Parsley, Chopped
- 1 Whole Egg
- 1 Egg White

FLOUR MIXTURE

- 2 cups Flour
- 2 tablespoons Corn Starch
- 1 teaspoon Cajun Seasoning
- 1 teaspoon Black Pepper
- 1 teaspoon Garlic Powder
- 1 teaspoon Onion Powder

WHISKEY GLAZE

- 1 tablespoon Vegetable Oil
- ½ cup White Onions, Chopped
- ½ teaspoon Minced Garlic
- ½ teaspoon Whiskey (optional)
- ½ cup Brown Sugar
- 1 ½ cup Canned Crushed Pineapple
- 1 teaspoon Soy Sauce
- 1 cup Teriyaki Sauce
- 1 teaspoon Cayenne Pepper
- ¼ teaspoon Garlic Salt
- 1 teaspoon Lemon Juice
- ¼ cup Water

UTENSILS/COOKWARE NEEDED:

- Large Frying Pan or Deep Fryer
- Mixing Bowls
- Saucepan
- Baking Dish
- Aluminum Foil

TURKEY STUFFED MEATBALLS

- 1 lb Ground Turkey
- ½ cup White Onions, Chopped
- 1 tablespoon Parsley, Chopped
- 1 tablespoon Garlic, Chopped
- ½ teaspoon Blackened Seasoning
- ½ teaspoon Garlic Powder
- ½ teaspoon Onion Powder
- ¼ teaspoon Black Pepper
- ½ teaspoon Paprika
- 1 teaspoon Crushed Red Pepper
- 1 teaspoon Garlic Paste
- 1 Egg, whisked
- ¾ cup Breadcrumbs
- ½ block Cheddar Cheese, Cut into Cubes
- ½ block Mozzarella Cheese, Cut into Cubes
- 1 teaspoon Olive Oil
- 1 cup Shredded Italian Style Blend Cheese

SAUCE

- 1 teaspoon Olive Oil
- ½ cup White Onions, Chopped
- 1 tablespoon Garlic, Chopped
- 1 tablespoon Parsley, Chopped
- 1-28 oz can Crushed Tomatoes
- 1-28 oz can Tomato Sauce
- 1 Tomato Bouillon Cube
- ½ teaspoon Onion Powder
- ½ teaspoon Garlic Powder
- ½ teaspoon Dried Oregano
- ½ teaspoon Dried Basil
- ½ teaspoon Black Pepper
- ⅛ teaspoon Garlic Salt

UTENSILS/COOKWARE NEEDED:

- Mixing Bowls
- Large Skillet
- Baking Dish

TOTAL TIME: 1 HR
SERVES: 8-10

STEP 1. Preheat the oven to 400 degrees.

STEP 2. Place the ground turkey in a mixing bowl with the chopped onions, parsley, garlic, blackened seasoning, garlic powder, onion powder, black pepper, paprika, crushed red pepper, garlic paste, the egg and breadcrumbs. Mix well. Roll of the mixture into balls, 1 ½ tablespoons at a time, and press a dent into the middle of each ball. Place a cube of cheese in the dent and close the meatball around the cheese, sealing the sides together to make sure the cheese doesn't come out while the meatballs cook. The mixture should make 7-9 large meatballs.

STEP 3. Warm a large skillet over medium heat. Pour in the olive oil and sear the meatballs for 5-8 mins or until they're nice and brown. Make sure to roll the meatballs around to get each side brown. Remove them from the pan and set aside.

STEP 4. FOR THE SAUCE: In the same pan the meatballs were cooked in, add the olive oil and sauté the chopped onions. Add in the garlic and parsley, then cook for 3-5 mins. Add in the crushed tomatoes, tomato sauce, bouillon cube and the remaining seasonings listed for the sauce and stir. Let the sauce simmer for 30 mins, stirring occasionally. If the sauce becomes too thick, add in ¼ cup of chicken stock.

STEP 5. Once the sauce is done simmering, pour a little in the bottom of a baking dish, then place the meatballs in the pan and cover them with ½ of the remaining sauce. Sprinkle on the shredded cheese and place the meatballs in the oven for 20 mins.

STEP 6. Remove the meatballs from the oven and let cool at least 10 mins before plating. Plate and serve over your favorite pasta with the rest of your sauce!

COOKIN' UP A BIRD

CHICKEN PARM

STEP 1. Preheat frying oil to 350 degrees.

STEP 2. Wash the chicken breasts using vinegar and water then butterfly them, cutting them all the way in half. Use a meat mallet or rolling pin to thin the chicken breasts to about ¼ inch thickness. Oil and season both sides of each piece of chicken with pollo seasoning, black pepper, Italian seasoning and garlic powder, Set aside.

STEP 3. FOR THE BREADING: In 3 separate bowls have your flour, egg, and breadcrumbs ready. Mix the parsley and parmesan cheese in with the breadcrumbs. Dip the chicken breasts in the flour, then egg, then breadcrumbs and place in the frying oil. Cook for 5-8 mins or until the chicken breasts are golden brown. Drain them on paper towels or over a wire rack and set to the side. Don't worry if the chicken isn't cooked all the way, they will finish in the oven.

STEP 4. FOR THE SAUCE: Warm a sauté pan over medium heat, then add the olive oil and sauté the chopped onions. Add in the garlic and parsley, then cook for 3-5 mins. Add in the crushed tomatoes, tomato sauce, bouillon cube and the remaining seasonings listed for the sauce and stir. Let the sauce simmer for 30 mins, stirring occasionally. If the sauce becomes too thick, add in ¼ cup of chicken stock.

STEP 5. Once the sauce is done, pour a little in the bottom of a baking dish, then layer the chicken breasts on the bottom of the dish and cover them with ½ of the remaining sauce. Sprinkle on the shredded cheese then place the pan in the oven on broil for 2-3 mins, or until the cheese is bubbly and starts to brown.

STEP 6. Remove the pan from the oven and let the chicken cool at least 10 mins before plating. Plate and serve over your favorite pasta with the rest of your sauce!

- Oil for Frying
- 2 Chicken Breasts
- 1 teaspoon Olive Oil
- ½ teaspoon Pollo Seasoning
- ½ teaspoon Black Pepper
- ½ teaspoon Italian Seasoning
- ½ teaspoon Garlic Powder
- 2 balls Fresh Mozzarella Cheese, Sliced

BREADING FOR CHICKEN

- 1 ½ cups Flour
- 2 Eggs, Beaten
- 1 cup Breadcrumbs
- 1 teaspoon parsley, fresh or dried
- ¼ cup Parmesan Cheese, Shredded or Grated

SAUCE

- 1 teaspoon Olive Oil
- ½ cup White Onions, Chopped
- 1 tablespoon Garlic, Chopped
- 1 tablespoon Parsley, Chopped
- 1-28 oz can Crushed Tomatoes
- 1-28 oz can Tomato Sauce
- 1 Tomato Bouillon Cube
- ½ teaspoon Onion Powder
- ½ teaspoon Garlic Powder
- ½ teaspoon Dried Oregano
- ½ teaspoon Dried Basil
- ½ teaspoon Black Pepper
- ⅛ teaspoon Garlic Salt

UTENSILS/COOKWARE NEEDED:

- Large Frying Pan
- Meat Mallet
- Mixing Bowls
- Sauté Pan
- Baking Dish

TOTAL TIME: 1 HR
SERVES: 6

SMOTHERED TURKEY WINGS

- 2 Turkey Wings
- 1 tablespoon Olive Oil
- 1 tablespoon Garlic Powder
- 1 tablespoon Onion Powder
- 1 tablespoon Black Pepper
- 1 tablespoon Italian Seasoning
- 1 tablespoon Paprika
- 1 tablespoon Mrs. Dash Seasoning
- Non-stick Cooking Spray
- 1 White Onion, Sliced
- 1 Green Bell Pepper, Sliced

GRAVY

- 2 tablespoons Unsalted Butter
- 1 Onion, Chopped
- 1 tablespoon Minced Garlic
- 3 tablespoons Flour
- ¼ teaspoon Black Pepper
- ¼ teaspoon Garlic Powder
- ¼ teaspoon Garlic Salt
- 1 tablespoon Crushed Red Pepper
- 3 cups Chicken Stock
- ½ cup Heavy Whipping Cream
- 1 teaspoon Browning Sauce
- 1 Chicken Bouillon Cube
- ⅓ cup Pan Drippings from the Turkey Wings

UTENSILS/COOKWARE NEEDED:

- Mixing Bowl
- Baking Dish
- Aluminum Foil
- Saucepan
- Small Rubber Spatula

TOTAL TIME: 3 ½ HRS
SERVES: 4

STEP 1. Preheat the oven to 400 degrees.

STEP 2. Wash the turkey wings using vinegar and water, then cut the wings so each wing is 1 drumstick and 1 flat. Place the wings in a bowl and drizzle them with olive oil, then season with garlic powder, onion powder, black pepper, Italian seasoning, paprika and Mrs. Dash. Mix well until the wings are coated in the seasonings.

STEP 3. Spray a baking dish with non-stick cooking spray and place the turkey wings in the dish along with the sliced onions and bell peppers. Cover the dish with foil and place it in the oven for 1-2 hours, making sure to baste the wings every 30 mins. After they cook, remove the foil from the pan, drain and reserve the drippings from the turkey wings (you will use this for your gravy so make sure to set aside).

STEP 4. FOR THE GRAVY: Warm a saucepan over medium heat and add the butter, then sauté the onions and garlic for 1-2 mins. Pour in the flour, 1 tablespoon at a time, stirring often. Add in all the other seasonings listed for the gravy along with the chicken stock, heavy cream, browning sauce, chicken bouillon and pan drippings. Simmer the gravy for 20 mins or until it thickens.

STEP 5. After the gravy has thickened, pour it over the turkey wings then cover the pan again and place them back in the oven to cook for another hour.

STEP 6. Remove the turkey wings from the oven and let cool 5 mins before serving. Plate and serve with jasmine rice (see pg. 176).

COOKIN' UP A BIRD

SALMON LINGUINI 120

SHRIMP LO MEIN 123

CRAB FETTUCCINI ALFREDO 124

CRAB GARLIC BREAD 127

BROCCOLI & CHEDDAR BREAD BOWL 128

STUFFED PASTA SHELLS 131

SEAFOOD RICE 134

SHRIMP PHO' 137

GARLIC NOODLES 138

SPICY RIGATONI FLORENTINE 141

MASHED POTATO & CHICKEN BOWL 142

LASAGNA ROLLS 145

CHICKEN ALFREDO LASAGNA 146

LOADED POTATO SOUP 149

SALMON LINGUINI

- 2 Salmon Filets, Skin Removed
- 1 teaspoon Minced Garlic
- 1 teaspoon Old Bay Seasoning
- ¼ Blackened Seasoning
- ¼ teaspoon Black Pepper
- ¼ teaspoon Garlic Powder
- ¼ teaspoon Onion Powder
- 2 tablespoons Unsalted Butter
- Alfredo Sauce
- ⅛ cup Parsley, Chopped
- ⅛ cup Cilantro, Chopped
- 3 cloves Fresh Garlic, Chopped
- 4 tablespoons Unsalted Butter
- 2 cups Heavy Whipping Cream
- 1 cup Shredded Parmesan
- 1 cup Shredded Mozzarella
- 1 cup Shredded Italian-Style Cheese Blend
- 1 teaspoon Blackened Seasoning
- 1 teaspoon Old Bay Seasoning
- ⅛ teaspoon Black Pepper
- ½ teaspoon Garlic Powder
- ⅛ teaspoon Garlic Salt

PASTA

- Pinch of Salt
- 1 tablespoon Olive Oil
- 1 lb box Linguini Pasta Noodles
- ¼ teaspoon Garlic Salt
- ½ stick Unsalted Butter

UTENSILS/COOKWARE NEEDED:

- Mixing Bowl
- Sauté Pan
- Whisk
- Spatula
- Large Pot

TOTAL TIME: 1 HR
SERVES: 6

STEP 1. Wash the salmon filets using vinegar and water then pat them dry so the seasonings stick. Rub with minced garlic on both sides of each filet, then season with Old Bay, blackened seasoning, black pepper, garlic powder and onion powder. Massage the filets and set aside, preferably on ice or in the fridge.

STEP 2. Heat a sauté pan over medium heat, then add butter and sear the salmon for 5-8 mins. Make sure to flip the filets over halfway through so each side gets seared well. Remove the salmon from the pan and set aside.

STEP 3. FOR THE SAUCE: In the same pan the salmon was cooked in, sauté the parsley, cilantro, and garlic over medium-low heat. Melt the butter in the pan, pour in the heavy cream then bring to a slow simmer. Whisk in the parmesan, mozzarella and Italian cheeses, a half cup at a time, until the sauce begins to thicken. Sprinkle in the blackened seasoning, Old Bay, black pepper, garlic powder and onion powder then stir well. Allow the sauce to continue thickening to a creamy consistency, which should take about 15 mins.

STEP 4. FOR THE PASTA: Boil a pot of water with a pinch of salt and add a tablespoon of olive oil to keep the pasta from sticking. Toss in the linguini noodles and boil for roughly 8 mins, or until the noodles are al dente then drain the pasta water. Add garlic salt and butter to the pasta and combine well.

STEP 5. Combine the pasta with the sauce in the sauté pan, then plate family-style topped with both salmon filets. Serve hot.

KRAV'N CARBS

SHRIMP LO MEIN

STEP 1. Wash the shrimp using vinegar and water, then place in a mixing bowl and season with black pepper and onion powder. Set aside, preferably over ice or in the fridge.

STEP 2. Warm a wok over medium-high heat then add some olive oil and sauté the minced garlic for 30 secs. Add the shrimp to the pan and sauté for 5-8 mins, then remove the cooked shrimp from the pan and set aside.

STEP 3. In the same wok the shrimp was cooked in, add more oil and cook the bell peppers for about 2-3 mins or until they're soft. Add the shredded cabbage, green onions and bean sprouts to the wok. Sauté for another 5 mins, then remove the pan from the heat.

STEP 4. FOR THE SAUCE: In a mixing bowl, combine all the ingredients listed for the sauce, mix well then set aside.

STEP 5. FOR THE PASTA: Boil a pot of water with a pinch of salt and add a tablespoon of olive oil to keep the noodles from sticking. Toss in the lo mein noodles and boil for roughly 8 mins, or until the noodles are al dente then drain the pasta water.

STEP 6. Add the noodles into the pan with the sautéed veggies. Sauté together for 1-2 mins, then add the sauce and cooked shrimp. Toss until the noodles are fully coated in the sauce, then plate and serve hot.

- 1lb Shrimp, Peeled and Deveined
- ¼ teaspoon Black Pepper
- ¼ teaspoon Onion Powder
- 2 teaspoons Olive Oil
- 1 tablespoon Minced Garlic
- 3 Bell Peppers, Sliced Thin
- 2 cups Shredded Cabbage
- 1 1/2 cups Green Onions
- 2 cups Fresh Bean Sprouts

SAUCE
- ¼ cup Hot Chili Crisp
- ¼ cup Garlic Chili Paste
- 1 tablespoon Sesame Oil
- 1/3 cup Oyster Sauce
- ½ cup Hoisin Sauce
- ¼ cup Soy Sauce

PASTA
- Pinch of Salt
- 1 tablespoon Olive Oil
- 1 lb Lo Mein Noodles

UTENSILS/COOKWARE NEEDED:
- 2 Mixing Bowls
- KitchenEnvy Wok
- Spatula
- Large Pot

TOTAL TIME:
SERVES: 12

CRAB FETTUCCINI ALFREDO

- 4 King Crab Legs
- 4 tablespoons Unsalted Butter
- ⅓ cup Parsley, Chopped
- ¼ cup Garlic, Chopped

ALFREDO SAUCE

- ⅛ cup Parsley, Chopped
- ⅛ cup Cilantro, Chopped
- 3 cloves Fresh Garlic, Chopped
- 4 tablespoons Unsalted Butter
- 2 cups Heavy Whipping Cream
- 1 cup Shredded Parmesan
- 1 cup Shredded Mozzarella
- 1 cup Shredded Italian-Style Cheese Blend
- 1 teaspoon Blackened Seasoning
- 1 teaspoon Old Bay Seasoning
- ⅛ teaspoon Black Pepper
- ½ teaspoon Garlic Powder
- ⅛ teaspoon Onion Powder

PASTA

- Pinch of Salt
- 1 tablespoon Olive Oil
- 1 lb Fettuccini Pasta Noodles
- ¼ teaspoon Garlic Salt
- ½ stick Unsalted Butter

UTENSILS/COOKWARE NEEDED:

- Scissors
- Sauté Pan
- Spatula
- Whisk
- Large Pot

TOTAL TIME: 30 MINA
SERVES: 6

STEP 1. Wash the crab legs thoroughly using vinegar and water, then remove the meat from the shell and dice it. Warm a sauté pan over medium heat then add the butter, parsley, and garlic. Stir in the chopped crab and cook for 5-8 mins. Remove the crab from the pan and set aside.

STEP 2. FOR THE SAUCE: In the same pan the crab was cooked in, sauté the parsley, cilantro, and garlic over medium-low heat. Melt the butter in the pan then pour in the heavy cream. Bring to a slow simmer. Whisk in the parmesan, mozzarella and Italian cheeses, a half cup at a time, until the sauce begins to thicken. Sprinkle in the blackened seasoning, Old Bay, black pepper, garlic powder and onion powder, stir well. Allow the sauce to continue thickening to a creamy consistency, which should take about 15 mins.

STEP 3. FOR THE PASTA: Boil a pot of water with a pinch of salt and add a tablespoon of olive oil to keep the pasta from sticking. Toss in the fettuccini noodles and boil for roughly 8 mins, or until the noodles are al dente then drain the pasta water. Add garlic salt and butter to the pasta and toss to combine well.

STEP 4. Combine the pasta with the sauce in the sauté pan, then add the crab back into the pan. Toss until the pasta is fully coated in the sauce, then plate family-style and serve hot.

KRAV'N CARBS

CRAB GARLIC BREAD

STEP 1. Preheat the oven to 400 degrees.

STEP 2. Wash crab legs thoroughly using vinegar and water, then remove the meat from the shell and chop it up. In a sauté pan, heat butter parsley and garlic then add the crab. Cook for 5-8 mins then remove from the pan and set aside.

STEP 3. FOR THE SPREAD: In a mixing bowl, use a wooden spoon or rubber spatula to press the olive oil, cilantro, parsley and garlic paste into the unsalted butter (the mixture should form a spread!)

STEP 4. FOR THE DIP (OPTIONAL): Sauté the parsley, cilantro, and garlic in a sauté pan over medium-low heat. Melt the butter in the pan then pour in the heavy cream. Bring to a slow simmer. Whisk in the parmesan, mozzarella and Italian cheeses, a half cup at a time, until the sauce begins to thicken. Sprinkle in the blackened seasoning, Old Bay, black pepper, garlic powder and onion powder and stir well. Allow the sauce to continue thickening to a creamy consistency, which should take about 15 mins.

STEP 5. FOR ASSEMBLY: Slice the French bread, then use a spatula to generously spread the butter mixture onto the bread. Sprinkle all the cheese onto the butter mixture then all the crab onto the top of the cheese. Bake the bread on a parchment-lined baking sheet for 5-8 mins, or until it's lightly toasted and golden-brown.

STEP 6. Remove the bread from the oven and cool at least 5 mins before cutting. Serve with alfredo dipping sauce on the side (optional).

NOTE: Add more or less cheese based on what you like, I like mine extra cheesy!

- 2 King Crab Legs
- 4 tablespoons Unsalted Butter
- 1/8 Chopped Parsley, Chopped
- 1/8 Chopped Garlic, Chopped
- 1 Medium-Sized Loaf Fresh French Bread
- 1 cup Shredded Parmesan Cheese
- 1 cup Shredded Mozzarella Cheese
- 1 cup Shredded Italian Cheese Blend

SPREAD
- 5 tablespoons Unsalted Butter, Softened
- 1/2 tablespoon Garlic Paste
- 1/2 tablespoon Olive Oil
- 1/2 tablespoon Cilantro, Chopped
- 1/2 tablespoon Parsley, Chopped

ALFREDO DIPPING SAUCE (OPTIONAL)
- 1/8 cup Parsley, Chopped
- 1/8 cup Cilantro, Chopped
- 3 cloves Fresh Garlic, Chopped
- 4 tablespoons Unsalted Butter
- 2 cups Heavy Whipping Cream
- 1 cup Shredded Parmesan
- 1 cup Shredded Mozzarella
- 1 cup Shredded Italian-Style Cheese Blend
- 1 teaspoon Blackened Seasoning
- 1 teaspoon Old Bay Seasoning
- 1/8 teaspoon Black Pepper
- 1/2 teaspoon Garlic Powder
- 1/8 teaspoon Onion Powder

UTENSILS/COOKWARE NEEDED:
- Scissors
- Sauté Pan
- Mixing Bowl
- Wooden Spoon or Rubber Spatula
- Whisk
- Spatula
- Parchment Paper
- Baking Sheet

TOTAL TIME: 10 MINS

SERVES: 6

BROCCOLI & CHEDDAR BREAD BOWL

- Sourdough Bread Bowl (or Bread Bowl of Your Choice)
- 3 tablespoons Unsalted Butter
- ½ cup Onions, Small Diced
- ⅛ cup Minced Garlic
- 2 cups Shredded Carrots
- ¼ cup Flour
- 3 cups Chicken Stock
- 2 ½ cups Broccoli
- ½ cup Heavy Whipping Cream
- ⅛ teaspoon Garlic Salt
- 1 teaspoon Garlic Powder
- 1 teaspoon Black Pepper
- 1 teaspoon Onion Powder
- ½ teaspoon Paprika
- 2 Chicken Bouillon Cubes
- 1 ½ cups Shredded Cheddar Cheese
- 2 tablespoons Unsalted Butter, Melted

UTENSILS/COOKWARE NEEDED:

- Large Pan
- Rubber Spatula
- Parchment Paper
- Baking Sheet

TOTAL TIME: 1 HR
SERVES: 6

STEP 1. Preheat the oven to 400 degrees.

STEP 2. Cut a circle from the top of the bread bowl down to the center of the bowl, making sure that you don't cut through the bottom of the bowl. Pull off the top and set it aside. Begin scooping out the inside of the bowl to make it hollow, then set aside.

STEP 3. Warm a large pan over medium-low heat, then melt the butter and sauté the onions and garlic for 3-5 mins or until the onions are soft. Add the shredded carrots and cook for 5 more minutes, then sprinkle in the flour, ⅛ cup at a time, creating a roux. Cook for 3-5 mins, stirring often to make sure the roux doesn't brown.

STEP 4. Pour in the chicken stock and stir, then add in the broccoli and heavy cream. Cover the pan and let the mixture simmer for 25-30 mins, stirring occasionally.

STEP 5. Add the seasonings (garlic salt, garlic powder, black pepper, onion powder, paprika, chicken bouillon) into the pan, then sprinkle in the cheddar cheese. Mix well and continue cooking for another 10-15 mins, stirring occasionally.

STEP 6. Brush some melted butter onto the bread bowl and bake on a parchment-lined baking sheet for 3-5 mins. Remove the bread bowl from the oven, then fill it with the broccoli cheddar soup and serve.

KRAV'N CARBS

STUFFED PASTA SHELLS (SEAFOOD EDITION)

STEP 1. Preheat the oven to 350 degrees.

STEP 2. Wash the salmon using vinegar and water then season the filets on both sides with black pepper, garlic powder and Old Bay. Add olive oil to a medium sized pan and warm over medium heat, then place the salmon in the pan. Cook for 2-3 mins then break the salmon apart with a spatula. Add the thawed-out spinach to the pan with the salmon and cook for another 2-3 mins. DO NOT overcook your salmon! Remove the salmon/spinach mixture from the pan and set aside to cool at least 5 mins.

STEP 3. FOR THE FILLING: Combine the softened cream cheese, salmon/spinach mixture, garlic paste and shredded cheeses in a mixing bowl. Mix well, then set aside.

STEP 4. FOR THE SAUCE: Sauté the parsley, cilantro, and garlic in a sauté pan over medium-low heat. Melt the butter in the pan then pour in the heavy cream. Bring to a slow simmer. Whisk in the parmesan, mozzarella and Italian cheeses, a half cup at a time, until the sauce begins to thicken. Sprinkle in the blackened seasoning, Old Bay, black pepper, garlic powder and onion powder and stir well. Allow the sauce to continue thickening to a creamy consistency, which should take about 15 mins.

STEP 5. FOR THE PASTA: Boil a pot of water with a pinch of salt and add a tablespoon of olive oil to keep the pasta from sticking. Toss in the shells and boil for roughly 8 mins, or until the noodles are al dente. Drain the pasta water and rinse with cold water.

- 2-3 Salmon Filets, Skin Removed
- ½ teaspoon Black Pepper
- ½ teaspoon Garlic Powder
- ½ teaspoon Old Bay Seasoning
- 1 tablespoon Olive Oil
- 1 ½ cups Frozen Spinach, Thawed Out
- ½ cup Shredded Mozzarella (for the top)
- Filling
- 8 oz Cream Cheese, Softened
- 1 tablespoon Garlic Paste
- 1 cup Shredded Mozzarella Cheese
- 1 cup Shredded Parmesan Cheese
- Alfredo Sauce
- ⅛ cup Parsley, Chopped
- ⅛ cup Cilantro, Chopped
- 3 cloves Fresh Garlic, Chopped
- 4 tablespoons Unsalted Butter
- 2 cups Heavy Whipping Cream
- 1 cup Shredded Parmesan
- 1 cup Shredded Mozzarella
- 1 cup Shredded Italian-Style Cheese Blend
- 1 teaspoon Blackened Seasoning
- 1 teaspoon Old Bay Seasoning
- ⅛ teaspoon Black Pepper
- ½ teaspoon Garlic Powder
- ⅛ teaspoon Onion Powder
- Noodles
- Pinch of Salt
- 1 tablespoon Olive Oil
- 1 lb Jumbo Shell Pasta Noodles

STEP 6. FOR ASSEMBLY: Fill the inside of the pasta shells with 1 tablespoon of the salmon/spinach/cream cheese mixture until all the shells are filled. Coat the bottom of the casserole dish with alfredo sauce and create one layer of the shells at the bottom of the pan. Drizzle another layer of alfredo sauce on the top of the stuffed shells then cover with the remaining mozzarella cheese. Cover the pan with foil and bake for 20 mins, then uncover and bake for 5 more mins or until the top is golden-brown and bubbly.

STEP 7. Remove the pan from the oven and let the stuffed shells cool at least 5-10 mins before serving.

UTENSILS/COOKWARE NEEDED:
- Medium Sized Pan
- Sauté Pan
- Spatula
- Mixing Bowl
- Whisk
- Large Pot
- Casserole Dish
- Aluminum Foil

TOTAL TIME: 50 MINS

SERVES: 4

KRAV'N CARBS

SEAFOOD RICE

- 2 Lobster Tails
- ½ lb Shrimp, Peeled and Deveined
- 2 Snow Crab Clusters
- 1 tablespoon Minced Garlic
- 1 tablespoon Parsley, Chopped
- 1 tablespoon Old Bay Seasoning
- 1 tablespoon Garlic Powder
- 1 tablespoon Black Pepper
- Rice
- 4 cups Jasmine Rice
- 2 teaspoons Melted Unsalted Butter
- ½ cup Onions, Small Diced
- 1 cup Bell Peppers, Small Diced
- 2 cups Frozen Mixed Vegetables
- 2 teaspoons Minced Garlic
- 1 teaspoon Garlic Powder
- ½ teaspoon Garlic Salt
- 1 teaspoon Onion Powder
- 1 teaspoon Black Pepper
- 1 teaspoon Blackened Seasoning
- 1 teaspoon Cajun Seasoning
- 2 tablespoons Turmeric
- 3 Bay Leaves, Crushed
- 2 cups Chicken Stock

UTENSILS/COOKWARE NEEDED:

- Scissors
- Mixing Bowl
- Spatula
- Colander
- KitchenEnvy Wok

TOTAL TIME: 45 MINS
SERVES: 12

STEP 1. Prep lobster tails by washing them using vinegar and water then cutting them in half lengthwise. Wash the shrimp and crab legs using vinegar and water as well. Place all the seafood in a mixing bowl and season with minced garlic, parsley, Old Bay, garlic powder and black pepper. Set aside, preferably on ice or inside the fridge.

STEP 2. FOR THE RICE: Rinse the rice using a colander or large pot, set aside. Warm a wok over medium-high heat, then melt the butter and sauté the onions, bell peppers, mixed vegetables and garlic for 5-8 mins, stirring occasionally. Add the clean rice and cook until it starts to brown, then season with the garlic powder, garlic salt, onion powder, black pepper, blackened seasoning, Cajun seasoning, turmeric and bay leaves. Stir until all the rice is coated in seasoning, then add the chicken stock. Cover the pan and let the rice cook for 15 mins.

STEP 3. When the rice is almost done, add the seasoned seafood to the pan and stir it into the rice. Cover the pan and cook for another 10 mins, or until the seafood is cooked through. Plate and serve hot.

KRAV'N CARBS

SHRIMP PHO'

STEP 1. Wash the shrimp using vinegar and water and set aside, preferably over ice or in the fridge.

STEP 2. Peel and slice the ginger then cut the green onions in half. Toss both ingredients into a large pot. Add the cinnamon sticks, star anise, coriander and peppercorns. Add the onion to the pot along with the garlic cloves. Sauté the ingredients for 5 mins over medium heat.

STEP 3. Pour in the boiling water and broth. Crumble in the bouillon cubes and bring to a boil. Turn the broth down to low and let it simmer for 25 mins.

STEP 4. Add the shrimp to the broth and cook for 3-5 mins, then remove the shrimp from the pot and set it aside. DO NOT overcook your shrimp! Strain the broth with a strainer or slotted spoon, then pour the broth back into the pot and return it to a simmer.

STEP 5. FOR THE NOODLES: Boil a pot of water with a pinch of salt and add a tablespoon of olive oil to keep the noodles from sticking. Toss in the rice noodles and boil for roughly 6 mins, or until the noodles are al dente then drain the water.

STEP 6. Plate the pho' in a bowl, starting with the noodles and broth, then add your favorite garnishes. Top with the cooked shrimp and serve!

- 8 pieces of Shrimp, Peeled and Deveined
- 5 slices Ginger
- 3 stalks Green Onions
- 2 Cinnamon Sticks
- 6 Star Anise Pods
- 4 Coriander Seeds
- 1 tablespoon Peppercorns
- ½ Whole White Onion, cut in half
- 6 Whole Garlic Cloves
- 3 cups Boiling Water
- 2 cups Broth (chicken, vegetable, beef)
- 2 Bouillon Cubes (chicken, vegetable, beef)
- Noodles
- Pinch of Salt
- 1 box Rice Noodles
- Garnish (Optional)
- Chili Oil
- Hoisin Sauce
- Fresh Mint Leaves
- Fresh Basil Leaves
- Garlic Chili Paste
- Sriracha Sauce
- Green Onions
- Fresh Bean Sprouts
- Jalapenos, Sliced Thin
- Limes, Cut Into Wedges
- White Onion, Sliced Thin

UTENSILS/COOKWARE NEEDED:

- 2 Large Pots
- Strainer
- Spatula

TOTAL TIME: 45 MINS
SERVES: 6

SPICY GARLIC NOODLES

- 1 teaspoon Olive Oil
- ¼ cup Garlic, Chopped
- Sauce
- 1 tablespoon Garlic Paste
- 1 tablespoon Minced Garlic
- ⅓ cup Soy Sauce
- 1 tablespoon Sriracha Sauce
- 2 teaspoons Sesame Oil
- 1 tablespoon Hot Sesame Oil
- 2 tablespoons Sesame Seeds
- 1 tablespoon Hot Chili Crisp
- 1 tablespoon Garlic Chili Sauce
- 1 teaspoon Red Pepper Flakes
- ¼ teaspoon Onion Powder
- ¼ teaspoon Black Pepper
- ¼ teaspoon Garlic Salt
- Noodles
- Pinch of Salt
- 1 tablespoon Olive Oil
- 1 lb Egg Noodles

UTENSILS/COOKWARE NEEDED:

- Mixing Bowl
- Sauté Pan
- Large Pot
- Tongs

TOTAL TIME: 20 MINS
SERVES: 6

STEP 1. FOR THE SAUCE: Combine all the ingredients listed for the sauce into a mixing bowl. Mix well and set aside.

STEP 2. Warm a sauté pan over medium heat then drizzle in olive oil and sauté the chopped garlic for 2-3 mins. Pour the sauce into the pan and bring to a boil, then reduce the heat to low and simmer.

STEP 3. FOR THE NOODLES: Boil a pot of water with a pinch of salt and add a tablespoon of olive oil to keep the noodles from sticking. Toss in the egg noodles and boil for roughly 8 mins, or until the noodles are al dente then drain the water.

STEP 4. Add the noodles into the garlic sauce and toss until the noodles are completely coated in the sauce. Plate and serve hot.

KRAV'N CARBS

SPICY RIGATONI FLORENTINE

STEP 1. Rinse the chicken breasts using vinegar and water then slice them into thin strips. Season the chicken with Cajun seasoning, garlic powder, paprika, black pepper and parsley and mix well. Warm a medium sized pan over medium heat, then drizzle in olive oil and sauté the chicken for 7-8 mins or until the chicken is cooked through and there is no more pink. Remove from the pan and set aside.

STEP 2. In the same pan the chicken was cooked in, combine all the ingredients listed for the sauce (onions, garlic, parsley, tomato paste, chicken stock, heavy cream, butter, crushed red pepper, black pepper, garlic salt, paprika). Simmer the sauce for 10-15 mins, stirring occasionally.

STEP 3. Boil a pot of water with a pinch of salt and add a tablespoon of olive oil to keep the pasta from sticking. Toss in the rigatoni noodles and boil for roughly 8 mins, or until the noodles are al dente then drain the pasta water. Add garlic salt and butter to the pasta and toss to combine well.

STEP 4. Toss the pasta in the sauce until it's completed coated, then add the chicken back into the pan. Add the spinach and wait for it to wilt, then sprinkle in the cheese. Mix well.

STEP 5. Plate and serve hot.

- 2 Chicken Breasts
- 1 teaspoon Cajun Seasoning
- ½ teaspoon Garlic Powder
- ½ teaspoon Paprika
- ½ teaspoon Black Pepper
- 1 teaspoon Parsley, Chopped
- 1 tablespoon Olive Oil
- 4 cups Fresh Spinach
- 2 cups Shredded Italian Blend Cheese

SAUCE
- ½ cup White Onions, Small Diced
- ⅓ cup Minced Garlic
- ⅓ cup Parsley, Chopped
- 1 cup Tomato Paste
- 1 ½ cups Chicken Stock
- 1 ½ cups Heavy Whipping Cream
- 2 tablespoons Unsalted Butter
- 2 tablespoons Crushed Red Pepper
- ½ teaspoon Black Pepper
- ½ teaspoon Garlic Salt
- ½ teaspoon Paprika

PASTA
- Pinch of Salt
- 1 tablespoon Olive Oil
- 1 lb Rigatoni Pasta Noodles
- ¼ teaspoon Garlic Salt
- ½ stick Unsalted Butter

UTENSILS/COOKWARE NEEDED:
- 2 Mixing Bowls
- Medium Sized Pan
- Spatula
- Large Pot

TOTAL TIME: 45 MINS
SERVES: 6

MASHED POTATO & CHICKEN BOWL

- Oil for Frying
- 2 Chicken Breasts
- 1 Egg
- ½ cup Buttermilk
- ¼ cup Hot Sauce
- ½ tablespoon Garlic Powder
- ½ tablespoon Onion Powder
- ½ tablespoon Black Pepper
- ½ tablespoon Paprika
- ½ tablespoon Chipotle Powder

FLOUR MIXTURE

- 3 cups Flour
- 1 teaspoon Black Pepper
- 1 teaspoon Garlic Powder
- 1 teaspoon Onion Powder
- 1 teaspoon Cajun Seasoning

CORN

- 2 tablespoons Unsalted Butter
- 1 can Corn, Drained
- 1 tablespoon Parsley, Chopped
- ½ tablespoon Garlic Salt

GRAVY

- 2 tablespoons Unsalted Butter
- ⅓ cup White Onions, Small Diced
- 1 tablespoon Minced Garlic
- ⅛ cup Flour
- 1 ½ cup Chicken Stock
- ⅓ Heavy Whipping Cream
- 1 teaspoon Crushed Red Pepper
- ½ tablespoon Black Pepper
- ½ Chicken Bouillon Cube
- ¼ tablespoon Browning Sauce

MASHED POTATOES

STEP 1. Preheat frying oil to 350 degrees.

STEP 2. Wash chicken breasts using vinegar and water then cut them into bite-sized pieces. Whisk together egg, buttermilk, hot sauce, garlic powder, onion powder, black pepper, paprika and chipotle powder in a mixing bowl. Place the sliced chicken into the mixture and set aside, preferably in the fridge.

STEP 3. FOR THE FLOUR MIXTURE: Mix together the flour and seasonings listed for the flour mixture and set aside.

STEP 4. FOR THE CORN: Heat the butter in a small saucepan over medium heat. Add the corn, parsley and garlic salt to the pan and cook for 5-10 mins, then remove the corn from the pan and set aside.

STEP 5. FOR THE GRAVY: In the same saucepan the corn was cooked in, melt the butter over medium heat then sauté the onions and garlic for 2-3 mins. Add in the flour and stir, then pour in the chicken stock and allow the gravy to simmer and thicken (about 5 mins). Pour in the heavy cream and add the crushed red pepper, black pepper, chicken bouillon cube and browning sauce. Stir and let the gravy cook for another 5 mins, then reduce the heat to low and simmer.

STEP 6. FOR THE POTATOES: Boil the peeled potatoes in a large pot of water until they are tender then drain the water. Pour the potatoes back into the pot and mash them with butter, heavy cream, garlic paste, garlic powder, garlic salt, black pepper and parsley until smooth. Set aside.

- 4 Small Potatoes, Peeled and Large diced
- 4 tablespoons Unsalted Butter
- 1/3 cup Heavy Whipping Cream
- 1/2 tablespoon Garlic Paste
- 1/2 teaspoon Garlic Powder
- 1/2 teaspoon Garlic Salt
- 3/4 teaspoon Black Pepper
- 1/2 tablespoon Fresh Parsley, Chopped

GARNISH
- Shredded cheese of Your Choice

UTENSILS/COOKWARE NEEDED:
- Frying Pan or Deep Fryer
- Whisk
- 2 Mixing Bowls
- Saucepan
- Large Pot
- Medium Sized Pan
- Potato Masher

STEP 7. Dip the marinated chicken in the flour, then submerge the pieces in the hot oil. Fry for 5-8 mins, or until the chicken is cooked through and there is no more pink. Drain the chicken on a wire rack or paper towels and set aside. Repeat until all the chicken is fried.

STEP 8. FOR ASSEMBLY: Plate in a bowl by starting with a layer of the mashed potatoes at the bottom and adding each cooked ingredient on top of the potatoes (corn, chicken, gravy). Sprinkle the top with cheese and serve hot!

TOTAL TIME: 45 MINS
SERVES: 6

KRAV'N CARBS

LASAGNA ROLLS

STEP 1. Preheat the oven to 400 degrees.

STEP 2. FOR MEAT SAUCE: In a medium sized pan, heat the olive oil on medium-low and sauté the onions and garlic for 2-3 mins. Add the ground turkey and cook for 7-9 mins, or until the meat is cooked through and there's no more pink. Drain the oil from the meat using a strainer, then pour the meat back in the pan and add the tomato sauce, tomato paste, diced tomatoes, garlic powder, onion powder, black pepper, fennel and oregano. Stir, then cover the pan and reduce the heat to low. Leave the sauce to simmer for 15 mins, then remove from heat.

STEP 3. FOR THE RICOTTA: In a mixing bowl combine the ricotta, parsley, parmesan cheese, garlic paste, garlic salt, black pepper and egg with a rubber spatula. Set aside, preferably in the fridge.

STEP 4. FOR THE PASTA: Boil a pot of water with a pinch of salt and add a tablespoon of olive oil to keep the pasta from sticking. Toss in the lasagna noodles and boil for roughly 8 mins, or until the noodles are al dente then drain the pasta water.

STEP 5. FOR ASSEMBLY: Lay out the lasagna noodles on a cutting board then on each individual noodle, spread a layer of the ricotta mixture then a layer of meat sauce, then sprinkle with cheese. Roll the noodles into pinwheel shapes, you should have enough for about 12 lasagna rolls. Spread a layer of meat sauce at the bottom of a casserole dish, then place the lasagna rolls side by side in the dish. Add another layer of cheese then meat sauce, then more cheese on top of the rolls. Cover with foil and bake for 30 mins.

STEP 6. Remove the rolls from the oven and let cool for at least 10 mins before serving.

SERVES: 8-10
TOTAL TIME: 1 HR

- Shredded Mozzarella Cheese, as desired
- Shredded Mild Cheddar Cheese, as desired

MEAT SAUCE
- 1 teaspoon Olive Oil
- ⅓ cup White Onions, Medium Diced
- ⅛ cup Garlic, Chopped
- 1 ½ lbs Ground Turkey or Beef
- ⅛ cup Parsley, Chopped
- 1 cup Tomato Sauce
- 1 cup Tomato Paste
- 2 cups Canned Diced Tomatoes
- 1 teaspoon Garlic Powder
- ½ teaspoon Onion Powder
- 1 teaspoon Black Pepper
- ½ teaspoon Fennel Seeds
- ½ teaspoon Oregano

RICOTTA MIXTURE
- 2 cups Ricotta Cheese
- ⅛ cup Parsley, Chopped
- ½ cup Grated Parmesan Cheese
- 1 tablespoon Garlic Paste
- 1 teaspoon Garlic Salt
- 1 teaspoon Black Pepper
- 1 Egg

PASTA
- Pinch of Salt
- 1 tablespoon Olive Oil
- 1 box Lasagna Pasta Noodles

UTENSILS/COOKWARE NEEDED:
- Medium Pan
- Strainer
- Mixing Bowl
- Spatula
- Small Rubber Spatula
- Large Pot
- Casserole Dish
- Aluminum Foil

CHICKEN ALFREDO LASAGNA

- 4 Large Chicken Breasts
- ¼ teaspoon Garlic Salt
- ¼ teaspoon Blackened Seasoning
- ¼ teaspoon Black Pepper
- 2 teaspoons Olive Oil
- 1 tablespoon Garlic, Chopped
- ½ tablespoon Parsley, Chopped
- 4 cups Spinach
- Shredded Mozzarella Cheese, as desired

ALFREDO SAUCE

- ⅛ cup Parsley, Chopped
- ⅛ cup Cilantro, Chopped
- 3 cloves Fresh Garlic, Chopped
- 4 tablespoons Unsalted Butter
- 2 cups Heavy Whipping Cream
- 1 cup Shredded Parmesan
- 1 cup Shredded Mozzarella
- 1 cup Shredded Italian-Style Cheese Blend
- ⅛ teaspoon Black Pepper
- ½ teaspoon Garlic Powder
- ⅛ teaspoon Garlic Salt

RICOTTA MIXTURE

- 2 cups Ricotta Cheese
- ⅛ cup Parsley, Chopped
- ½ cup Parmesan Cheese, Grated or Shredded
- 1 cup Shredded Mozzarella Cheese
- 1 tablespoon Garlic Paste
- 1 teaspoon Garlic Salt
- 1 teaspoon Black Pepper
- 1 Egg

STEP 1. Preheat the oven to 400 degrees.

STEP 2. Wash the chicken breasts using vinegar and water then cut into thin slices. Place the chicken into a mixing bowl and season with garlic salt, blackened seasoning and black pepper. In a large pan add the olive oil, chopped garlic and parsley and cook over medium heat. Add the chicken and cook 7-9 mins or until the chicken is cooked through and there is no more pink. Toss in the spinach and wilt, then remove everything from the pan and set aside.

STEP 3. FOR THE SAUCE: In the same pan that the chicken and spinach were cooked in, sauté the parsley, cilantro, and garlic over medium-low heat. Melt the butter in the pan then pour in the heavy cream and bring to a slow simmer. Whisk in the parmesan, mozzarella and Italian cheeses, a half cup at a time, until the sauce begins to thicken. Sprinkle in the black pepper, garlic powder and onion powder and stir well. Allow the sauce to continue thickening to a creamy consistency, which should take about 15 mins.

STEP 4. FOR THE RICOTTA: In a mixing bowl combine ricotta, parsley, parmesan cheese, mozzarella cheese, garlic paste, garlic salt, black pepper and egg with a rubber spatula. Set aside, preferably in the fridge.

STEP 5. FOR THE PASTA: Boil a pot of water with a pinch of salt and add a tablespoon of olive oil to keep the pasta from sticking. Toss in the lasagna noodles and boil for roughly 8 mins, or until the noodles are al dente then drain the pasta water.

STEP 6. FOR ASSEMBLY: Spread a layer of alfredo sauce at the bottom of the casserole dish, then lay out lasagna noodles in a single layer and spread a layer of the ricotta mixture. Add a layer of the chicken and spinach mixture then cheese, then alfredo sauce. Repeat for 2-3 more layers, making the final layer noodles, then sauce, then cheese.

PASTA:
- Pinch of Salt
- 1 tablespoon Olive Oil
- 1 box Lasagna Noodles

UTENSILS/COOKWARE NEEDED:
- Mixing Bowls
- Large Sauté Pan
- Spatula
- Whisk
- Small Rubber Spatula
- Large Pot
- Casserole Dish
- Aluminum Foil

TOTAL TIME: 1 HR
SERVES: 6

Cover with foil and bake for 30 mins, remove foil and broil for 5 mins. Keep an eye on it to make sure the top of the lasagna doesn't burn!

STEP 7. Remove the lasagna from the oven and let cool for at least 10-15 mins before serving.

KRAV'N CARBS

LOADED POTATO SOUP

STEP 1. Warm a large pot over medium-low heat. Dice and sauté the bacon until crispy, then remove from the pan and set aside, keeping ⅓ cup of the bacon grease in the pot.

STEP 2. Chop the onions and sauté in the large pot until they're soft, then add the garlic and the flour to create a roux. Cook for 2-3 mins then stir in the heavy cream, chicken stock, butter and sour cream. Small dice the potatoes and pour them into the pot, then season with black pepper, garlic salt, garlic powder, onion powder and bouillon cube. Continue cooking for another 20 mins or until the potatoes are cooked through, stirring occasionally.

STEP 3. Lightly mash the potatoes in the soup, making sure to leave a few chunks. Sprinkle in the cheese and stir until it's melted, then add ½ of the cooked bacon bits back into the pot, leaving the other half for garnish.

STEP 4. Plate the soup in a bowl and garnish with the remaining bacon and more cheddar, serve hot.

- 10-12 slices Bacon (Pork or Turkey)
- ½ cup White Onions, Chopped
- ⅛ cup Garlic, Chopped
- ¼ cup Flour
- 2 cups Heavy Whipping Cream
- 4 cups Chicken Stock
- 2 tablespoons Unsalted Butter
- ⅓ cup Sour Cream
- 4 Small Potatoes
- ½ teaspoon Black Pepper
- ½ teaspoon Garlic Salt
- ½ teaspoon Garlic Powder
- ½ teaspoon Onion Powder
- 1 Bouillon Cube (chicken, vegetable or beef)
- 1 cup Shredded Sharp Cheddar

GARNISH:

- Remaining Bacon
- Shredded Sharp Cheddar

UTENSILS/COOKWARE NEEDED:

- Large Pot
- Spatula
- Potato Masher

TOTAL TIME: 45 MINS

SERVES: 6

ROASTED POTATOES & GREEN BEANS 152

CREAMY SCALLOPED POTATOES 155

GARLIC CHILI GREEN BEANS 156

LOADED MASHED POTATOES 159

POUTINE FRIES 160

BAKED BEANS 163

YELLOW RICE 164

BROCCOLI CHEDDAR RICE CASSEROLE 167

CREAMED SPINACH 168

FRIED CORN 171

RED BEANS AND RICE 172

BLACK EYED PEAS 175

JASMINE RICE 176

GRANNY'S POTATO SALAD 179

ROASTED POTATOES & GREEN BEANS

- 6-10 Red Potatoes
- 1 teaspoon Olive Oil
- ½ teaspoon Garlic Salt
- 4 teaspoons Italian Seasoning
- 2 teaspoons Paprika
- 3 cups Fresh Green Beans
- ½ teaspoon Garlic Powder
- ½ teaspoon Onion Powder
- ½ teaspoon Black Pepper

UTENSILS/COOKWARE NEEDED:

- Baking Dish
- Aluminum Foil
- Mixing Bowl

TOTAL TIME: 40 MINS
SERVES: 3

STEP 1. Preheat the oven to 400 degrees.

STEP 2. Wash and dry the potatoes, then medium dice them and pour the potatoes into a baking dish. Drizzle the potatoes with olive oil and season them with the garlic salt, Italian seasoning and paprika. Mix well, then cover the dish with foil and bake the potatoes for 15-20 mins.

STEP 3. Before adding the green beans, season them in a mixing bowl with the remaining seasonings (garlic powder, onion powder, black pepper) then add the green beans into the baking dish with the potatoes. Roast the potatoes and green beans together for another 20 mins.

STEP 4. Remove the pan from the oven and serve alongside your favorite main dish!

YOU'RE JUST A SIDE

CREAMY SCALLOPED POTATOES

STEP 1. Preheat the oven to 400 degrees.

STEP 2. Wash and dry the potatoes, then slice them and place them into a mixing bowl. Set aside.

STEP 3. FOR THE SAUCE: Warm a saucepan over medium heat, then add the butter and sauté the onions and garlic for 3-5 mins. Sprinkle in the flour, 1 tablespoon at a time, stirring often to create a roux. Pour in the heavy whipping cream and stir, then season the sauce with black pepper, onion powder, garlic powder, garlic salt and parsley. Simmer the sauce for 10-12 more mins, stirring often, until it thickens.

STEP 4. FOR ASSEMBLY: Coat the bottom of the casserole dish with olive oil, then place a layer of the sliced potatoes at the bottom of oiled pan. Sprinkle some mozzarella, parmesan and chives over the potatoes then repeat the layering until all the potatoes are used. On the last layer of cheese and chives, pour the sauce over the potatoes and sprinkle with more cheese.

STEP 5. Cover the pan with foil and bake for 20 mins, then uncover and sprinkle on more cheese. Bake the potatoes another 20-25 mins, or until the potatoes are cooked through and the top is golden-brown and bubbly.

STEP 6. Remove the scalloped potatoes from the oven and let cool for at least 10 mins before serving.

- 10-12 Russet Potatoes, Thinly Sliced
- ½ teaspoon Olive Oil
- Shredded Mozzarella Cheese, As Desired
- Shredded Parmesan Cheese, As Desired
- Grated Parmesan Cheese, As Desired
- Chopped Chives, As Desired

SAUCE

- 4 tablespoons Unsalted Butter
- ½ White Onion, Small Diced
- 1 tablespoon Minced Garlic
- 2 tablespoons Flour
- 2 cups Heavy Whipping Cream
- 1 tablespoon Black Pepper
- 1 tablespoon Onion Powder
- 1 tablespoon Garlic Powder
- ½ tablespoon Garlic Salt
- 1 teaspoon Parsley, Chopped

UTENSILS/COOKWARE NEEDED:

- Mixing Bowl
- Saucepan
- Casserole Dish
- Aluminum Foil

TOTAL TIME: 1 HR
SERVES: 4

GARLIC CHILI GREEN BEANS

- 1 tablespoon Olive Oil
- 4 cups Green Beans
- ⅓ cup Garlic, Chopped
- 3 teaspoons Soy Sauce
- 2 teaspoons Oyster Sauce
- 1 teaspoon Garlic Chili Paste

UTENSILS/COOKWARE NEEDED:
- KitchenEnvy Wok

TOTAL TIME: 20 MINS
SERVES: 3

STEP 1. Warm a wok over medium-high heat, then add the olive oil and green beans to the pan. Sauté for 5-8 mins then add the chopped garlic, soy sauce, oyster sauce and garlic chili paste. Stir and continue cooking another 3-5 mins.

STEP 2. Remove the green beans from the pan and serve hot.

YOU'RE JUST A SIDE

LOADED MASHED POTATOES

STEP 1. Preheat oven to 400 degrees.

STEP 2. Wash the shrimp (in the ingredients section labeled *shrimp*) using vinegar and water, then place them in a mixing bowl. Set aside, preferable over ice or in the fridge.

STEP 3. Peel and dice the potatoes then place them in a pot of water with the bouillon cubes, garlic salt and parsley. Boil the potatoes for 25-35 mins, or until they are fork tender then drain the water and place the cooked potatoes into a separate mixing bowl.

STEP 4. Mash the cooked potatoes with butter and heavy cream, then season them with the garlic paste, garlic powder, and black pepper. Mix well then add ½ cup of the cheddar cheese, the sour cream and ¼ cup of the chives and stir until well-combined. Set aside.

STEP 5. FOR THE SHRIMP: Warm a sauté pan over medium heat then add the butter and parsley. Pour the cleaned shrimp into the pan then season them with Old Bay and garlic and herb seasoning. Cook the shrimp for 3-5 mins, then remove the pan from the heat.

STEP 6. FOR ASSSEMBLY: Coat the bottom of a baking dish with softened butter or spray with non-stick cooking spray, then spread a layer of ½ the mashed potatoes in the pan. Sprinkle on ¼ cup of cheddar cheese, then ⅛ cup of chives and ½ of the cooked shrimp. Repeat the layering one more time with the remaining ingredients (remaining mashed potatoes, ¼ cup cheddar, ⅛ cup chives, remaining shrimp) then place the dish in the oven for 15 mins.

STEP 7. Remove the pan from the oven and let the loaded mashed potatoes cool at least 10 mins before serving.

- 8 Potatoes, Medium Diced
- 2 Chicken Bouillon Cubes
- ¼ teaspoon Garlic Salt
- ½ teaspoon Parsley, Chopped
- ½ stick Unsalted Butter
- ½ cup Heavy Cream
- 1 tablespoon Garlic Paste
- ½ teaspoon Garlic Powder
- ½ teaspoon Black Pepper
- 1 cup Shredded Sharp Cheddar Cheese
- ¼ cup Sour Cream
- ½ cup Chives, Chopped
- Non-stick Cooking Spray

SHRIMP

- ½ lb Shrimp, Peeled and Deveined
- 2 tablespoons Unsalted Butter
- 2 tablespoons Parsley, Chopped
- ½ teaspoon Old Bay Seasoning
- 1 teaspoon Garlic and Herb Seasoning

UTENSILS/COOKWARE NEEDED:

- Mixing Bowls
- Large Pot
- Sauté Pan
- Baking Dish

TOTAL TIME: 1 HR

SERVES: 4

YOU'RE JUST A SIDE

POUTINE FRIES

- 10-12 Potatoes
- 1 teaspoon Olive Oil
- ½ teaspoon Black Pepper
- ½ teaspoon Garlic Salt
- Non-stick Cooking Spray
- 1 bag Cheese Curds

GRAVY

- 4 tablespoons Unsalted Butter
- ⅓ cup Onions, Chopped
- 2 tablespoons Minced Garlic
- 2 tablespoons Flour
- 2 cups Beef Stock
- ¼ cup Worcestershire Sauce
- ¼ teaspoon Black Pepper
- ¼ teaspoon Garlic Powder
- 1 Beef Bouillon Cube

UTENSILS/COOKWARE NEEDED:

- Mixing Bowl
- Baking Sheet
- Parchment Paper
- Saucepan

TOTAL TIME: 45 MINS
SERVES: 4

STEP 1. Preheat the oven to 400 degrees.

STEP 2. Slice the potatoes into fries then place them in a mixing bowl. Drizzle the fries with olive oil and season them with the black pepper and garlic salt.

STEP 3. Line a baking sheet with parchment paper then coat with non-stick cooking spray and pour the fries onto the baking sheet. Roast the fries for 25-30 mins, or until the potatoes are cooked through.

STEP 4. FOR THE GRAVY: Warm a saucepan over medium heat and melt the butter, then sauté the onions and garlic for 3-5 mins. Sprinkle in the flour and stir continuously to create a roux, then pour in the beef stock and Worcestershire sauce. Season the gravy with black pepper, garlic powder and the bouillon cube then stir until the gravy is thickened to your liking.

STEP 5. FOR ASSEMBLY: Plate the fries then place the cheese curds on top of the fries and pour the gravy over the cheese. Serve hot!

YOU'RE JUST A SIDE

FULLY LOADED BAKED BEANS

STEP 1. Warm a large pan over medium heat and drizzle in the olive oil, then sauté the onions, bell pepper and garlic. Add the ground turkey to the pan and season it with paprika, onion powder, garlic powder, black pepper and blackened seasoning. Cook the turkey for 10-12 mins, or until it's cooked through and there is no more pink. Drain the meat and set aside.

STEP 2. Pour the cans of baked beans into a casserole dish add the brown sugar then season them with the Worcestershire sauce, BBQ sauce, Dijon mustard, garlic salt, garlic powder, onion powder, black pepper and cinnamon. Mix well, then add in the cooked ground turkey and stir until well-combined. Cover the casserole dish with foil and bake for 30-35 mins.

STEP 3. Remove the baked beans from the oven and let cool at least 10 mins before serving.

- 2 teaspoons Olive Oil
- 1 cup White Onions, Small Diced
- 1 Bell Pepper, Small Diced
- 2 cloves Garlic, Minced
- 1 lb Ground Turkey or Beef
- 1 teaspoon Paprika
- 1 teaspoon Onion Powder
- 1 teaspoon Garlic Powder
- 1 teaspoon Black Pepper
- 2 teaspoons Blackened Seasoning
- 3-4 cans Baked Beans
- 2 cups Brown Sugar
- 1/3 cup Worcestershire Sauce
- 2 1/2 cups BBQ Sauce
- 1/3 cup Dijon Mustard
- 1/2 tablespoon Garlic Salt
- 1/2 tablespoon Garlic Powder
- 1/2 tablespoon Onion Powder
- 1/2 tablespoon Black Pepper
- 1 teaspoon Ground Cinnamon

UTENSILS/COOKWARE NEEDED:
- Large Pan
- Spatula
- Casserole Dish
- Aluminum Foil

TOTAL TIME: 45
SERVES: 4

YELLOW RICE

- 1 teaspoon Olive Oil
- 1 tablespoon Minced Garlic
- 2 Bay Leaves, Crushed
- 1 teaspoon Mrs. Dash Seasoning
- 1 teaspoon Cumin
- 1 teaspoon Italian Seasoning
- 2 teaspoons Turmeric Powder
- ⅛ teaspoon Garlic Salt
- 3 cups Chicken Stock
- 4 cups Jasmine Rice
- 3 tablespoons Unsalted Butter
- 1 Chicken Bouillon Cube

UTENSILS/COOKWARE NEEDED:

- Saucepan

TOTAL TIME: 30 MINS
SERVES: 4-6

STEP 1. Warm a saucepan over medium heat, then drizzle in the olive oil and sauté the minced garlic for 1 minute. Add the crushed bay leaves, Mrs. Dash, cumin, Italian seasoning, turmeric and garlic salt then stir the ingredients together.

STEP 2. Pour the chicken stock into the pan and continue stirring. Add the rice, butter and chicken bouillon and mix well, then simmer for 1-2 mins. Reduce the heat, cover the pan and continue cooking the rice for 20-25 mins, stirring occasionally. Make sure not to overcook your rice!

STEP 3. Plate and serve hot alongside oxtails or curry.

YOU'RE JUST A SIDE

BROCCOLI CHEDDAR RICE CASSEROLE

STEP 1. Preheat the oven to 400 degrees.

STEP 2. Pour the rice, water and chicken stock into a large pot over medium heat. Add the butter, parsley, garlic salt, black pepper and garlic powder then stir the ingredients together and reduce the heat to low. Cover the pan and simmer the rice for 20 mins, then uncover and add the broccoli into the pan. Stir the broccoli and rice together, then cover the pan again and cook for another 5 mins.

STEP 3. FOR THE CHEESE SAUCE: Warm a saucepan over medium heat, add in the olive oil and butter then sauté the celery, onions and garlic for 3-5 mins. Add in the flour and stir, then pour in the water and heavy cream. Bring to a simmer then season with the chicken bouillon, black pepper, parsley, paprika and onion powder. Add in 3 cups of the cheddar then cook for 5-8 mins, whisking often, until the cheese is melted, and the sauce has thickened.

STEP 4. Pour the cheese sauce into the pot with the broccoli and rice and mix well, then spray a casserole dish with non-stick cooking spray and transfer the mixture into the dish. Sprinkle the top of the casserole with the remainder of the cheese, then cover the casserole dish and bake for 30 mins. The cheese should be melty and the rice and broccoli should be cooked through.

STEP 5. Remove the casserole from the oven and let it cool at least 10 mins before serving.

NOTES: if you don't have chicken bouillon paste, use 1 bouillon cube or 1 tablespoon of bouillon powder instead!

- 3 cups Jasmine Rice
- 2 ½ cups Water
- 3 cups Chicken Stock
- ½ stick Unsalted Butter
- ½ tablespoon Parsley, Chopped
- ½ teaspoon Garlic Salt
- ½ teaspoon Black Pepper
- ½ teaspoon Garlic Powder
- 5 cups Chopped Broccoli, Fresh or Frozen
- Non-stick Cooking Spray
- Cheese Sauce
- 2 teaspoons Olive Oil
- 2 tablespoons Unsalted Butter
- ½ cup Celery, Small Diced
- ½ cup White Onion, Small Diced
- 1 tablespoon Garlic, Chopped
- 3 tablespoons Flour
- 2 cups Water
- 2 cups Heavy Whipping Cream
- 1 tablespoon Chicken Bouillon Paste
- ½ teaspoon Black Pepper
- ½ tablespoon Parsley, Chopped
- ½ teaspoon Paprika
- ½ teaspoon Onion Powder
- 4 cups Shredded Sharp Cheddar Cheese

UTENSILS/COOKWARE NEEDED:
- Large Pot
- Saucepan
- Whisk
- Casserole Dish

TOTAL TIME: 1 ½ HRS
SERVES: 6

CREAMED SPINACH

- 1 teaspoon Olive Oil
- 1/3 cup White Onions, Small Diced
- 1/2 tablespoon Minced Garlic
- 2 tablespoons Unsalted Butter
- 3 tablespoons Flour
- 2 cups Half & Half
- 1 cup Heavy Whipping Cream
- ½ teaspoon Black Pepper
- ½ teaspoon Garlic Salt
- ½ teaspoon Garlic Powder
- 2 Bay Leaves
- 2-10 oz bags Spinach
- ½ cup Parmesan Cheese, Shredded or Grated

UTENSILS/COOKWARE NEEDED:

- Sauté Pan
- Small Pot
- Casserole Dish

TOTAL TIME: 30 MINS

SERVES: 6

STEP 1. Preheat the oven to 400 degrees.

STEP 2. Warm a sauté pan over medium heat, drizzle in the olive oil and sauté the onions and garlic for 3-5 mins. Add the butter and flour then cook for 2 more minutes.

STEP 3. Pour in the half & half and heavy cream and mix well. Season the sauce with the black pepper, garlic salt and garlic powder. Place the bay leaves into the sauce and simmer another 5-8 mins, remembering to remove the bay leaves before adding the spinach.

STEP 4. Boil a pot of water and add in the spinach. Cook for about 1 minute or until it wilts, then drain the spinach and add it to the pan with the sauce. Stir until well combined then pour the creamed spinach into a casserole dish. Sprinkle the top with parmesan cheese and bake for 5-10 mins, or until the cheese is melted.

STEP 5. Remove the creamed spinach from the oven and let cool at least 5 mins before serving!

YOU'RE JUST A SIDE

FRIED CORN

STEP 1. Use a knife to remove the corn kernels from the cob, then place the cut corn into a mixing bowl along with the other chopped veggies (bell peppers, onions, garlic) and set aside.

STEP 2. Warm a large cast iron pan over medium heat and cook the chopped bacon until it's crispy, then drain the bacon bits on paper towels and set aside. Keep the bacon grease in the pan, you'll be using it to fry the corn in!

STEP 3. In the same pan the bacon was cooked in, pour in the corn and veggies from the mixing bowl and add the butter. Season the corn and veggies with the black pepper, garlic powder, onion powder, Cajun seasoning, garlic salt and parsley. Mix well and fry for 10-15 mins, stirring occasionally, then pour in the heavy cream and cook for another 10-15 mins.

STEP 4. Stir in the bacon bits and serve hot!

- 6-8 ears Fresh Corn
- 1 Red Bell Pepper, Small Diced
- 1 Green Bell Pepper, Small Diced
- 1 White Onion, Small Diced
- 1 tablespoon Garlic, Chopped
- 4-8 slices Bacon, Chopped
- 3 tablespoons Unsalted Butter
- 1 tablespoon Black Pepper
- 1 tablespoon Garlic Powder
- 1 tablespoon Onion Powder
- 1 teaspoon Cajun Seasoning
- 1/4 tablespoon Garlic Salt
- 1 tablespoon Parsley, Chopped
- 1/3 cup Heavy Whipping Cream

UTENSILS/COOKWARE NEEDED:

- Mixing Bowl
- Large Cast Iron Pan

TOTAL TIME: 45 MINS

SERVES: 6

HOME-COOKED MEALS CAN BE EASY, FUN, AND VERY REWARDING.

YOU'RE JUST A SIDE

RED BEANS AND RICE

- 1 bag Dried Red Kidney Beans, Soaked
- 1 teaspoon Vegetable Oil
- 1 pack Andouille or Turkey Smoked Sausage, Sliced into Half-Moons
- 1 White Onion, Small Diced
- 3 stalks Celery, Small Diced
- 1 Bell Pepper, Small Diced
- 1 tablespoon Minced Garlic
- 1 Smoked Turkey Leg or Smoked Hamhock
- 5 cups Water
- 5 cups Chicken or Beef Stock
- 2 teaspoons Paprika
- 1 teaspoon Dried Oregano
- 1 teaspoon Garlic Powder
- 1 teaspoon Onion Powder
- 1 teaspoon Black Pepper
- 1 teaspoon Italian Seasoning
- 1 teaspoon Blackened Seasoning
- ¼ teaspoon Cayenne Pepper
- 1 tablespoon Crushed Red Pepper
- 1 teaspoon Cumin
- 2 teaspoons Tomato Bouillon Powder or 1 ½ Tomato Bouillon Cubes
- 3-4 Bay Leaves
- ½ cup Tomato Paste
- 2 cups Cooked White Rice

UTENSILS/COOKWARE NEEDED:

- Mixing Bowl
- Stock Pot

TOTAL TIME: 3 HRS
SERVES: 6

STEP 1. Pour the red kidney beans into a mixing bowl and soak them in water overnight, then drain them the next day and set aside.

STEP 2. Warm a stock pot over medium heat then drizzle in the vegetable oil and sauté the sliced sausage for 10-12 mins, or until the sausage is golden-brown. Remove the sausage from the pot and set aside.

STEP 3. In the same pot the sausage was cooked in sauté the onions, celery, bell peppers and minced garlic for 3-5 mins then add the soaked beans, smoked meat, 3 cups of the water and 3 cups of the chicken stock.

STEP 4. Season the beans with the paprika, oregano, garlic powder, onion powder, black pepper, Italian seasoning, blackened seasoning, cayenne pepper, crushed red pepper, cumin and tomato bouillon then add the bay leaves and tomato paste.

STEP 5. Stir the pot and bring the beans to a boil, then reduce the heat to low and cook for 1 ½-2 hrs, stirring every 30 mins. As the beans cook the liquid will reduce, so make sure to check it and add 1 cup of chicken stock and 1 cup of water as needed.

STEP 6. Once the beans are tender, take the smoked meat out of the pot and remove the meat from the bone then add it back into the pot and stir. Serve over white rice.

YOU'RE JUST A SIDE

BLACK EYED PEAS

STEP 1. Pour the black-eyed peas in a mixing bowl and soak in water at least 3-4 hrs before cooking. Drain the water and rinse the peas.

STEP 2. Pour the black-eyed peas, chicken stock and water into a stockpot. Warm the pot over medium-high heat then add the butter, onions, bell peppers, minced garlic and smoked turkey. Stir the ingredients until well-combined.

STEP 3. Season the black-eyed peas with garlic salt, paprika, black pepper, Old Bay and onion powder. Use a large spoon to thoroughly mix the ingredients in the pot. Cover the stockpot and simmer over medium-low heat for 1 hr, then once the peas are tender, remove the stockpot from the heat.

STEP 4. Use a ladle to scoop the black-eyed peas into serving bowls.

- 1lb bag Dried Black-Eyed Peas, Soaked
- 5 cups Chicken Stock
- 2 ½ cups Water
- 4 tablespoons Unsalted Butter
- ¼ cup White Onions, Chopped
- ¼ cup Bell Peppers, Chopped
- 1 tablespoon Minced Garlic
- 1 Smoked Turkey Leg
- 1 tablespoon Garlic Salt
- ½ tablespoon Paprika
- ½ tablespoon Black Pepper
- 1 tablespoon Old Bay Seasoning
- ½ tablespoon Onion Powder

UTENSILS/COOKWARE NEEDED:

- Mixing Bowl
- Stock Pot
- Long-Handled Spoon

TOTAL TIME: 1 ½ HRS
SERVES: 6

YOU'RE JUST A SIDE

JASMINE RICE

- 6 cups Jasmine Rice
- 6 ½ cups Water
- 3 tablespoons Unsalted Butter
- 4 sprigs Fresh Thyme
- ½ teaspoon Italian Seasoning

UTENSILS/COOKWARE NEEDED:
- Large Pot

TOTAL TIME: 30 MINS

SERVES: 6-10

NOTE: if you don't have fresh thyme, substitute with 1 tablespoon of dried thyme or another teaspoon of Italian seasoning.

STEP 1. Pour the jasmine rice into a large pot. Rinse the rice by filling the pot with water then draining it, continue rinsing until the water runs clear.

STEP 2. Fill a large pot with the 6 ½ cups of water then add the butter, thyme and Italian seasoning. Cover the rice and simmer over medium-low heat for 15-20 mins.

STEP 3. Remove the lid when all the water has evaporated, and the rice looks fluffy. Serve immediately.

GRANNY'S POTATO SALAD

STEP 1. Wash, peel, and medium dice the potatoes. Set aside in a stockpot filled with water and once all the potatoes are diced, drain the water and rinse the diced potatoes.

STEP 2. Refill the pot with more water, enough to cover the potatoes. Add 1 tablespoon of garlic salt to the pot and place it on the stove over medium heat. Boil the diced potatoes for 30-40 mins, or until they're fork-tender, then drain the pot. Pour the potatoes into a large mixing bowl and set them in the freezer or fridge for 10-15 mins, or until the potatoes have cooled down.

STEP 3. Place the eggs in a separate pot of water with 1 tablespoon of salt and boil them for 5-10 mins, then drain the pot and run the boiled eggs under cold water for at least 5 mins. Crack and peel the shells off the boiled eggs then sit them on a paper towel to dry. Once the eggs are peeled, small dice most of them and set aside. Save 2-3 eggs to slice into rounds and set aside for garnish.

STEP 4. Pull the bowl of potatoes out of the fridge or freezer and add in the chopped eggs, bell peppers and onions. Stir everything together using a large spoon or rubber spatula, then pour in the relish, Miracle Whip, mayo and mustard. Season the potato salad with the dill, black pepper, garlic powder, Accent (optional), sugar (optional) and salt (optional). Mix well.

STEP 5. Plate the potato salad family-style and garnish with the sliced egg, paprika and some extra dill. Serve room temp or cold with your favorite BBQ dish!

- 12-15 Small Russet Potatoes
- 1 tablespoon Garlic Salt
- 8-12 Eggs
- 1 tablespoon Salt
- 1 cup Green Bell Pepper, Minced
- ¼ White Onion, Minced
- 2 cups Sweet Relish
- 1 ½ cups Miracle Whip
- ¼ cup Mayonnaise
- 2 tablespoons Yellow Mustard
- 1 tablespoon Dill, Fresh or Dried
- 1 tablespoon + 1 teaspoon Black Pepper
- 1 tablespoon Garlic Powder
- 1 tablespoon Accent Seasoning (optional)
- ½ tablespoon Sugar (optional)
- ½ tablespoon Salt (optional)
- Paprika for Garnish

UTENSILS/COOKWARE NEEDED:

- Large Pot
- Mixing Bowls
- Medium Pot
- Large Spoon or Rubber Spatula

TOTAL TIME: 1 HR

SERVES: 6-10

SWEET HEAT CHICKEN TENDERS 182

CHICKEN & CHEESE ENCHILADAS 185

CHICKEN & CHEESE TAQUITOS 186

BUFFALO CHICKEN DIP 189

BUFFALO CHICKEN FRIES 190

JERK CHICKEN FLATBREAD PIZZA 193

LOADED POTATO SKIN 194

SALMON FLATBREAD PIZZA 197

BIRRIA TACOS 198

CHICKEN BIRRIA TACOS 201

SALMON BOWL 202

MOZZARELLA STICKS 205

LOADED CRUNCH WRAP 206

CRAB CAKES 209

TACO SALAD 210

SPINACH & ARTICHOKE DIP 213

SWEET HEAT CHICKEN TENDERS

- Oil for Frying
- 1 pack Chicken Breast Tenderloins
- ½ teaspoon Garlic Powder
- ½ teaspoon Onion Powder
- ½ teaspoon Black Pepper
- ½ teaspoon Chipotle Powder
- ½ teaspoon Paprika
- 1 cup Buttermilk
- 1 Egg
- ¼ cup Hot Sauce
- Flour Mixture:
- 2 cups Flour
- ½ cup Cornstarch
- ½ teaspoon Garlic Powder
- ½ teaspoon Garlic Salt
- ½ teaspoon Cajun Seasoning
- ½ teaspoon Black Pepper
- Sauce:
- 4 tablespoons Unsalted Butter
- 1 cup Ketchup
- ½ cup Sriracha Sauce
- 1 cup Sweet Chill Sauce
- 1 tablespoon Crushed Red Pepper

UTENSILS/COOKWARE NEEDED:

- Large Frying Pan or Deep Fryer
- Mixing Bowls
- Whisk
- Saucepan
- Tongs

TOTAL TIME: 30 MINS
SERVES: 6

STEP 1. Preheat frying oil to 350 degrees.

STEP 2. Wash the chicken using water and vinegar, then place the chicken in a bowl and season with garlic powder, onion powder, black pepper, chipotle powder and paprika. Set aside, preferably over ice or in the fridge.

STEP 3. In a separate bowl, whisk together the buttermilk, egg and hot sauce. Pour the egg mixture into the bowl with the chicken and mix well.

STEP 4. FOR THE FLOUR MIXTURE: In a Ziplock bag or another bowl, combine all the ingredients listed for the flour mixture and stir. Add the chicken strips into the flour, 4-5 at a time, then back into the egg mixture and back into the flour so the chicken strips have a double coating.

STEP 5. Place the breaded chicken strips into the frying oil for 5-8 mins or until golden brown and cooked through (no more pink). Drain on paper towels or a wire rack and set aside. Repeat until all the chicken strips are cooked. If you start running low on the flour mixture, add more flour and seasonings to the bag.

STEP 6. FOR THE SAUCE: in a small saucepan, mix together the butter, ketchup, sriracha, sweet chili sauce and crushed red pepper. Simmer for 3-5 mins, then toss the cooked chicken strips in the pan with the sauce until they're fully coated.

STEP 7. Plate and serve hot.

NOTE: If you want the sauce spicier, add more sriracha. If you want it thinner, add more butter.

SIMPLY SNACKIN'

CHICKEN & CHEESE ENCHILADAS

STEP 1. Preheat the oven to 375 degrees.

STEP 2. Wash the chicken using water and vinegar, then dice the chicken into small pieces and place them in a mixing bowl. Season the pieces of chicken with salsa verde, black pepper, garlic powder, onion powder, garlic salt, parsley and pollo seasoning. Mix well and set aside, preferably over ice or in the fridge.

STEP 3. Warm a sauté pan with olive oil over medium heat, then place the seasoned chicken in the pan. Cook for 8-12 mins or until the chicken is cooked through (no more pink). Remove the chicken from the pan and place it in a bowl with a teaspoon of the enchilada sauce.

STEP 4. FOR ASSEMBLY: Pour some enchilada sauce in the bottom of a baking dish then warm the tortillas in the microwave before rolling the enchiladas, this will help the tortillas roll easier and not break. Lay the tortillas down and add a tablespoon of the chicken mixture, then a tablespoon of cheese and roll the tortillas around the filling. Place the enchiladas tightly next to each other inside the baking dish. Repeat until all the filling is used. Pour the remaining enchilada sauce over top then add more cheese and the green onions/cilantro.

STEP 5. Bake for 35 mins or until the cheese is melted and bubbly. Remove the enchiladas from the oven and let cool for at least 10 mins, then plate and serve hot.

- 1 lb Chicken Breast Tenderloins
- 1 cup Salsa Verde
- ½ teaspoon Black Pepper
- ½ teaspoon Garlic Powder
- ½ teaspoon Onion Powder
- ⅛ teaspoon Garlic Salt
- 1 tablespoon Parsley, Chopped
- ½ teaspoon Pollo Seasoning
- 1 tablespoon Olive Oil
- 1 block Oaxaca Cheese
- 1 can Enchilada Sauce, Green or Red Small Tortillas, Corn or Flour
- 2 tablespoons Green Onions or Cilantro, Chopped

UTENSILS/COOKWARE NEEDED:

- 2 Mixing Bowls
- Sauté Pan
- Small Rubber Spatula
- Large Baking Dish

TOTAL TIME: 1 HR
SERVES: 6

NOTE: If desired, you can add beans to the chicken mixture before rolling your enchiladas!

SIMPLY SNACKIN'

CHICKEN & CHEESE TAQUITOS

- Oil for Frying
- 1 lb Chicken Breast Tenderloins
- 1 cup Salsa Verde
- ½ teaspoon Black Pepper
- ½ teaspoon Garlic Powder
- ½ teaspoon Onion Powder
- ⅛ teaspoon Garlic Salt
- 1 tablespoon Parsley, Chopped
- ½ teaspoon Pollo Seasoning
- 1 tablespoon Olive Oil
- Corn Tortillas
- 1 block Oaxaca Cheese, shredded
- Garnish (optional):
- Sour cream
- Cilantro
- Guacamole
- Salsa
- Nacho cheese

UTENSILS/COOKWARE NEEDED:

- Large frying pan or deep fryer
- Mixing Bowl
- Sauté Pan
- Small Rubber Spatula
- Tongs

TOTAL TIME: 45 MINS
SERVES: 6

STEP 1. Preheat frying oil to 350 degrees.

STEP 2. Wash the chicken using water and vinegar, then dice the chicken into small pieces and place them in a mixing bowl. Season the pieces of chicken with salsa verde, black pepper, garlic powder, onion powder, garlic salt, parsley and pollo seasoning. Mix well and set aside, preferably over ice or in the fridge.

STEP 3. Warm a sauté pan with olive oil over medium heat, then place the seasoned chicken in the pan. Cook for 8-12 mins or until the chicken is cooked through (no more pink). Remove from the pan and set aside.

STEP 4. FOR ASSEMBLY: Warm the tortillas in the microwave before rolling the taquitos, this will help the tortillas roll easier and not break. Lay the tortillas down and add a tablespoon of the chicken mixture, then a tablespoon of cheese and roll the tortillas around the filling. Repeat until all the filling is used.

STEP 5. Place the rolled taquitos in the frying oil and cook until golden brown. Plate with garnish and serve hot.

SIMPLY SNACKIN'

BUFFALO CHICKEN DIP

STEP 1. Preheat oven to 350 degrees.

STEP 2. Wash the chicken breasts using water and vinegar, then place them in a pot with the bouillon cubes and parsley. Add enough water to the pot to cover the chicken, then put a lid on the pot and cook over medium heat for 25-30 mins or until the chicken is cooked through (no more pink). The chicken should also be tender enough to shred.

STEP 3. Remove the chicken from the pot, transfer it to a bowl and shred it using 2 forks. Add in the cream cheese, buffalo sauce, green onions, 1 cup of mozzarella cheese, 1 cup of Colby jack cheese, and the ranch seasoning. Mix well until all the chicken is coated.

STEP 4. Pour the mixture into a baking dish and top with the remaining cheese, then bake for 15 mins or until the dip is bubbly and the cheese is fully melted.

STEP 5. Plate and serve with tortilla chips.

- 3 Chicken Breasts
- 2 Chicken Bouillon Cubes
- 1 tablespoon Parsley, Chopped
- 4-6 cups Water
- 1-8 oz stick Cream Cheese, Softened
- 1 cup Buffalo Sauce
- ½ cup Green Onions, Chopped
- 1 ⅓ cup Shredded Mozzarella Cheese
- 1 ⅓ cup Shredded Colby Jack Cheese
- 1 Ranch Seasoning Packet

UTENSILS/COOKWARE NEEDED:

- Small Pot
- Baking Dish
- Small Rubber Spatula
- Mixing bowl

TOTAL TIME: 45 MINS
SERVES: 6

I DEVELOPED A LOVE AND PASSION FOR COOKING IN MY GRANDMOTHER'S KITCHEN.

SIMPLY SNACKIN'

BUFFALO CHICKEN FRIES

- 3 Chicken Breasts
- 2 Chicken Bouillon Cubes
- 1 tablespoon Parsley, Chopped
- 4-6 cups Water
- 1-8 oz stick Cream Cheese, Softened
- 1 cup Buffalo Sauce
- ½ cup Green Onions, Chopped
- 1 cup Shredded Mozzarella Cheese
- 1 cup Shredded Colby Jack Cheese
- 1 Ranch Seasoning Packet
- Oil for Frying
- Breading:
- 3 eggs
- 1 ½ cups flour
- 1 ½ cups breadcrumbs

UTENSILS/COOKWARE NEEDED:

- Large Pot
- Mixing Bowl
- Small Rubber Spatula
- Glass Baking Dish
- Parchment Paper
- Large Frying Pan or Deep Fryer

TOTAL TIME: 1 HR
SERVES: 6

STEP 1. Wash the chicken breasts using water and vinegar, then place them in a pot with the bouillon cubes and parsley. Add enough water to the pot to cover the chicken, then put a lid on the pot and cook over medium heat for 25-30 mins or until the chicken is cooked through (no more pink). The chicken should also be tender enough to shred.

STEP 2. Remove the chicken from the pot, transfer it to a bowl and shred it using 2 forks. Add in the cream cheese, buffalo sauce, green onions, mozzarella cheese, colby jack cheese, and the ranch seasoning. Mix well until all the chicken is coated.

STEP 3. Line a glass baking dish with parchment paper then press the chicken mixture into the dish, creating one flat layer. Freeze for 1-2 hrs or until the mixture is completely stiff.

STEP 4. Preheat frying oil to 350 degrees.

STEP 5. Take the chicken mixture out of the freezer, then pull it out of the parchment paper and place it on a cutting board. Cut the mixture into rectangles, similar to the size of mozzarella sticks, and set aside.

STEP 6. FOR THE BREADING: Pour the flour, egg, and breadcrumbs into 3 separate bowls to bread the fries. Dip the fries into the flour, then the egg then the breadcrumbs and fry for 2-3 mins or until golden-brown. Drain on paper towels or a wire rack and set aside. Repeat the process until all the chicken fries are done.

STEP 7. Plate and serve hot.

SIMPLY SNACKIN'

JERK CHICKEN FLATBREAD PIZZA

STEP 1. Preheat the oven to 375 degrees.

STEP 2. FOR THE JERK MARINADE: Use gloves to remove the seeds and chop the scotch bonnets, if you like really spicy jerk sauce, leave the seeds in. Toss the scotch bonnets into a blender, then add the green onions, thyme, white onions, pimento seeds, brown sugar, garlic cloves, ginger, cinnamon, nutmeg, garlic salt, black pepper, browning sauce, lemon juice, olive oil and water. Blend until the sauce is smooth then pour the marinade into a mixing bowl and set 1 cup of the marinade to the side in a separate bowl.

STEP 3. Chop the red onions and bell peppers then place them in the bowl with the jerk marinade.

STEP 4. Wash the chicken tenderloins using water and vinegar, then cut them into small chunks. Place the diced chicken in the bowl with the veggies and jerk marinade, then mix until all the chicken is coated in the sauce. Marinate at least 15 mins.

STEP 5. Warm a large pan over medium-low heat, then add the olive oil to sauté the veggies and marinated chicken for 10-15 mins or until the chicken is cooked through (no more pink).

STEP 6. Place the flatbread on a baking sheet then brush it with olive oil and the jerk sauce that was set aside. Sprinkle ½ of the cheese on top of the jerk sauce, then layer on the jerk chicken and veggies and top with more cheese. Bake for 15 mins or until the cheese is melted.

STEP 7. Cut, plate and serve hot.

- ½ Red Onion, Small Diced
- ½ Red Bell Pepper, Small Diced
- ½ Green Bell Pepper, Small Diced
- 3 Chicken Tenderloins
- 1 teaspoon Olive Oil
- 1 Flatbread
- ½ cup Shredded Mozzarella Cheese
- ½ cup Shredded Cheddar Cheese
- Jerk Marinade:
- 4 Scotch Bonnet Peppers
- 4 Green Onions, Cut in Half
- 6-8 sprigs Fresh Thyme, Stem Removed
- ½ White Onion, Sliced
- ⅛ cup Pimento Seeds or Black Peppercorns
- ¾ cup Brown Sugar
- 6-8 Garlic Cloves
- 1 ½ tablespoons Fresh Ginger, Sliced
- 1 tablespoon Cinnamon
- 1 tablespoon Nutmeg
- ½ teaspoon Garlic Salt
- 1 tablespoon Black Pepper
- ½ tablespoon Browning Sauce
- ½ tablespoon Lemon Juice
- 1 tablespoon Olive Oil
- ¼ cup Water

UTENSILS/COOKWARE NEEDED:

- Blender
- Mixing Bowls
- Large Pan
- Small Rubber Spatula
- Baking Sheet
- Pastry Brush

TOTAL TIME: 45 MINS
SERVES: 4

SIMPLY SNACKIN'

LOADED POTATO SKIN

- 5 Small-Medium Sized Potatoes
- 1 tablespoon Olive Oil
- ¼ cup Heavy Whipping Cream
- ½ cup Shredded Cheddar Cheese
- 2 tablespoons Unsalted Butter
- ⅛ teaspoon Garlic Salt
- 1 teaspoon Garlic Paste
- ½ teaspoon Black Pepper
- Garnish
- Sprinkle of Shredded Cheddar Cheese
- Sprinkle of Bacon Bits, Fresh or Store-Bought
- Sprinkle of Green Onions, Sliced

UTENSILS/COOKWARE NEEDED:

- Aluminum Foil
- Mixing Bowls
- Baking Dish
- Potato Masher

TOTAL TIME: 1 HR
SERVES: 5

STEP 1. Preheat the oven to 400 degrees. Wash and poke the potatoes with a fork, then rub them with oil and roll them loosely in foil. Bake for 30-35 mins or until the potatoes are soft. Remove the potatoes from the oven and let them cool for at least 10 mins, or until they are cool enough for you to hold in your hand.

STEP 2. Cut the potatoes in half and scoop out most of the white flesh of the potato into a mixing bowl, leaving about half an inch still in the skins. Set the skins to the side in a baking dish. To the bowl of cooked potatoes, add the heavy cream, cheese, butter and seasonings. Mash together until the potatoes are smooth.

STEP 3. FOR ASSEMBLY: Put 2-3 tablespoons of the potato filling back into the skins, then top with more cheddar cheese, bacon bits, and green onions. Bake for 25 mins or until the cheese is melted and bubbly.

STEP 4. Plate and serve hot!

SIMPLY SNACKIN'

SALMON FLATBREAD PIZZA

STEP 1. Preheat the oven to 375 degrees

STEP 2. Wash the salmon using water and vinegar, then pat dry. Warm a large pan over medium heat then place the salmon in the pan with the butter. Cook for 5 mins, flipping the salmon over halfway through. Start to break up the salmon with a spatula, then add the seasonings. Sauté the salmon for another 2-3 mins, then remove it from the pan and set aside.

STEP 3. FOR THE SAUCE: In the same pan the salmon was cooked in, pour in all the ingredients listed for the sauce and whisk until well-blended.

STEP 4. FOR ASSEMBLY: Place the flatbread on a baking sheet then brush with olive oil and some of the cream sauce. Sprinkle ½ of the shredded cheese on top of the cream sauce, then sprinkle on the red onions and green bell peppers. Add the salmon and arugula, then top with the sliced mozzarella cheese. Bake for 15 mins or until the cheese is melted.

STEP 5. Cut, plate and serve hot.

- 1 Salmon Filet, Skin Removed
- 2 tablespoons Unsalted Butter
- ½ teaspoon Cajun Seasoning
- ½ teaspoon Garlic Powder
- ½ teaspoon Onion Powder
- ½ teaspoon Black Pepper
- 1 Flatbread
- 1 teaspoon Olive Oil
- ¼ cup Shredded Mozzarella Cheese
- ¼ cup Red Onion, Small Diced
- ½ cup Green Bell Peppers, Small Diced
- Sprinkle of Arugula
- 1-8 oz ball Fresh Mozzarella Cheese, Sliced
- Cream Sauce
- ¾ cup Heavy Whipping Cream
- 2 tablespoons Unsalted Butter
- ½ teaspoon Cajun Seasoning
- ½ teaspoon Garlic Powder
- ½ teaspoon Onion Powder
- ½ teaspoon Black Pepper
- ¾ cup Shredded Mozzarella Cheese

UTENSILS/COOKWARE NEEDED:

- Large Pan
- Spatula
- Whisk
- Baking Sheet

SERVES: 6
TOTAL TIME: 30 MINS

SIMPLY SNACKIN'

BIRRIA TACOS

- 1 Whole Beef Chuck Roast
- 8 Whole Garlic Cloves
- ½ White Onion
- 4-5 Bay Leaves
- 1 tablespoon Garlic Salt
- 4-6 cups Water
- Corn Tortillas
- Oaxaca Cheese, Shredded

SAUCE:
- 2 cups Dried Chile de Arbol
- 2 cups Dried California Chiles
- 2 cups Dried Guajillo Chiles
- 5 Roma Tomatoes
- 8 Whole Garlic Cloves
- ¼ cup Fresh Ginger, Sliced
- 1 Tomato Bouillon Cube
- 1 Cinnamon Stick
- 5 Whole Cloves
- 1 teaspoon Paprika
- 2 teaspoons Cumin
- 1 teaspoon Pollo Seasoning
- 1 teaspoon Chili Powder
- 1 teaspoon Italian Seasoning
- 1 teaspoon Black Pepper
- 2 teaspoons Garlic Salt
- 2 teaspoons Garlic Powder
- Liquid from Rehydrating the Chiles
- Garnish
- Diced Onion
- Cilantro

UTENSILS/COOKWARE NEEDED:
- Large Pot
- Medium Pot
- Blender
- Strainer
- Mixing Bowls
- Large Skillet or Griddle

TOTAL TIME: 3-4 HRS
SERVES: 8-10

STEP 1. Wash the beef roast using vinegar and water, then pat dry and cut into 6 large pieces. Place the beef in a large pot then add the garlic cloves, onion, bay leaves and garlic salt. Pour enough water in the pot to cover the beef. Put a lid on the pot and cook for 45 mins-1 hr.

STEP 2. FOR THE SAUCE: Warm a medium sized pot of water over medium heat. Cut and remove the seeds from the dried chilis, then place them in the pot of water along with the Roma tomatoes and garlic cloves. Boil for 20-25 mins or until the tomatoes and garlic are soft and the chilis are rehydrated. Remove everything but the liquid from the pot and place the chilis, garlic and tomatoes in a blender. Add all the other ingredients listed for the sauce into the blender, pouring in some of the liquid from the chilis and tomatoes, 1 cup at a time until the sauce is smooth. The sauce should not be the consistency of a soup, so make sure not to add too much liquid.

STEP 3. Remove the garlic cloves, bay leaves and onion from the pot the beef is cooking in then strain the blended chili sauce over the pot the beef is in. Stir, cover, and continue cooking the beef for another 1-2 hrs or until the beef is fork tender. Skim the fat off the top of the sauce using a large spoon and remove the beef from the pot, then place it in a large mixing bowl and use 2 forks to shred the meat. You can also chop it up on a cutting board.

STEP 4. FOR ASSEMBLY: Oil a large skillet or griddle pan and warm over medium-high heat, then lay down the corn tortillas. Pour 2 tablespoons of the sauce onto each tortilla and sprinkle some cheese onto half of the tortilla, then place some of the shredded beef on top of the cheese and fold the other half of the tortilla over it, forming a taco. Cook for 3-5 mins then flip the tacos over to ensure they get brown on both sides. Remove the tacos from the pan and set aside, then repeat the process until you've used all but about 2 cups of the shredded beef.

STEP 5. Place the remaining shredded beef into small side bowls then pour some sauce over the top to fill the bowl. Garnish with diced onions and fresh cilantro and serve as a dipping sauce on the side of your tacos.

SIMPLY SNACKIN'

CHICKEN BIRRIA TACOS

STEP 1. Wash the chicken breast using vinegar and water, then pat dry and place it in a large pot. Add the garlic cloves, onion, bay leaves and garlic salt, then pour enough water in the pot to cover the chicken. Put a lid on the pot and cook for 30-45 mins.

STEP 2. FOR THE SAUCE: Warm a medium sized pot of water over medium heat. Cut and remove the seeds from the dried chilis, then place them in the pot of water along with the Roma tomatoes and garlic cloves. Boil for 20-25 mins or until the tomatoes and garlic are soft and the chilis are rehydrated. Remove everything but the liquid from the pot and place the chilis, garlic and tomatoes in a blender. Add all the other ingredients listed for the sauce into the blender, pouring in some of the liquid from, the chilis and tomatoes, 1 cup at a time until the sauce is smooth. The sauce should not be the consistency of a soup, so make sure not to add too much of the liquid.

STEP 3. Remove the garlic cloves, bay leaves and onion from the pot the chicken is cooking in then strain the blended chili sauce over the chicken. Stir, cover the soup and continue cooking the chicken for another 30 mins-1 hr or until the chicken is fork tender. Skim the fat off the top of the soup using a large spoon and remove the chicken from the pot, then place it in a large mixing bowl and use 2 forks to shred the meat. You can also chop it up on a cutting board.

STEP 4. FOR ASSEMBLY: Oil a large skillet or griddle pan and warm over medium-high heat, then lay down the corn tortillas. Pour 2 tablespoons of the sauce onto each tortilla and sprinkle some cheese onto half of the tortilla, then place some of the shredded chicken on top of the cheese and fold the other half of the tortilla over it, forming a taco. Cook for 3-5 mins then flip the tacos over to ensure they get brown on both sides. Remove the tacos from the pan and set aside, then repeat the process until you've used all but about 2 cups of the shredded chicken.

STEP 5. Place the remaining shredded chicken into small side bowls then pour some sauce over the top to fill the bowl. Garnish with diced onions and fresh cilantro and serve as a dipping sauce on the side of your tacos.

- 2 Large Chicken Breasts
- 8 Whole Garlic Cloves
- ½ White Onion
- 4-5 Bay Leaves
- 1 tablespoon Garlic Salt
- 3-4 cups Water
- Oaxaca Cheese, Shredded
- Corn Tortillas

SAUCE:

- 2 cups Dried Chile de Arbol
- 2 cups Dried California Chiles
- 2 cups Dried Guajillo Chiles
- 5 Roma Tomatoes
- 8 Whole Garlic Cloves
- ¼ cup Fresh Ginger, Sliced
- 1 Tomato Bouillon Cube
- 1 Cinnamon Stick
- 5 Whole Cloves
- 1 teaspoon Paprika
- 2 teaspoons Cumin
- 1 teaspoon Pollo Seasoning
- 1 teaspoon Chili Powder
- 1 teaspoon Italian Seasoning
- 1 teaspoon Black Pepper
- 2 teaspoons Garlic Salt
- 2 teaspoons Garlic Powder
- Liquid from Rehydrating the Chiles
- Garnish
- Diced Onion
- Cilantro

UTENSILS/COOKWARE NEEDED:

- Large Pot
- Medium Pot
- Blender
- Strainer
- Small Rubber Spatula
- Mixing Bowls
- Large Skillet or Griddle

TOTAL TIME: 2-3 HRS

SERVES: 8-10

SIMPLY SNACKIN'

SALMON BOWL

- 2 Salmon Filets
- 1 teaspoon Blackened Seasoning
- 1 teaspoon Black Pepper
- 1 teaspoon Garlic Powder
- 1 teaspoon Onion Power
- 1 teaspoon Lemon Juice
- 1 teaspoon Olive Oil
- 2 cups Cooked White or Jasmine Rice (see pg. 176)
- 1 cup Shredded Carrots
- ½ English Cucumber, Sliced
- 1 Avocado, Sliced
- 1 teaspoon Parsley, Chopped
- Sauce:
- ½ cup Mayonnaise
- ¼ cup Sriracha Sauce
- 2 teaspoons Sesame Oil

UTENSILS/COOKWARE NEEDED:

- Mixing Bowls
- Sauté Pan
- Spatula

TOTAL TIME: 20 MINS
SERVES: 2

NOTE: Every part of this bowl is beautiful yet simple, so don't be afraid to get creative with your plating

STEP 1. Wash the salmon using water and vinegar, then cut it into medium chunks and place the chunks in a mixing bowl. Season the salmon with blackened seasoning, black pepper, garlic powder, onion powder and lemon juice.

STEP 2. Warm a sauté pan over medium-high heat and add the olive oil, then cook the salmon chunks for 5-8 mins or until they are cooked through. Remove the salmon from the pan and set aside.

STEP 3. FOR THE SAUCE: In a small mixing bowl combine the mayo, sriracha and sesame oil. Mix well and set aside.

STEP 4. FOR ASSEMBLY: Plate the cooked rice at the bottom of a serving bowl then place some salmon, shredded carrots, sliced cucumber, avocado and parsley over the rice. Drizzle on the sauce and serve.

SIMPLY SNACKIN'

MOZZARELLA STICKS

STEP 1. Preheat frying oil to 350-375 degrees.

STEP 2. In 3 separate bowls have your flour, egg and breadcrumbs ready. Dip the mozzarella sticks in the flour, then egg, then breadcrumbs and place them in the frying oil. Cook for 5-8 mins or until the cheese sticks are golden-brown. Drain them on paper towels or over a wire rack and set aside. Repeat until all the mozzarella sticks are fried.

STEP 3. Plate and serve with marinara sauce.

- Oil for Frying
- 2 cups Flour
- 3 Eggs
- 2 cups Breadcrumbs
- 1 pack Mozzarella Cheese Sticks

UTENSILS/COOKWARE NEEDED:

- Large Frying Pan or Deep Fryer
- Mixing Bowls

TOTAL TIME: 20 MINS
SERVES: 4

> MY PLEASURE COMES FROM GIVING. **I LOVE TO COOK FOR OTHERS** AND SEE THE SATISFACTION ON THEIR FACES **WHEN THEY TAKE A BITE** OF MY FOOD.

SIMPLY SNACKIN'

LOADED CRUNCH WRAP

- 1 lb Ground Turkey or Beef
- 1 teaspoon Paprika
- ¼ teaspoon Garlic Salt
- 1 teaspoon Cumin
- 1 teaspoon Chili Powder
- 1 teaspoon Onion Powder
- 1 teaspoon Old Bay Seasoning
- 1 teaspoon Cajun Seasoning
- 1 teaspoon Cayenne Pepper
- 1 teaspoon Olive Oil
- 4-6 Tostada Shells
- Large Flour Tortillas
- Nacho Cheese Sauce
- Sour Cream
- Shredded Cheese
- Shredded Lettuce

UTENSILS/COOKWARE NEEDED:

- Mixing Bowls
- Sauté Pan
- Spatula

TOTAL TIME: 40 MINS
SERVES: 4

NOTES: This is a great way to spice up your Taco Tuesday leftovers!

STEP 1. .In a mixing bowl, combine the ground turkey with all the seasonings listed and mix well. Warm a sauté pan over medium heat and add the olive oil, then cook the seasoned ground turkey for 10-12 mins or until the meat is cooked through and there's no more pink. Remove from the pan and set aside.

STEP 2. FOR ASSEMBLY: Take a tostada shell and place it in the center of a large flour tortilla then use a knife to cut around the tostada shell, creating a small flour tortilla that's the same size as the tostada shell. On another large flour tortilla, place ¼ cup of ground turkey in the middle then pour 2 tablespoons of the nacho cheese on top and spread it around. Place the tostada shell on top of the meat and cheese, then spread a thin layer of sour cream on top of the tostada shell. Add about 3 tablespoons of shredded cheese and shredded lettuce, then place the small flour tortilla cut-out on top. Fold the sides of the larger flour tortilla around the filling, flipping it over to ensure the crunch wrap stays together.

STEP 3. Warm a clean sauté pan or griddle over medium heat, coat the pan with olive oil then sear the crunch wrap. Make sure to place it in the pan with the folded side down first to seal the tortilla around the filling. Once both sides are golden brown, remove the crunch wrap from the pan.

STEP 4. Cut, plate and serve with your favorite toppings.

SIMPLY SNACKIN'

CRAB CAKES

STEP 1. Preheat frying oil to 350 degrees.

STEP 2. In a mixing bowl, whisk together all the wet ingredients (egg, Worcestershire sauce, mayo, Dijon and lemon juice) then add the Old Bay, garlic salt and chives, mix well.

STEP 3. Pour in the crab meat and crackers and stir, then add in the breadcrumbs. Form the mixture into balls and flatten them in your hands, forming the crab cakes.

STEP 4. Place the cakes into the frying oil and cook for 3-5 mins on each side. Drain on paper towels or a wire rack and set aside. Repeat until all the crab cakes are cooked.

STEP 5. Plate and serve hot.

- Oil for Frying
- 1 Egg
- 1 tablespoon Worcestershire Sauce
- ½ cup Mayonnaise
- ⅓ cup Dijon Mustard
- 1 teaspoon Lemon Juice
- 1 tablespoon Old Bay Seasoning
- 1 teaspoon Garlic Salt
- 1 tablespoon Chives
- 2 cans Jumbo Lump Crab
- 1 cup Crushed Butter Crackers
- ½ cup Breadcrumbs

UTENSILS/COOKWARE NEEDED:

- Large Frying Pan or Deep Fryer
- Spatula
- Mixing bowl

TOTAL TIME: 30 MINS
SERVES: 4

NOTE: If you want the crab cakes to be extra crispy, crush up some extra crackers and dip the crab cakes into the breadcrumbs.

SIMPLY SNACKIN'

TACO SALAD

- 1 lb Ground Turkey or Beef
- 1 teaspoon Paprika
- ¼ teaspoon Garlic Salt
- 1 teaspoon Cumin
- 1 teaspoon Chili Powder
- 1 teaspoon Onion Powder
- 1 teaspoon Old Bay Seasoning
- 1 teaspoon Cajun Seasoning
- 1 teaspoon Cayenne Pepper
- 1 teaspoon Olive Oil
- 1 pack Ready-Made Corn Tortilla Taco Bowls
- Toppings (optional)
- Shredded Lettuce
- Shredded Cheese
- Cherry Tomatoes, Sliced in Half
- Sour Cream
- Guacamole

UTENSILS/COOKWARE NEEDED:

- Mixing Bowls
- Spatula
- Sauté Pan
- Small Rubber Spatula

TOTAL TIME: 30 MINS

SERVES: 4

NOTE: All the toppings are optional, so choose your favorites!

STEP 1. In a mixing bowl, combine the ground turkey with all the seasonings listed and mix well. Warm a sauté pan over medium heat and add the olive oil, then cook the seasoned ground turkey for 10-12 mins or until the meat is cooked through and there's no more pink. Remove from the pan and set aside.

STEP 2. FOR ASSEMBLY: Place one of the ready-made taco bowls on a plate then add some lettuce, ground turkey, shredded cheese, tomatoes and top with sour cream and guacamole. Serve with a side of black beans or Spanish rice.

SIMPLY SNACKIN'

SPINACH & ARTICHOKE DIP

STEP 1. Preheat the oven to 400 degrees.

STEP 2. Drain the liquid from the spinach and chop into bite-sized pieces, then place the chopped spinach into a mixing bowl. Repeat the same process for the artichoke hearts, placing the chopped artichokes in the same mixing bowl as the spinach.

STEP 3. Add the remaining ingredients listed into the mixing bowl and stir everything together until well-combined.

STEP 4. Pour the mixture into a small cast iron pan or baking dish and place the pan in the oven for 15 mins, or until the dip is bubbly and starting to brown on the top.

STEP 5. Remove the dip from the oven and let cool at least 5 mins before plating, serve with tortilla chips.

- 1 bag Frozen Spinach, Thawed
- 1 can of Artichoke Hearts
- 8 oz Cream Cheese, Softened
- 1 cup Shredded Mozzarella Cheese
- ½ cup Shredded Parmesan Cheese
- ½ teaspoon Garlic Powder
- ½ teaspoon Onion Powder

UTENSILS/COOKWARE NEEDED:

- Mixing bowl
- Small Rubber Spatula
- Small Cast Iron Pan or Small Baking Dish

TOTAL TIME: 30 MINS

SERVES: 4

SIMPLY SNACKIN'

SWEET POTATO PIE 216

CORNBREAD DRESSING 219

GARLIC & HERB TURKEY 220

HONEY PINEAPPLE BAKED HAM 223

COLLARD GREENS 224

MAC AND CHEESE 227

CANDIED YAMS 228

SOUTHERN GRAVY 231

HONEY BUTTER CORNBREAD 232

HERB ROASTED CORNISH HENS 235

BEEF POT ROAST 236

GRANNY'S FRIED CHICKEN 239

WHOLE SPICED CHICKEN 240

SWEET POTATO PIE

- 3 Large Sweet Potatoes
- 4 tablespoons Unsalted Butter
- 1 ½ cups White Sugar
- 1 ⅓ cup Brown Sugar
- 1 ½ tablespoons Vanilla Extract
- 1 ½ teaspoon Ground Nutmeg
- 1 tablespoon Ground Cinnamon
- ⅓ cup Melted Unsalted Butter
- ⅔ cup Self-Rising Flour
- ¾ cup Sweetened Condensed Milk
- ⅓ cup Half & Half
- 3 Eggs
- 3-4 Pre-Made Pie Crusts

UTENSILS/COOKWARE NEEDED:

- Large Pot
- Mixing Bowl
- Masher
- Hand Mixer
- Small Rubber Spatula
- Baking Sheet

TOTAL TIME: 1 HR
SERVES: 8-10

STEP 1. Preheat the oven to 350 degrees.

STEP 2. Wash the sweet potatoes then place them in a large pot of water. Add the 4 tablespoons of butter and cook the sweet potatoes for 45 mins-1 hr, or until they are fork tender.

STEP 3. Drain the water and allow the sweet potatoes to cool at least 10 mins, or until they are cool enough for you to peel off the skins. Remove the skins and place the cooked peeled sweet potatoes in a large mixing bowl. Mash the sweet potatoes with a masher then use the hand mixer to make them smooth.

STEP 4. Add in the white sugar, brown sugar, vanilla extract, nutmeg, and cinnamon. Continue mixing the ingredients together, then scrape down the sides of the bowl and pour in the melted butter. Stir the filling again, making sure to scrape down the sides of the bowl again, then mix in the flour, condensed milk, and half & half. Continue stirring the filling and scraping down the sides and be sure to taste the filling to make sure it's sweet enough and that you can taste the spices (if not, add more brown sugar and cinnamon/nutmeg to taste). Once the filling is to your liking, add in the eggs and continue mixing the batter until it's completely smooth and has no strings.

STEP 5. Pour the filling into the pre-made pie crusts then place them on a baking sheet to bake for 30-45 mins or until the filling is firm. Let the pies cool at least 15 mins before cutting. Plate and serve with whipped cream!

HOLIDAY ESSENTIALS

CORNBREAD DRESSING

STEP 1. Preheat the oven to 350 degrees.

STEP 2. Pour the cornbread mix into a bowl and follow the package instructions for baking. Once the cornbread is golden brown, remove it from the oven and set it aside to cool.

STEP 3. Chop the onions, celery and bell peppers then cook the veggies with oil in a small sauté pan for 10-15 mins over medium heat. Remove the veggies from the pan and set aside.

STEP 4. Remove the bones from the rotisserie chicken, then chop it up and pour it into the same bowl as the sautéed veggies. Set aside.

STEP 5. Once the cornbread is cool, crumble it in a large mixing bowl then add the box of stove-top dressing and mix thoroughly. Pour in the sautéed veggies and rotisserie chicken and continue mixing. Season the dressing with thyme, rosemary, sage, poultry seasoning, onion powder, black pepper and garlic salt. Stir in the seasonings then add the chicken stock, ¼ cup at a time (the mixture should not be soupy!) Then add in the cans of cream of chicken and cream of celery soup. Mix the ingredients together, then pour in the beaten eggs and stir everything together one more time. Place the ingredients into a long baking dish.

STEP 6. Bake for 40-55 mins or until the dressing is golden brown. Plate and serve with your favorite holiday protein or eat it by itself!

- Cornbread Mix, Enough for 1 Pan of Cornbread
- 1 White Onion, Small Diced
- 4 stalks Celery, Small Diced
- 1 Green Bell Pepper, Small Diced
- 1 teaspoon Vegetable Oil
- 1 whole Rotisserie Chicken
- 1 box Stove Top Stuffing Mix, Any Flavor
- 1 tablespoon Dried Thyme
- 1 tablespoon Rosemary
- 1 tablespoon Dried Sage
- 1 tablespoon Poultry Seasoning
- ½ tablespoon Onion Powder
- ½ tablespoon Black Pepper
- 1 teaspoon Garlic Salt
- 1 ½ cups Chicken Stock
- 1 can Cream of Chicken Soup
- 1 can Cream of Celery Soup
- 2 Eggs, Beaten

UTENSILS/COOKWARE NEEDED:

- Mixing Bowls
- Sauté Pan
- Spatula
- Long Baking Dish

TOTAL TIME: 2 HRS
SERVES: 6

GARLIC & HERB TURKEY

- 1 Whole Turkey
- 1 Lemon, Cut in Half
- 1 White Onion, Cut in Half
- 6-7 Whole Garlic Cloves
- 4 sprigs Fresh Thyme
- 4 sprigs Fresh Rosemary
- 4 sprigs Fresh Sage
- 2 Chicken Bouillon Cubes
- Garlic & Herb Butter
- 2 sticks Unsalted Butter, Softened
- 1 tablespoon Olive Oil
- ½ tablespoon Dried Rosemary
- ½ tablespoon Dried Thyme
- ½ tablespoon Garlic Salt
- ½ tablespoon Onion Powder
- ½ tablespoon Garlic Powder
- 1 tablespoon Poultry Seasoning
- ½ tablespoon Black Pepper
- 1 tablespoon Cajun Seasoning
- ½ tablespoon Dried Sage
- 1 tablespoon Parsley, Chopped
- 1 tablespoon Cilantro, Chopped
- 1 tablespoon Garlic Paste
- 1 tablespoon Minced Garlic
- 1 tablespoon Lemon Juice

UTENSILS/COOKWARE NEEDED:

- Mixing Bowl
- Small Rubber Spatula
- Roasting Pan
- Turkey Bag

TOTAL TIME: 5 HRS
SERVES: 6

STEP 1. Preheat the oven to 375 degrees.

STEP 2. FOR THE GARLIC & HERB BUTTER: In a mixing bowl, combine all the ingredients for the garlic and herb butter and mix well. Set aside.

STEP 3. Wash the turkey using water and vinegar, then remove the innards and pat dry (if the turkey skin isn't dry, the garlic and herb butter won't stick). Place the turkey on the roasting pan and stuff it with the lemon, onion, garlic cloves, fresh thyme, fresh rosemary, fresh sage and bouillon cubes.

STEP 4. Rub the turkey with the garlic and herb butter, making sure to rub the butter underneath the skin around the breast, legs and thighs. Cover the turkey in a plastic oven-safe turkey bag and allow to cook for 3-4 hrs. Baste the turkey every 30-45 mins by dripping the juices from the pan over the top and inside of the turkey. To get the turkey a nice golden-brown color, remove it from the bag and allow the turkey to continue roasting for another 20-30 mins.

STEP 5. Let the turkey rest at least 15 mins before cutting, then plate and serve with your favorite holiday sides!

HOLIDAY ESSENTIALS

Holiday Essentials | 223

HONEY PINEAPPLE BAKED HAM

STEP 1. Preheat the oven to 350 degrees.

STEP 2. Place the ham on a large baking dish or roasting pan, set aside.

STEP 3. Drain the juice from the pineapples into a mixing bowl and set aside the slices to use later. In the mixing bowl with the pineapple juice, add the brown sugar, white sugar, honey, melted butter, ginger, cinnamon, nutmeg and paprika. Mix well and brush the mixture onto the ham, making sure to brush in between each slice to get the flavor all over the ham. Place the pineapple slices onto the top and sides of the ham and use toothpicks to secure the pineapple slices in place. Put the ham in the oven and bake for 30-45 mins.

STEP 4. FOR THE GLAZE: Pour the remainder of the mixture that was brushed onto the ham into a saucepan, then add the brown sugar and simmer over medium heat for 5-8 mins then remove the glaze from the pan and set aside.

STEP 5. Once the ham has baked for 30-45 mins, uncover it and pour the glaze over the top. Turn the oven to 400 degrees and continue baking the ham for 5-10 more mins.

STEP 6. Remove the ham from the oven and allow to cool at least 5 mins before plating, serve with your favorite holiday sides.

- 1 Pre-Sliced Bone-In Ham
- 1 can of Sliced Pineapple
- ½ cup Brown Sugar
- ⅓ cup White Sugar
- 2 tablespoons Honey
- 2 tablespoons Melted Unsalted Butter 1 teaspoon Ground Ginger
- 1 teaspoon Ground Cinnamon
- 1 teaspoon Ground Nutmeg
- 1 teaspoon Paprika
- Glaze
- Remaining Pineapple Juice Mixture for the Ham
- ½ cup Brown Sugar

UTENSILS/COOKWARE NEEDED:
- Large Baking Dish or Roasting Pan
- Mixing Bowls
- Small Rubber Spatula
- Pastry Brush
- Toothpicks

TOTAL TIME: 1 ½ HRS
SERVES: 6

NOTE: If you prefer an unsliced bone-in ham you can use that too, I use the pre-sliced ham as a quick trick to have one less thing to worry about for the holidays!

HOLIDAY ESSENTIALS

COLLARD GREENS

- 4 bunches Collard Greens
- 2 bunches Mustard Greens
- 4 tablespoons Olive Oil
- 1 tablespoon Minced Garlic
- ¾ cup Bell Peppers, Medium Diced
- ¼ cup White Onions, Medium Diced
- 1-2 Smoked Turkey Tegs
- 5 cups Chicken Stock
- 2 ½ cups Water
- 1 tablespoon Garlic Salt
- ½ tablespoon Black Pepper
- ½ tablespoon Paprika
- 1 tablespoon Old Bay Seasoning
- ½ tablespoon Onion Powder
- 1 teaspoon Crushed Red Pepper
- 4 tablespoons Unsalted Butter

UTENSILS/COOKWARE NEEDED:

- Mixing Bowl
- Stockpot
- Tongs

TOTAL TIME: 1 ½ HRS
SERVES: 10-12

STEP 1. Remove the stems from the collard and mustard greens. Rinse the leaves of the greens with cool water then chop them into bite-sized pieces. Place the greens into a large mixing bowl and set aside.

STEP 2. Warm the olive oil over high heat in a stockpot. Add the minced garlic, bell peppers, onions and smoked turkey legs to the pot. Sauté the ingredients for 6 mins.

STEP 3. Deglaze the pot by pouring in 1 cup of the chicken stock. Transfer the cut greens to the pot then pour in the water and remaining chicken stock. Simmer the greens for 30 mins.

STEP 4. Season the greens with the garlic salt, black pepper, paprika, Old Bay, onion powder, crushed red pepper and butter. Use a pair of tongs to toss the greens in the pot, making sure to get the seasonings throughout. Simmer the greens over medium heat for another 45-50 mins. Serve hot with your favorite comfort food!

HOLIDAY ESSENTIALS

MAC & CHEESE

STEP 1. Preheat the oven to 350 degrees. In a large pot, boil the macaroni to al dente.

STEP 2. Drain the noodles using a strainer then pour the macaroni into a casserole dish. Season the noodles with Old Bay, black pepper and garlic salt then stir the ingredients until they are well combined.

STEP 3. Crack the egg into a bowl and whisk it, then stir the beaten egg and milk into the seasoned macaroni noodles.

STEP 4. Add the cream of mushroom (optional), butter and heavy cream then sprinkle in all but 2 cups of the cheeses. Using a large spoon, stir all the ingredients together until they're well combined then sprinkle the remaining cheese on top.

STEP 5. Cover the casserole dish with foil then place the mac and cheese in the oven to bake. After 20-25 mins, remove the foil and allow the top of the mac and cheese to brown for 5 more minutes.

STEP 6. Remove the pan from the oven and allow the mac and cheese to cool at least 10 mins before serving.

- 1-1 ½ lbs Elbow Macaroni Noodles
- ¼ teaspoon Old Bay Seasoning
- ¼ teaspoon Black Pepper
- ¼ teaspoon Garlic Salt
- 1 Egg
- 2 cups Milk
- 1 can of Cream of Mushroom, Chicken or Celery Soup (optional)
- ½ stick Unsalted Butter
- ¼ cup Heavy Whipping Cream
- 2 cups Extra Sharp Cheddar, Grated
- 2 cups Regular Sharp Cheddar, Grated
- 2 cups Medium Cheddar, Grated
- 2 cups Colby Jack, Grated
- 2 cups Monterrey Jack, Grated

UTENSILS/COOKWARE NEEDED:

- Large Pot
- Strainer
- Casserole Dish
- Large Spoon
- Aluminum Foil

TOTAL TIME: 45

SERVES: 6

HOLIDAY ESSENTIALS

CANDIED YAMS

- 4 Sweet Potatoes
- ½ stick Unsalted Butter
- 1 teaspoon Ground Cinnamon
- ¾ cup Brown Sugar
- ½ cup White Sugar
- ¼ teaspoon Ground Nutmeg

UTENSILS/COOKWARE NEEDED:

- Large Pot
- Saucepan
- Baking Dish
- Aluminum Foil

TOTAL TIME: 45 MINS
SERVES: 6

STEP 1. Preheat the oven to 350 degrees.

STEP 2. Peel the sweet potatoes, then rinse them and cut the potatoes into 1-inch slices. Place the sweet potatoes in a large pot of water and boil them over medium-high heat until they have softened. Drain the water and place the sweet potatoes in a baking dish.

STEP 3. Combine the butter, cinnamon, brown sugar, white sugar and nutmeg in a saucepan and warm the mixture over high heat until it thickens into a syrup.

STEP 4. Pour the syrup over the sweet potatoes and mix well, making sure the sweet potatoes are completely coated in the sauce. Cover the baking dish with foil and place it in the oven to bake for 30 mins, or until the yams are fork-tender and golden-brown on top.

STEP 5. Remove the candied yams from the oven and allow them to cool at least 10 mins before serving.

WHENEVER SOMEONE ASKS WHAT MY PASSION IS, I SAY FASHION IS MY FIRST LOVE, BUT COOKING IS WHERE MY HEART IS.

HOLIDAY ESSENTIALS

SOUTHERN GRAVY

STEP 1. Warm a large saucepan over medium heat and melt the butter and pan drippings, then sauté the onions and garlic for 5-8 mins, stirring occasionally.

STEP 2. Add in the flour, 1 tablespoon at a time, to create a roux. Pour in the chicken stock and heavy cream and stir. Season the gravy with browning sauce, crushed red pepper, garlic powder, onion powder, black pepper, garlic salt and the chicken bouillon cube. Continue simmering the gravy for 8-10 more mins, stirring occasionally. Make sure to taste the gravy and if it needs more flavor, add a second bouillon cube.

STEP 3. Once the gravy has thickened, remove it from the pan and serve with poultry or mashed potatoes!

- 3 tablespoons Unsalted Butter
- 1 cup Pan Drippings, from the Meat You Cook with the Gravy
- 1 White Onion, Sliced
- 1 tablespoon Minced Garlic
- ⅓ cup Flour
- 4 cups Chicken Stock
- ½ cup Heavy Whipping Cream
- 1 teaspoon Browning Sauce
- 1 teaspoon Crushed Red Pepper
- 1 teaspoon Garlic Powder
- 1 teaspoon Onion Powder
- 1 teaspoon Black Pepper
- 1 teaspoon Garlic Salt
- 1 Chicken Bouillon Cube

UTENSILS/COOKWARE NEEDED:

- Large Saucepan
- Large Spoon

TOTAL TIME: 25 MINS

SERVES: 6

NOTE: If you do not have pan drippings, use 1 tablespoon of vegetable oil and 1 extra cup of chicken stock

HOLIDAY ESSENTIALS

HONEY BUTTER CORNBREAD

- 1 cup Flour, Leveled
- ¾ cup Cornmeal
- ½ teaspoon Kosher Salt
- ½ teaspoon Baking Soda
- 1 teaspoon Baking Powder
- 1 stick Unsalted Butter
- ¼ cup Vegetable Oil
- 1 cup White Sugar
- ⅓ cup Honey
- 2 Eggs
- 1 ¼ cups Buttermilk
- Non-stick Cooking Spray

UTENSILS/COOKWARE NEEDED:

- Mixing Bowls
- Small Rubber Spatula
- 8x8 Baking Pan

TOTAL TIME: 40 MINS
SERVES: 6

STEP 1. Preheat the oven to 375 degrees.

STEP 2. In a small mixing bowl combine the flour, cornmeal, kosher salt, baking soda and baking powder. Set aside.

STEP 3. Melt the butter in a separate bowl, making sure it's microwave safe. Add the vegetable oil, sugar and honey to the bowl with the melted butter. Stir until well-combined. Crack the eggs into the bowl, then pour in the buttermilk and whisk thoroughly.

STEP 4. Stir the dry ingredients from the small mixing bowl (flour, cornmeal, kosher salt, baking soda, baking powder) into the large mixing bowl with the melted butter mixture. Make sure all the ingredients are completely combined but do not overmix! It's okay if there are a few lumps.

STEP 5. Spray the bottom and sides of a baking pan with non-stick cooking spray, then pour the batter into the pan and smooth out the top. Bake for 30 mins, you'll know the cornbread is done when a toothpick is inserted through the center and comes out clean with no batter.

STEP 6. Allow the cornbread to cool for at least 10 mins before slicing and serving.

HOLIDAY ESSENTIALS

HERB ROASTED CORNISH HENS

STEP 1. Preheat the oven to 400 degrees.

STEP 2. Wash the Cornish hens with vinegar and water, then pat dry and set aside.

STEP 3. In a mixing bowl combine the melted butter, olive oil, lemon juice, Old Bay, garlic powder, onion powder, black pepper, minced garlic and Italian seasoning. Mix well, then brush the mixture onto the Cornish hens.

STEP 4. Line a baking sheet with foil then coat the foil with non-stick cooking spray then place the Cornish hens on the pan. Stuff the Cornish hens with the lemon, garlic cloves, onion, butter and thyme then place the pan in the oven. Roast the hens for 35-40 mins, uncovered.

STEP 5. Remove the Cornish hens from the oven and allow them to rest for at least 10 mins before cutting into them. Plate and serve with your favorite holiday sides!

- 2 Cornish Game Hens
- 2 tablespoons Melted Unsalted Butter
- 1 tablespoon Olive Oil
- 2 teaspoons Lemon Juice
- 1 teaspoon Old Bay Seasoning
- 1 teaspoon Garlic Powder
- 1 teaspoon Onion Powder
- ½ tablespoon Black Pepper
- 1 teaspoon Minced Garlic
- 1 teaspoon Italian Seasoning
- Non-stick Cooking Spray
- ½ Lemon, Cut in Half
- 4-5 Whole Garlic cloves
- 1 White Onion, Cut into 4ths
- 4 tablespoons Unsalted Butter
- 4-5 sprigs Fresh Thyme

UTENSILS/COOKWARE NEEDED:

- Mixing Bowl
- Baking Sheet
- Aluminum Foil

TOTAL TIME: 50 MINS
SERVES: 6

BEEF POT ROAST

- 1 Beef Chuck Roast
- 4 tablespoons Worcestershire Sauce
- 2 tablespoons Minced Garlic
- 1 teaspoon Garlic Powder
- 1 teaspoon Onion Powder
- 1 teaspoon Paprika
- 1 teaspoon Black Pepper
- 1 teaspoon Blackened Seasoning
- ½ teaspoon Garlic Salt
- 1 teaspoon Cilantro, Chopped
- 1 teaspoon Parsley, Chopped
- 1 tablespoon Beef Bouillon Powder or 1 Beef Bouillon Cube
- 2 teaspoons Olive oil
- 4 Carrots
- 6-8 Potatoes
- 1 White Onion
- 4 sprigs Fresh Rosemary
- 2 tablespoons Unsalted Butter
- 3 cups Beef Stock

UTENSILS/COOKWARE NEEDED:

- Large Pan or Dutch Oven
- Casserole Dish or Dutch Oven
- Aluminum Foil

TOTAL TIME: 4 HRS
SERVES: 6

STEP 1. Preheat the oven to 400 degrees.

STEP 2. Wash the chuck roast using water and vinegar and pat dry. Rub half the Worcestershire sauce and half the minced garlic onto the roast then sprinkle on the garlic powder, onion powder, paprika, black pepper, blackened seasoning, garlic salt, cilantro, parsley and bouillon powder. Massage the seasonings into the beef.

STEP 3. Place a large pan or Dutch oven over medium-high heat and add olive oil to the pan. Sear the roast for 5 mins on each side, then transfer the roast to a casserole dish if you aren't using a Dutch oven.

STEP 4. Peel the carrots and potatoes, then dice them along with the onion into medium-sized pieces. Arrange the veggies around the roast and place the rosemary on top. Cover everything in the pan with the beef broth, then cover the pan with foil and place it in the oven for about 2-3 hrs or until everything is tender.

STEP 5. Remove the roast from the oven and allow to cool at least 10 mins before serving. Plate family-style and serve with mashed potatoes.

HOLIDAY ESSENTIALS

GRANNY'S FRIED CHICKEN

STEP 1. Preheat frying oil to 350 degrees.

STEP 2. Wash the chicken using vinegar and water then place the chicken in a mixing bowl and season with the seasoned salt, pollo seasoning, garlic powder, onion powder and black pepper. Mix well and set aside.

STEP 3. Pour the flour into a bag (Ziplock, plastic or paper) and season to taste or leave the flour as is.

STEP 4. Dip the seasoned chicken in the flour, then shake the bag to ensure the chicken is fully coated. Shake the excess flour off the chicken before submerging it in the oil then fry for 12-15 mins, flipping the chicken over halfway through. Remove the chicken from the oil and drain it on a wire rack or paper towels.

STEP 5. Plate and serve with your favorite hot sauce!

- Oil for Frying
- 1 pack Chicken Legs or Thighs
- 1 teaspoon Seasoned Salt
- 1 teaspoon Pollo Seasoning
- 1 teaspoon Garlic Powder
- 1 teaspoon Onion Powder
- 1 teaspoon Black Pepper
- 4 cups Flour

UTENSILS/COOKWARE NEEDED:

- Large Pot or Deep Fryer
- Mixing Bowl
- Bag (Ziplock, plastic or paper)

TOTAL TIME: 30 MINS

SERVES: 6

WHOLE SPICED CHICKEN

- 1 Whole Chicken
- ¼ cup Olive Oil
- 2 tablespoons Melted Unsalted Butter
- 1 tablespoon Garlic, Chopped
- 1 tablespoon Cilantro, Chopped
- 1 tablespoon Parsley, Chopped
- 1 tablespoon Onion Powder
- 1 tablespoon Garlic Powder
- 1 tablespoon Black Pepper
- 1 tablespoon Paprika
- ½ tablespoon Chipotle Powder
- ½ tablespoon Garlic Salt
- 1 tablespoon Blackened Seasoning
- 1 tablespoon Chicken Bouillon Powder

UTENSILS/COOKWARE NEEDED:

- Mixing Bowl
- Roasting Pan
- Aluminum Foil

TOTAL TIME: 3 HRS
SERVES: 6

STEP 1. Preheat the oven to 400 degrees.

STEP 2. Wash the chicken using vinegar and water, then cut the chicken in half and pat it dry (this is to make sure the seasonings stick to the chicken). Mix together the olive oil, butter, chopped garlic, cilantro, parsley and all the seasoning listed in a bowl then massage the seasoning mix all over the chicken, inside and out and underneath the skin.

STEP 3. Place the chicken in a roasting pan and cover the pan with foil. Roast the chicken for 1 ½-2 hrs depending on the size of the chicken. When there's 15 mins left, uncover the chicken and put the oven on broil to get the skin nice and crispy.

STEP 4. Let the chicken rest at least 15 mins before cutting into it. Plate and serve with your favorite sides!

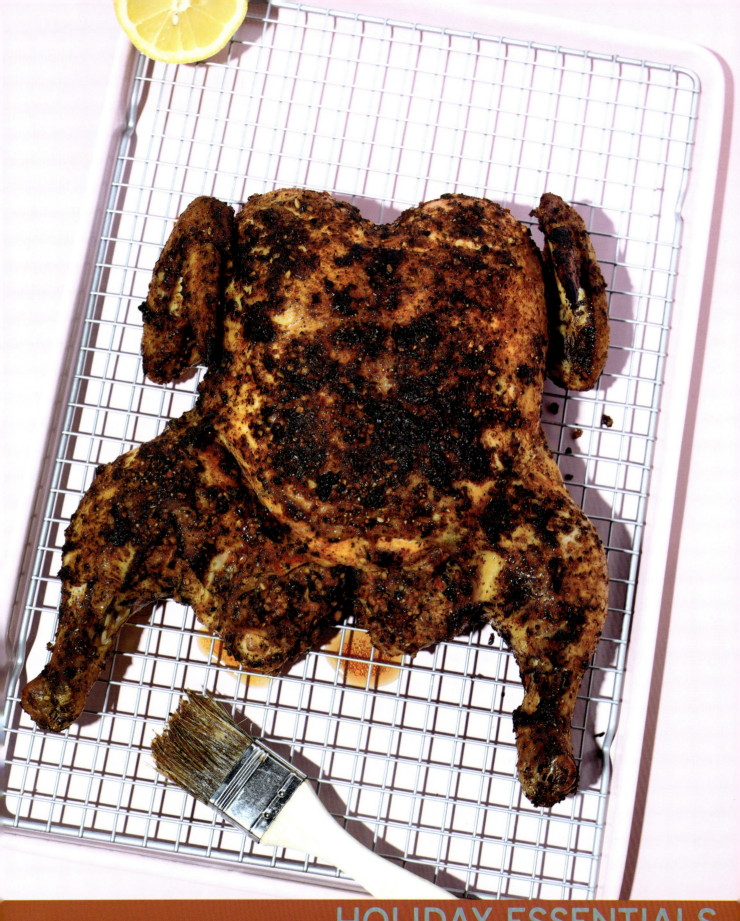

HOLIDAY ESSENTIALS

Air Fryer
ESSENTIALS

BACON WRAPPED JALAPENO POPPERS 244

GARLIC STEAK BITES 247

GARLIC PARM BRUSSEL SPROUTS 248

CHIPOTLE SHRIMP FAJITAS 251

STUFFED MEATBALLS 252

SALMON CAKES 255

BEEF & CHEESE EMPANADAS 256

AIR FRIED SALMON BITES 259

BACON WRAPPED SHRIMP 260

PIGS IN A BLANKET 263

AIR FRYER CORNISH HENS 264

PORK CHOPS WITH ROASTED POTATOES 267

COCONUT SHRIMP 268

STUFFED MUSHROOM CHICKEN 271

BACON WRAPPED JALAPENO POPPERS

- 4-5 Jalapenos
- 1 pack Sliced Bacon
- Non-stick Cooking Spray
- Filling:
- 1-8 oz Cream Cheese, Softened
- 1/3 cup Shredded Cheese of Your Choice
- 1/3 cup Cooked Ground Beef or Turkey
- 1/2 teaspoon Garlic Powder
- 1/2 teaspoon Black Pepper
- 1/2 teaspoon Onion Powder

UTENSILS/COOKWARE NEEDED:

- Mixing Bowl
- Small Rubber Spatula
- KitchenEnvy Air Fryer

TOTAL TIME: 30 MINS
SERVES: 4

NOTE: If you don't want to wrap the jalapeno poppers in bacon, sprinkle more shredded cheese on top of the filling before placing the poppers in the air fryer.

STEP 1. Cut the tops off the jalapenos then cut them in half lengthwise and remove the seeds. Set aside.

STEP 2. FOR THE FILLING: In a mixing bowl place the cream cheese, shredded cheese and ground beef. Cream the mixture together with a rubber spatula until it's smooth. Add in the seasonings listed for the filling and stir them into the mixture.

STEP 3. FOR ASSEMBLY: Lay the jalapenos flat then place 1 tablespoon of filling in the open halves and wrap a piece of bacon around the filled jalapenos. Repeat until all the jalapeno poppers are made.

STEP 4. Spray the air fryer pan with non-stick cooking spray then place the jalapeno poppers in the pan and cook at 400 degrees for 10 mins.

STEP 5. Plate and serve hot!

AIR FRYER ESSENTIALS

GARLIC STEAK BITES

STEP 1. Clean the steak using vinegar and water then cut it into medium sized chunks and place them in a mixing bowl. Season the steak bites with garlic and herb seasoning, parsley, onion powder, paprika and Worcestershire sauce. Mix well.

STEP 2. Spray the air fryer pan with non-stick cooking spray then pour the steak bites into the pan and place the butter on top. Set the air fryer to 400 degrees and cook the steak bites for 10-15 mins, checking the steak bites halfway through to give them a stir.

STEP 3. Remove the steak bites from the air fryer and serve with your favorite side!

- 1 Steak
- 1 teaspoon Garlic and Herb Seasoning
- 1 teaspoon Parsley, Chopped
- ½ teaspoon Onion Powder
- ½ teaspoon Paprika
- 1 teaspoon Worcestershire Sauce
- Non-stick Cooking Spray
- 1 tablespoon Unsalted Butter

UTENSILS/COOKWARE NEEDED:

- Mixing Bowl
- Spatula
- KitchenEnvy Air Fryer

TOTAL TIME: 20 MINS
SERVES: 4

AIR FRYER ESSENTIALS

GARLIC PARM BRUSSEL SPROUTS

- 1 bag Brussel Sprouts
- Non-stick Cooking Spray
- 1 teaspoon Soy Sauce
- ½ teaspoon Mrs. Dash Seasoning
- ½ teaspoon Garlic Powder
- ½ teaspoon Italian Seasoning
- Shredded Parmesan Cheese

UTENSILS/COOKWARE NEEDED:
- KitchenEnvy Air Fryer

TOTAL TIME: 30 MINS
SERVES: 4

STEP 1. Cut the Brussel sprouts in half, then spray the air fryer pan with non-stick cooking spray and place the Brussel sprouts in the pan.

STEP 2. Season the Brussel sprouts with soy sauce, Mrs. Dash, garlic powder and Italian seasoning. Mix well.

STEP 3. Set the air fryer to 400 degrees and cook the Brussel sprouts for 20 mins.

STEP 4. Remove the Brussel sprouts from the pan then sprinkle them with parmesan cheese and serve hot!

> **I LOVE COOKING FOR THE SAME REASON THAT I LOVE FASHION – THE THRILL OF CREATING SOMETHING NEW.**

AIR FRYER ESSENTIALS

CHIPOTLE SHRIMP FAJITAS

STEP 1. Slice the onion and bell peppers and place them in a mixing bowl. Set aside.

STEP 2. Wash the shrimp using vinegar and water, then place them in the bowl with the veggies and season everything with chipotle powder, black pepper, blackened seasoning, garlic powder and parsley. Mix well.

STEP 3. Spray the air fryer with non-stick cooking spray then place the seasoned shrimp and veggies in the air fryer pan. Set the air fryer to 400 degrees for 7 mins.

STEP 4. Remove the fajitas from the air fryer, plate and serve with tortillas and your favorite taco toppings!

- ½ White Onion
- ½ Green Bell Pepper
- ½ Red Bell Pepper
- 1/2 lb Shrimp, Peeled and Deveined
- ½ teaspoon Chipotle Powder
- ½ teaspoon Black Pepper
- ½ teaspoon Blackened Seasoning
- ½ teaspoon Garlic Powder
- 1 tablespoon Parsley, Chopped
- Non-stick Cooking Spray
- 4-6 Tortillas

UTENSILS/COOKWARE NEEDED:

- Mixing Bowl
- KitchenEnvy Air Fryer

SERVES: 2
TOTAL TIME: 15 MINS

STUFFED MEATBALLS

- 1 lb Ground Beef or Turkey
- ½ cup White Onions, Chopped
- 1 tablespoon Parsley, Chopped
- 1 tablespoon Garlic, Chopped
- ½ teaspoon Blackened Seasoning
- ½ teaspoon Garlic Powder
- ½ teaspoon Onion Powder
- ¼ teaspoon Black Pepper
- ½ teaspoon Paprika
- 1 teaspoon Crushed Red Pepper
- 1 teaspoon Garlic Paste
- 1 Egg
- ¾ cup Breadcrumbs
- 1 block Cheddar Cheese, Cut into Cubes
- 1 block Mozzarella Cheese, Cut in Cubes
- Non-stick Cooking Spray

UTENSILS/COOKWARE NEEDED:

- Mixing Bowl
- Spatula
- KitchenEnvy Air Fryer

TOTAL TIME: 1 HR
SERVES: 6

STEP 1. Place the ground turkey in a mixing bowl with the chopped onions, parsley, chopped garlic, blackened seasoning, garlic powder, onion powder, black pepper, paprika, crushed red pepper, garlic paste, the egg and breadcrumbs. Mix well.

STEP 2. Roll 1 ½ tablespoons of the mixture into balls and press a dent into the middle of each ball. Place a cube of cheese in the dent and close the meatball around the cheese, sealing the sides together to make sure the cheese doesn't come out while the meatballs cook. The mixture should make 7-9 large meatballs.

STEP 3. Spray the air fryer pan with non-stick cooking spray, then place the meatballs in the pan and cook them in the air fryer at 400 degrees for 25 mins, or until the meatballs are brown and completely cooked through.

STEP 4. Remove the stuffed meatballs from the air fryer, plate and serve over your favorite pasta with your favorite spaghetti sauce!

AIR FRYER ESSENTIALS

SALMON CAKES

STEP 1. Place the salmon into a large mixing bowl. Using your hands, crumble the salmon while also removing all the bones, fat, and skin. Season the salmon with the black pepper, onion powder, minced garlic, onion salt, Old Bay and garlic powder then mix well.

STEP 2. In a separate bowl, crack the eggs and whisk them, then pour the beaten eggs into the mixing bowl with the seasoned salmon along with the mayonnaise. Mix well until everything is combined, then pour in ½ cup of the breadcrumbs.

STEP 3. FOR ASSEMBLY: Shape the salmon cakes by placing ¼ cup of the mixture into your hand and using both your hands to squeeze it into a ball, then gently flatten the ball to your desired thickness. Pour the remaining breadcrumbs into a bowl and fully coat the outside salmon cakes.

STEP 4. Spray the air fryer pan with non-stick spray, then place the salmon cakes in the pan and cook them in the air fryer at 400 degrees for 30 mins.

STEP 5. Remove the salmon cakes from the air fryer, plate and serve hot!

- 2-14.75 oz cans of Pink Salmon
- ¼ teaspoon Black Pepper
- ½ teaspoon Onion Powder
- 1 tablespoon Minced Garlic
- ¼ teaspoon Onion Salt
- ½ tablespoon Old Bay Seasoning
- ½ tablespoon Garlic Powder
- 2 Eggs
- 1 tablespoon Mayonnaise
- 1 ½ cups Panko Breadcrumbs
- Non-stick Cooking Spray

UTENSILS/COOKWARE NEEDED:

- Mixing Bowls
- Whisk
- Small Rubber Spatula
- KitchenEnvy Air Fryer

TOTAL TIME: 45 MINS
SERVES: 6

AIR FRYER ESSENTIALS

BEEF & CHEESE EMPANADAS

- 1 lb Ground Beef
- ¼ cup White Onions, Chopped
- ½ teaspoon Garlic Powder
- ½ teaspoon Onion Powder
- ½ teaspoon Black Pepper
- 1 ½ cups Shredded Cheddar Cheese
- ⅓ cup Tomato Paste
- 2 packs of Pre-Made Pie Crust
- 1 Egg + 1 tablespoon Water (Egg Wash)
- Non-stick Cooking Spray

UTENSILS/COOKWARE NEEDED:

- Sauté Pan
- Spatula
- KitchenEnvy Air Fryer

TOTAL TIME: 40 MINS
SERVES: 4

STEP 1. Warm a sauté pan over medium-high heat then add in the ground beef and chopped onions. Season the ground beef with garlic powder, onion powder and black pepper, then use a spatula to break up the beef into small pieces. Cook 10-12 mins or until the meat is completely brown. Sprinkle in 1 cup of the shredded cheese into the pan of ground beef, then add in the tomato paste. Cook until the cheese is melted, then remove the mixture the pan from the heat and set aside.

STEP 2. FOR ASSEMBLY: Roll out the pie crust on a floured surface then use a bowl to cut out a smaller circle from the center of the pie crust. Repeat on the remaining pie crusts. Brush the edges of the crusts with egg wash, then place 2 tablespoons of the beef mixture on the pie crust rounds, leaving half of the pie crust open so it can be folded over the filling (almost like a taco). Sprinkle another teaspoon of shredded cheese on top of the beef mixture, then fold the crust over the filling and seal the edges using a fork.

STEP 3. Brush the tops of the empanadas with more egg wash, then spray the air fryer pan with non-stick cooking spray and place the empanadas in the pan. Cook them in the air fryer at 400 degrees for 15 mins.

STEP 4. Remove the empanadas from the air fryer, then plate and serve hot!

AIR FRYER ESSENTIALS

AIR FRIED SALMON BITES

STEP 1. Wash the salmon filet using vinegar and water, then pat it dry and cut the filet into medium sized chunks. Place the chunks in a mixing bowl then pour the olive oil on them and season with the garlic and herb seasoning, paprika, black pepper, Italian seasoning, blackened seasoning and parsley. Mix well.

STEP 2. Spray the air fryer pan with non-stick cooking spray then place the salmon bites in the pan and cook them in the air fryer at 400 degrees for 15 mins.

STEP 3. Remove the salmon bites from the air fryer, plate and serve with jasmine rice (see pg. 176).

- 1 Salmon Filet, Skin Removed
- ½ teaspoon Olive Oil
- ½ teaspoon Garlic and Herb Seasoning
- ½ teaspoon Paprika
- ½ teaspoon Black Pepper
- ½ teaspoon Italian Seasoning
- ½ teaspoon Blackened Seasoning
- 1 teaspoon Parsley, Chopped
- Non-stick Cooking Spray

UTENSILS/COOKWARE NEEDED:

- Mixing Bowl
- Small Rubber Spatula
- KitchenEnvy Air Fryer

TOTAL TIME: 25 MINS

SERVES: 6

> THE KITCHEN IS A PLACE TO EXPERIENCE HAPPY VIBES, MAKE GREAT MEMORIES AND BOND WITH LOVED ONES.

BACON WRAPPED SHRIMP

- ½ lb Shrimp, Peeled and Deveined
- 1 pack Sliced Bacon
- 1 teaspoon Blackened Seasoning
- 1 teaspoon Garlic and Herb Seasoning
- Non-stick Cooking Spray

UTENSILS/COOKWARE NEEDED:
- KitchenEnvy Air Fryer

TOTAL TIME: 30 MINS
SERVES: 6

STEP 1. Wash the shrimp using vinegar and water, then pat them dry and wrap each piece of shrimp with half a slice of bacon. Season the shrimp with blackened seasoning and garlic & herb seasoning.

STEP 2. Spray the air fryer pan with non-stick cooking spray then place the bacon wrapped shrimp in the pan. Cook them in the air fryer at 400 degrees for 10-15 mins.

STEP 3. Remove the bacon wrapped shrimp from the air fryer, plate and serve hot!

AIR FRYER ESSENTIALS

PIGS IN A BLANKET

STEP 1. Roll out the crescent dough and separate the triangles, then place 2 sausage links end-to-end on each triangle. Roll the dough around the sausages, creating the pigs in a blanket, then brush the tops with melted butter.

STEP 2. Spray the air fryer pan with non-stick cooking spray then place the pigs in a blanket in the pan and cook them in the air fryer at 400 degrees for 15 mins.

STEP 3. Remove the pigs in a blanket from the air fryer, plate and serve hot!

- 1 roll Crescent Roll Dough
- 1 pack Li'l Smokies Sausage Links
- 2 tablespoons Melted Unsalted Butter
- Non-stick Cooking Spray

UTENSILS/COOKWARE NEEDED:
- KitchenEnvy Air Fryer

TOTAL TIME: 25 MINS
SERVES: 4

AIR FRYER ESSENTIALS

AIR FRYER CORNISH HENS

- 2 Cornish Game Hens
- 2 tablespoons Melted Unsalted Butter
- 1 tablespoon Olive Oil
- 2 teaspoons Lemon Juice
- 1 teaspoon Old Bay
- 1 teaspoon Garlic Powder
- 1 teaspoon Onion Powder
- ½ tablespoon Black Pepper
- 1 teaspoon Minced Garlic
- 1 teaspoon Italian Seasoning
- ½ Lemon, Cut in Half
- 4-5 Whole Garlic Cloves
- 1 White Onion, Cut into 4ths
- 4 tablespoons Unsalted Butter
- 4-5 sprigs Fresh Thyme
- Non-stick Cooking Spray

UTENSILS/COOKWARE NEEDED:

- Mixing Bowl
- KitchenEnvy Air Fryer

SERVES: 6
TOTAL TIME: 50 MINS

STEP 1. Wash the Cornish hens with vinegar and water, then pat them dry.

STEP 2. In a mixing bowl combine the melted butter, olive oil, lemon juice, Old Bay, garlic powder, onion powder, black pepper, minced garlic and Italian seasoning. Mix well and brush the mixture onto the Cornish hens, then stuff them with the lemon, garlic cloves, onion, butter and thyme.

STEP 3. Spray the air fryer pan with non-stick cooking spray then place the Cornish hens in the pan. Cook them in the air fryer at 400 degrees for 35-40 mins.

STEP 4. Remove the hens from the air fryer and let them rest at least 10 mins before cutting into them. Plate and serve with your favorite sides!

AIR FRYER ESSENTIALS

PORK CHOPS WITH ROASTED POTATOES

STEP 1. Wash the pork chops using vinegar and water, then pat them dry and season them with 1 teaspoon of Mrs. Dash and garlic powder on both sides.

STEP 2. Cut the potatoes into 4ths and place them in a mixing bowl, then season them with 1 teaspoon of Mrs. Dash and 1 teaspoon garlic powder.

STEP 3. Spray the air fryer pan with non-stick cooking spray then place the pork chops and potatoes in the pan. Pour in the broccoli and season with the rest of the Mrs. Dash and garlic powder. Place the pan in the air fryer and cook at 400 degrees for 30 mins.

STEP 4. Remove the meal from the air fryer, plate and serve hot!

- 2 Pork Chops
- 3 teaspoons Mrs. Dash Seasoning
- 1 teaspoon Garlic Powder
- 3-4 Red Potatoes, Cut into 4ths
- Non-stick Cooking Spray
- 1 cup Broccoli
- 2 teaspoons Garlic Salt

UTENSILS/COOKWARE NEEDED:

- Mixing Bowl
- KitchenEnvy Air Fryer

TOTAL TIME: 35 MINS

SERVES: 2

AIR FRYER ESSENTIALS

COCONUT SHRIMP

- ½ lb Shrimp, Peeled and Deveined
- 1 teaspoon Garlic Powder
- 1 teaspoon Italian Seasoning
- 1 teaspoon Old Bay Seasoning
- 2 cups Shredded Coconut
- 2 Eggs
- Non-stick Cooking Spray

UTENSILS/COOKWARE NEEDED:

- Mixing Bowls
- Whisk
- KitchenEnvy Air Fryer

TOTAL TIME: 30 MINS
SERVES: 6

STEP 1. Wash the shrimp using vinegar and water, then pat them dry and place them in a mixing bowl. Season the shrimp with garlic powder, Italian seasoning and Old Bay. Mix well and set aside.

STEP 2. FOR THE BREADING: Crack the eggs into a mixing bowl and whisk them, then in a separate bowl pour the shredded coconut. Dip the seasoned shrimp into the egg, then the coconut. Repeat until all the shrimp are breaded. If you start to run low on egg or coconut to bread the shrimp, add more as needed.

STEP 3. Spray the air fryer pan with non-stick cooking spray then place the coconut shrimp in the pan and cook them in the air fryer at 400 degrees for 15 mins.

STEP 4. Remove the coconut shrimp from the air fryer, plate and serve hot!

AIR FRYER ESSENTIALS

STUFFED MUSHROOM CHICKEN

STEP 1. Wash the chicken using vinegar and water, then pat dry and slice a pocket on the side of the chicken to have an opening for the filling. Place the chicken in a bowl, drizzle with 1 teaspoon of olive oil then season with the garlic powder, onion powder, Italian seasoning, pollo seasoning and chipotle powder. Make sure the seasonings completely coat the chicken, then set aside preferably in the fridge or over ice.

STEP 2. Warm a sauté pan over medium heat, drizzle in the remaining olive oil then sauté the mushrooms, bell peppers and onions. Season the veggies with garlic salt and continue cooking for 3-5 mins, or until the veggies have cooked down. Remove everything from the pan and let cool at least 10 mins before stuffing the chicken breasts.

STEP 3. FOR ASSEMBLY: Lay out the seasoned chicken breasts and stuff each one with a ¼ cup - ½ cup of the cooked veggie mixture and ¼ cup of shredded cheese.

STEP 4. Spray the air fryer pan with non-stick cooking spray, then place the stuffed chicken breasts in the pan and cook them in the air fryer at 400 degrees for 15-20 mins, or until the chicken is cooked through (no more pink).

STEP 5. Remove the mushroom stuffed chicken breasts from the air fryer and allow them to rest at least 10 mins before slicing. Plate and serve hot!

- 2 Chicken Breasts
- 2 teaspoons Olive Oil
- 1 teaspoon Garlic Powder
- 1 teaspoon Onion Powder
- 1 teaspoon Italian Seasoning
- 1 teaspoon Pollo Seasoning
- 1 teaspoon Chipotle Powder
- 1 cup Mushrooms, Sliced
- ½ cup Bell Peppers, Small Diced
- ½ Cup White Onions, Small Diced
- ¼ cup Garlic Salt
- ½ cup Shredded Cheese of Your Choice
- Non-stick Cooking Spray

UTENSILS/COOKWARE NEEDED:

- Mixing Bowl
- Spatula
- Sauté Pan

TOTAL TIME: 35 MINS
SERVES: 6

GRILLED CHEESE SLOPPY JOE'S 274

BAKED SPAGHETTI 277

SLIDERS 278

CHICKEN FRIES 281

GARLIC BREAD PIZZA 282

MAC & CHEESE BALLS 285

JERK CHICKEN STIR FRY 286

LOADED NACHOS 289

CHOPPED CHEESE SANDWICH 290

FLAMIN' HOT WINGS 292

MINI PANCAKE SANDWICHES 294

GRILLED CHEESE SLOPPY JOE'S

- 1 Bell Pepper, Small Diced
- ½ Small White Onion, Small Diced
- 1 lb Ground Turkey or Beef
- 1 teaspoon Garlic Salt
- 1 tablespoon Garlic Powder
- 1 tablespoon Onion Powder
- ½ tablespoon Black Pepper
- ¼ teaspoon Paprika
- 1 teaspoon Olive Oil
- 2-8 oz cans Tomato Sauce
- ½ cup Ketchup
- Sliced Mozzarella Cheese, As Needed
- Sliced Cheddar Cheese, As Needed
- Sliced Thick Bread, As Needed

UTENSILS/COOKWARE NEEDED:

- Mixing Bowl
- Large Pan
- Spatula
- Pan or Griddle

TOTAL TIME: 30 MINS
SERVES: 6

STEP 1. Wash and chop the bell peppers and onions, then set aside.

STEP 2. Put the ground turkey in a mixing bowl and season with the garlic salt, garlic powder, onion powder, black pepper and paprika. Mix well.

STEP 3. Warm a large pan over medium heat and drizzle in the olive oil, then add the turkey and chopped veggies into the pan and cook 10-12 mins, or until the turkey is completely cooked through and there is no more pink. Make sure to use a spatula to break the meat into smaller pieces, then pour in the tomato sauce and ketchup, mix well.

STEP 4. FOR ASSEMBLY: Lay a slice of cheese on each piece of bread then pour ½ cup of the sloppy joe mix on top of one of the pieces of bread. Sandwich the bread together then warm a pan or griddle over medium heat and sear the bread for 2-3 mins on each side, or until it's golden-brown and the cheese is melted.

STEP 5. Plate and serve hot!

30-MIN MEALS

BAKED SPAGHETTI/ SPAGHETTI CASSEROLE

STEP 1. Preheat the oven to 350 degrees.

STEP 2. Wash and chop the bell peppers and onions, then set aside.

STEP 3. Put the ground turkey in a mixing bowl and season with the garlic salt, garlic powder, black pepper, onion powder, Cajun seasoning and Worcestershire sauce. Mix well.

STEP 4. Warm a large pan over medium heat and drizzle in the olive oil, then add the turkey and chopped veggies into the pan and cook 10-12 mins, or until the turkey is completely cooked through and there is no more pink. Make sure to use a spatula to break the meat into smaller pieces, then pour in the tomato and spaghetti sauces and mix well.

STEP 5. Boil a large pot of water over medium-high heat and cook the pasta to al dente. Drain

STEP 6. FOR ASSEMBLY: Spray a casserole dish with non-stick cooking spray then pour a layer of the meat sauce on the bottom of the dish. Place a layer of the cooked spaghetti noodles on top of the sauce then sprinkle on some cheese. Repeat until you use all the noodles and sauce, making sure that the final layer is cheese.

STEP 7. Bake for 10-15 mins then let the casserole cool at least 5 mins before serving.

- ½ Bell Pepper, Small Diced
- ½ Small White Onion, Small Diced
- 1lb Ground Turkey or Beef
- ½ teaspoon Garlic Salt
- ½ tablespoon Garlic Powder
- ½ teaspoon Black Pepper
- ½ teaspoon Onion Powder
- ½ teaspoon Cajun Seasoning
- 1 tablespoon Worcestershire Sauce
- 1 teaspoon Olive Oil
- 1-15 oz can Tomato Sauce
- 1 jar of Your Favorite Spaghetti Sauce
- 1 lb Spaghetti Noodles
- Non-stick Cooking Spray
- 2 cups Shredded Cheddar Cheese

UTENSILS/COOKWARE NEEDED:
- Mixing Bowl
- Large Pan
- Spatula
- Large Pot
- Casserole Dish

TOTAL TIME: 30 MINS
SERVES: 6

30-MIN MEALS

SLIDERS

- 1 lb Ground Turkey or Beef
- ½ teaspoon Garlic Salt
- ½ teaspoon Black Pepper
- ½ teaspoon Onion Powder
- ½ tablespoon Garlic Powder
- ½ teaspoon Cajun Seasoning
- 1 tablespoon Worcestershire Sauce
- ¼ cup Minced White Onions (optional)
- 1 teaspoon Olive Oil
- Sliced Cheese of Your Choice
- Slider Buns

UTENSILS/COOKWARE NEEDED:

- Mixing Bowl
- Spatula
- Large Skillet or Griddle

TOTAL TIME: 30 MINS
SERVES: 6

STEP 1. Place the ground turkey in a mixing bowl and season with garlic salt, black pepper, onion powder, garlic powder, Cajun seasoning and Worcestershire sauce. Mince the onions then toss into the mixing bowl. Mix all the ingredients together until well-combined.

STEP 2. Take a ¼ cup of the mixture and form it into a ball, then flatten it in your hands to form a patty. Repeat until you turn all the turkey mixture is used.

STEP 3. Warm a large skillet or griddle over medium heat, drizzle in the olive oil and sear the patties on each side for 3-5 mins. Top with sliced cheese and cover the pan to allow the cheese to melt on the patties.

STEP 4. Serve on toasted slider buns with your favorite burger toppings!

30-MIN MEALS

CHICKEN FRIES

STEP 1. Preheat frying oil to 350 degrees.

STEP 2. Wash the chicken breast using vinegar and water, then slice them into the shape of thick fries and place them in a mixing bowl. Season the chicken fries with seasoned salt and garlic powder, mix well.

STEP 3. Lay the seasoned chicken fries flat on a baking sheet or plate and place them in the freezer for 20 mins, this will firm the fries so they don't curl up when you fry them.

STEP 4. FOR THE BREADING: In 3 separate bowls have your flour, eggs and panko ready. Dip the chilled chicken fries in the flour, then egg, then panko and place them in the frying oil. Cook for 3-5 mins or until the chicken fries are golden-brown and cooked through (no more pink). Drain them on paper towels or a wire rack and repeat until all the chicken fries are cooked.

STEP 5. Plate and serve with your favorite side and dipping sauce.

- Oil for Frying
- 3 Chicken Breasts
- ¼ teaspoon Seasoned Salt
- ½ tablespoon Garlic Powder
- Breading
- 2 cups Flour
- 2 Eggs, Beaten
- 2 cups Panko Breadcrumbs

UTENSILS/COOKWARE NEEDED:
- Large Frying Pan or Deep Fryer
- Mixing Bowls
- Baking Sheet

TOTAL TIME: 30 MINS

SERVES: 4

HOME-COOKED MEALS CAN BE EASY, FUN, AND VERY REWARDING.

30-MIN MEALS

GARLIC BREAD PIZZA

- 8-12 Slices of Pre-Made Garlic Bread
- 1 tablespoon Pizza Sauce
- 1 cup Shredded Parmesan Cheese
- 1 cup Shredded Italian Style Cheese Blend
- 3 oz Pre-Sliced Pepperoni

UTENSILS/COOKWARE NEEDED:
- Baking Sheet
- Parchment Paper
- Small Rubber Spatula
- Mixing Bowls

TOTAL TIME: 20 MINS
SERVES: 6

STEP 1. Preheat the oven to 350 degrees.

STEP 2. FOR ASSEMBLY: Lay out the slices of garlic bread on a parchment-lined baking sheet in one flat layer, then spread 1 ½ tablespoons of the pizza sauce on each slice. Sprinkle 1 tablespoon or parmesan and 1 tablespoon of Italian style cheese on top of the pizza sauce, then layer the sliced peperoni on top of the cheese.

STEP 3. Bake the pizzas for 10-15 mins, or until the cheese is melted and bubbly.

STEP 4. Plate and serve hot!

30-MIN MEALS

MAC & CHEESE BALLS

STEP 1. Preheat frying oil to 350 degrees.

STEP 2. Boil a pot of water with a pinch of salt. Add a tablespoon of olive oil to keep the pasta from sticking. Toss in the macaroni noodles and boil for roughly 8 mins or until the noodles are al dente. Drain the water and pour the noodles back into the pot, then add the butter and seasonings (chicken bouillon, paprika, garlic salt, Old Bay, onion powder, garlic powder and black pepper). Mix well then add the shredded cheeses and stir until everything is well-combined. Set aside to cool at least 15 mins, or until it is cool enough to hold in your hands.

STEP 3. Once the mac and cheese has cooled, scoop out a ¼ cup of the macaroni and cheese at a time and roll it into a ball. Place the mac & cheese balls on a parchment-lined baking sheet and sit them in the freezer for 20-30 mins, this is a crucial step to make sure that the mac and cheese balls do not fall apart in the fryer!

STEP 4. FOR THE BREADING: Whisk together the eggs and heavy cream in a large mixing bowl. Pour the flour into a Ziplock or plastic bag and season the flour with garlic powder, onion powder, black pepper, and seasoned salt. Mix well. In another bag, pour the breadcrumbs and season with the parsley and blackened seasoning. Mix well. Start dipping the cold mac & cheese balls in the seasoned flour then egg, then flour and egg again, and finish with breadcrumbs.

STEP 5. Fry the mac & cheese balls for 5-10 mins, then drain them on paper towels or a wire rack.

STEP 6. Plate and serve hot!

NOTE: For added cheesy flavor, you can blend up a bag of Cheeto puffs and use them in place of the breadcrumbs!

- Oil for Frying
- Pinch of Salt
- 1 teaspoon Olive Oil
- 1lb Elbow Macaroni Noodles
- 2 tablespoons Unsalted Butter
- ½ Chicken Bouillon Cube
- ½ teaspoon Paprika
- ¼ teaspoon Garlic Salt
- ¼ teaspoon Old Bay Seasoning
- ½ teaspoon Onion Powder
- ½ teaspoon Garlic Powder
- ¼ teaspoon Black Pepper
- ½ cup Shredded Cheddar Cheese
- ½ cup Shredded Mozzarella Cheese
- ½ cup Shredded Colby Jack Cheese
- Breading
- 5-6 Eggs, Beaten
- ⅓ cup Heavy Whipping Cream
- 2 cups Flour
- ½ teaspoon Garlic Powder
- ½ teaspoon Onion Powder
- ¼ teaspoon Black Pepper
- 1 teaspoon Seasoned Salt
- 2 cups Breadcrumbs
- 2 tablespoons Parsley, Chopped
- 1 teaspoon Blackened Seasoning

UTENSILS/COOKWARE NEEDED:

- Large Frying Pan or Deep Fryer
- Stockpot
- Mixing Bowl
- Baking Sheet
- Parchment Paper
- Ziplock or Plastic Bags

TOTAL TIME: 1 ½ HRS
SERVES: 6

30-MIN MEALS

JERK CHICKEN STIR FRY

- 1 pack Chicken Breasts
- Jerk Marinade
- 1 tablespoon Olive Oil
- 1 Bell Pepper, Sliced
- 1 Medium White Onion, Sliced
- 1 teaspoon Minced Garlic
- ½ cup Brussels Sprouts, Cut in Half
- 1 cup Green Beans
- ½ cup Carrots, Sliced
- ½ cup Snap Peas
- ½ cup Broccoli Florets
- ½ cup Kale
- Jerk Marinade
- 4 Scotch Bonnet Peppers
- 6-8 Garlic Cloves
- 4 Green Onions, Cut in Half
- ½ White Onion, Sliced
- 6-8 sprigs Fresh Thyme, Stem Removed
- ⅛ cup Pimento Seeds or Black Peppercorns
- ¾ cup Brown Sugar
- 1 ½ tablespoons Fresh Ginger, Sliced
- 1 tablespoon Cinnamon
- 1 tablespoon Nutmeg
- ½ teaspoon Garlic Salt
- 1 tablespoon Black Pepper
- ½ tablespoon Browning Sauce
- ½ tablespoon Lemon Juice
- 1 tablespoon Olive Oil
- ¼ cup Water

UTENSILS/COOKWARE NEEDED:

- Mixing Bowls

SERVES: 6

STEP 1. Wash the chicken breast using vinegar and water, then slice the chicken into short strips and place the chicken in a mixing bowl.

STEP 2. FOR THE JERK MARINADE: Use gloves to remove the seeds and slice the scotch bonnets, if you like really spicy jerk sauce, you can leave the seeds in. Throw the scotch bonnets into a blender, then add in the garlic cloves, green onions, white onion, thyme, pimento seeds or black peppercorns, brown sugar, ginger, cinnamon, nutmeg, garlic salt, black pepper, browning sauce, lemon juice, olive oil and water. Blend until the sauce is smooth then pour the marinade into the bowl with the sliced chicken breast and mix well. Marinate for at least 15 mins.

STEP 3. Warm a wok over medium heat, drizzle in the olive oil then cook the jerk-marinated chicken breast for 10-12 mins or until it is cooked through (no more pink). Add the sliced bell peppers, onions and minced garlic into the wok with the chicken and sauté for 2 more mins, then add in the remaining stir fry veggies (brussels sprouts, green beans, carrots, snap peas, broccoli, kale). Mix everything together and cook another 5-8 mins, or until the veggies have softened slightly.

STEP 4. Remove the stir fry from the pan, plate family-style and serve over jasmine rice (see pg.169)

30-MIN MEALS

LOADED NACHOS

STEP 1. Warm a sauté pan over medium heat, drizzle in the olive oil and add the ground turkey. Season with the cumin, paprika, garlic powder, onion powder, blackened seasoning, chili powder and chipotle powder. Mix well, then pour in the chopped onions. Cook for 10-12 mins, or until the turkey is cooked through and there's no more pink. Remove the meat from the pan and set aside.

STEP 2. Drain the canned corn and pour it into a saucepan, sauté over medium-high heat. Add the butter, garlic powder and parsley and stir. Cook for 3-5 mins or until the corn starts to brown a little. Remove from the pan and set aside.

STEP 3. Heat up the nacho cheese sauce, pinto beans and black beans and set aside.

STEP 4. FOR ASSEMBLY: Pour the tortilla chips onto a plate then pile high with all the toppings (ground turkey, beans, corn, sour cream, jalapenos, guac and your favorite salsa).

STEP 5. Serve immediately!

- 1 teaspoon Olive Oil
- 1lb Ground Turkey or Beef
- 1 teaspoon Cumin
- 1 teaspoon Paprika
- 1 teaspoon Garlic Powder
- 1 teaspoon Onion Powder
- 1 teaspoon Blackened Seasoning
- 1 teaspoon Chili Powder
- 1 teaspoon Chipotle Powder
- ¼ White Onion, Chopped
- 1 can Corn, Drained
- 1 tablespoon Unsalted Butter
- ¼ teaspoon Garlic Powder
- ½ teaspoon Parsley, Chopped
- 1 can Nacho Cheese Sauce
- 1 can Pinto Beans, Drained
- 1 can Black Beans, Drained
- Tortilla chips
- Toppings (optional)
- Sour Cream
- Pickled Sliced Jalapenos
- Guacamole
- Salsa

UTENSILS/COOKWARE NEEDED:

- Sauté pan
- Saucepan

TOTAL TIME: 20 MINS
SERVES: 6

30-MIN MEALS

CHOPPED CHEESE SANDWICH

- 1 teaspoon Olive Oil
- ½ White Onion, Small Diced
- ½ Green Bell Pepper, Small Diced
- 1lb Ground Turkey or Beef
- 1 teaspoon Paprika
- 1 teaspoon Onion Powder
- 1 teaspoon Garlic Powder
- 1 teaspoon Black Pepper
- 1 teaspoon Blackened Seasoning
- 4 Slices of Cheese of Your Choice
- 4 Hoagie or Sub Rolls (toasting is optional)
- Mayonnaise (optional)
- Ketchup (optional)
- 1 cup Shredded Lettuce
- 2 Roma Tomatoes, Sliced

UTENSILS/COOKWARE NEEDED:

- Large Pan
- Spatula

TOTAL TIME: 30 MINS

SERVES: 4

NOTE: this dish is a New York staple that's simple and quick to make!

STEP 1. Warm a large pan over medium heat. Drizzle in the olive oil, then sauté the diced onions and bell peppers. Add the ground turkey and season with paprika, onion powder, garlic powder, black pepper and blackened seasoning. Cook the turkey for 10-12 mins, or until it's cooked through, making sure to break up the meat using a spatula.

STEP 2. In the pan, gather the ground turkey into a line across the middle then melt the cheese slices over the top.

STEP 3. FOR ASSEMBLY: Place the hoagie rolls on plates, then smear with mayo and ketchup (optional). Top with the ground turkey and melted cheese, then add the shredded lettuce and tomato.

STEP 4. Serve immediately!

30-MIN MEALS

FLAMIN' HOT WINGS

STEP 1. Wash the chicken wings in vinegar and water, then pat them dry and place the wings in a mixing bowl. Season the chicken with garlic salt, black pepper, garlic powder and onion powder. Mix well.

STEP 2. FOR THE BREADING: In 3 separate bowls have your flour, egg and crushed Hot Cheetos ready. Dip the chicken wings in the flour, then egg, then crushed Hot Cheetos.

STEP 3. Spray the air fryer pan with non-stick cooking spray then place the breaded chicken wings in the pan. Cook at 400 degrees for 15-20 mins, or until the chicken wings are cooked through.

STEP 4. Plate and serve with your favorite dipping sauce.

- 1 bag Chicken Party Wings
- ½ teaspoon Garlic Salt
- ½ teaspoon Black Pepper
- 1 tablespoon Garlic Powder
- 1 tablespoon Onion Powder
- Non-stick Cooking Spray

BREADING

- 2 cups Flour
- 3 Eggs
- 2 cups Flamin' Hot Cheeto Puffs, Crushed

UTENSILS/COOKWARE NEEDED:

- Mixing Bowls
- KitchenEnvy Air Fryer

TOTAL TIME: 40 MINS
SERVES: 6

30-MIN MEALS

MINI PANCAKE SANDWICHES

- 1 teaspoon Olive Oil
- 4 Eggs, Cooked Your Way
- 4 Turkey Sausage Patties

PANCAKE MIX

- 2 cups Flour
- 5 tablespoons White Sugar
- 3 teaspoons Baking Powder
- 2 teaspoons Baking Soda
- 1/8 teaspoon Salt
- 5 tablespoons Melted Unsalted Butter
- 2 teaspoons Vanilla Extract
- 3 cups Buttermilk
- 3 Eggs
- Non-stick Cooking Spray

UTENSILS/COOKWARE NEEDED:

- Medium Pan
- Mixing Bowls
- Whisk
- Spatula
- KitchenEnvy Breakfast Pan

TOTAL TIME: 30 MINS
SERVES: 4

STEP 1. Warm a pan over medium-low heat and drizzle with oil, then cook the eggs to your liking (scrambled, sunny-side up, over easy, etc). Remove the eggs from the pan and set aside.

STEP 2. In the same pan the eggs were cooked in, sear the sausage patties for 5-8 mins or until they are golden-brown and cooked through. Remove them from the pan and set aside.

STEP 3. FOR THE PANCAKES: Combine the dry ingredients (flour, sugar, baking powder, baking soda, and salt) in a mixing bowl and mix well. Make a well in the middle of the dry ingredients then add the wet (butter, vanilla, buttermilk and eggs) to the mixing bowl. Whisk the ingredients together to create the pancake batter. Spray a pan (the same pan the eggs and sausage were cooked in) with non-stick cooking spray then place over medium heat. Pour on a ¼ cup of batter for each pancake and when bubbles cover the surface of the pancake, it's ready to flip. DO NOT flip the batter until it has set (bubbled). Flip the pancake with a spatula, the top side of the pancake should be golden-brown and the edges should be slightly crispy. Continue cooking on the other side for 2-4 mins then remove from the pan and set aside. Repeat until all the pancakes are made.

STEP 4. FOR ASSEMBLY: Use a pancake as the bottom bun of the sandwich, then place a piece of sausage on the pancake and top the sausage with an egg. Use another pancake as the top bun of the sandwich.

STEP 5. Plate and serve!

30-MIN MEALS

VEGAN FRENCH TOAST 298

VEGAN BURRITO 301

AVOCADO TOAST 302

VEGAN BREAKFAST PLATE 305

BUFFALO CAULIFLOWER WRAP 306

BBQ OYSTER MUSHROOM SLIDERS 309

CALLALOO WRAP 310

GENERAL TSO'S CAULIFLOWER 313

BUTTER BEAN STEW/PUMPKIN STEW 314

EGGPLANT PARMESAN 317

VEGAN LASAGNA ROLLS 318

VEGGIE FRIED RICE 321

CHILI MARINATED TOFU PLATE 322

THE LOVE BOWL 325

VEGAN BISCOFF BROWNIES 326

BLUEBERRY BANANA NUT LOAF 329

ZUCCHINI BREAD 330

VEGAN FRENCH TOAST

- 1 cup Dairy-Free Milk
- 2 teaspoons Vanilla Extract
- 2 tablespoons Corn Starch, Leveled
- ½ teaspoon Cinnamon
- 4 tablespoons Vegan Butter
- 6 slices of Thick Bread
- Caramelized Apples
- 1 Apple, Peeled and Sliced
- 2 tablespoons Vegan Butter
- 1 cup Brown Sugar
- 2 teaspoons Vanilla Extract
- 1 teaspoon Honey

UTENSILS/COOKWARE NEEDED:

- Mixing Bowl
- Sauté Pan or Griddle
- Saucepan

TOTAL TIME: 35 MINS
SERVES: 2

STEP 1. Pour the milk in a mixing bowl and add the vanilla extract, corn starch and cinnamon. Mix well and set aside.

STEP 2. Warm a sauté pan or griddle over medium heat and add 1 tablespoon of vegan butter. Dip the bread in the milk mixture and place the bread in the pan with the melted butter. Sear the French toast for 1-2 mins then flip and cook another 2 mins. Remove from the pan and set aside, preferably in the oven or microwave so the French toast stays warm.

STEP 3. FOR THE APPLES: Peel and slice the apple then pour the slices in a saucepan with the butter and simmer over medium heat for 2-3 mins. Add the brown sugar, vanilla extract and honey and cook 5 more mins or until the apples have softened.

STEP 4. Plate the French toast and serve with the caramelized apples on top.

> I DEVELOPED A LOVE AND PASSION FOR COOKING IN MY GRANDMOTHER'S KITCHEN.

VEGAN VIBES

VEGAN BURRITO

STEP 1. Wash, peel and small dice the potatoes. Pour the pieces into a bowl, then drizzle with 1 teaspoon of the vegetable oil, season to taste and mix well. Warm a sauté pan over medium heat and cook the potatoes for 10-15 mins, or until they are fork tender and golden-brown. Remove the potatoes from the pan and set aside.

STEP 2. Cut the vegan sausage into small pieces and place the pieces in the same pan that the potatoes were cooked in. Brown the sausage for 3-5 mins then remove from the pan and set aside.

STEP 3. Wash and chop the onions and bell peppers then sauté them in the same pan the potatoes and sausage were cooked in, making sure to drizzle more oil into the pan. Cook the onions and bell peppers for 5-8 mins, or until the veggies have softened and lightly browned. Leave the veggies in the pan but remove the pan from heat.

STEP 4. FOR THE TOFU SCRAMBLE: Remove the tofu from its packaging, then press out any remaining liquid. Crumble the drained tofu into a mixing bowl and season with salt, pepper, turmeric, paprika and cumin. In the same pan the veggies are still in, drizzle with more oil and add the seasoned tofu and spinach to the pan. Sauté everything together over medium heat for 5 mins, or until the tofu changes color.

STEP 5. Sprinkle with the vegan cheese and pour in 1 tablespoon of water to help the cheese melt. Remove the tofu scramble from the pan and set aside

STEP 6. FOR ASSEMBLY: Warm a flour tortilla and place 2 tablespoons of each .Cut, plate and serve hot!

- 2 Large Russet Potatoes
- 2 teaspoons Vegetable Oil
- ½ cup Vegan Sausage Links
- ½ cup White Onions, Small Diced
- ½ cup Bell Peppers, Small Diced
- 1 Avocado, Diced
- Large Flour Tortillas
- Tofu Scramble
- ½ cup Firm Tofu, Patted Dry
- ½ teaspoon Salt
- ½ teaspoon Black Pepper
- ¼ teaspoon Turmeric
- ¼ teaspoon Paprika
- ¼ teaspoon Cumin
- 1 cup Fresh Spinach
- 1 cup Vegan Cheese
- 1 tablespoon Water

UTENSILS/COOKWARE NEEDED:
- Mixing Bowl
- Sauté Pan
- Spatula

TOTAL TIME: 30 MINS
SERVES: 2

VEGAN VIBES

AVOCADO TOAST

- 3 tablespoons Vegan Butter
- 4-6 Slices of Thick Bread
- 3 ripe Avocados
- ½ teaspoon Salt
- ¼ teaspoon Pepper
- 1 teaspoon Lime or Lemon Juice
- Garnish (optional)
- Sesame Seeds
- Paprika
- Sliced Radish

UTENSILS/COOKWARE NEEDED:

- Mixing Bowl
- Spatula
- Griddle

TOTAL TIME: 10 MINS

SERVES: 3

STEP 1. Melt the butter on a griddle over medium heat, then toast the bread on both sides. Place the bread on plates and set aside.

STEP 2. Remove the pits and scoop out the avocados into a mixing bowl then, using a fork, mash them together with salt, pepper and lime juice. Smear 3 tablespoons-¼ cup of the mixture onto the top of each piece of toast, choose your favorite garnishes and serve!

VEGAN VIBES

VEGAN BREAKFAST PLATE

STEP 1. Wash, peel and medium dice the potatoes. Pour the pieces into a bowl, drizzle with 1 teaspoon of the vegetable oil and season with salt, black pepper, rosemary, and garlic powder. Mix well. Warm a sauté pan over medium heat and cook the potatoes for 10-15 mins, or until they are fork tender and golden-brown. Remove the potatoes from the pan and set aside.

STEP 2. Place the vegan sausage in the same pan that the potatoes were cooked in and brown the sausage for 3-5 mins. Remove from the pan and set aside.

STEP 3. Wash and chop the onions and bell peppers and sauté them in the same pan the potatoes and sausage were cooked in, and make sure to drizzle more oil into the pan. Cook the onions and bell peppers for 5-8 mins, or until the veggies have softened and lightly browned. Leave the veggies in the pan but remove the pan from heat.

STEP 4. FOR THE TOFU SCRAMBLE: Remove the tofu from its packaging, then press out any remaining liquid. Crumble the drained tofu into a mixing bowl and season with salt, pepper, turmeric, paprika and cumin. In the same pan the veggies are still in, drizzle with more oil and add the seasoned tofu and spinach to the pan. Sauté everything together over medium heat for 5 mins, or until the tofu changes color. Heat the oven to 400 degrees and toast the bread until golden-brown, then set on a plate and place the tofu scramble, potatoes and sausage on the plate with the toast. Serve hot!

- 2-4 Medium-Sized Russet Potatoes, Medium Diced
- 1 tablespoon Vegetable Oil
- ¼ teaspoon Salt
- ¼ teaspoon Black Pepper
- ¼ teaspoon Dried Rosemary
- ¼ teaspoon Garlic Powder
- 4 Vegan Sausage Links
- ½ cup White Onions, Small Diced
- ½ cup Bell Peppers, Small Diced
- 4-6 slices of Thick Bread
- Tofu Scramble
- ½ cup Firm Tofu, Patted Dry
- ½ teaspoon Salt
- ½ teaspoon Black Pepper
- ¼ teaspoon Turmeric
- ¼ teaspoon Paprika
- ¼ teaspoon Cumin
- 1 cup Fresh Spinach
- 1 cup Vegan Cheese
- 1 tablespoon Water

UTENSILS/COOKWARE NEEDED:

- Mixing Bowls
- Sauté Pan
- Spatula

TOTAL TIME: 35 MINS
SERVES: 3

BUFFALO CAULIFLOWER WRAP

- Oil for Frying
- 1 head Cauliflower
- 2 cups Panko Breadcrumbs
- 1 cup Buffalo Sauce
- Large Flour Tortillas
- Vegan Blue Cheese, As Desired
- Shredded Romaine Lettuce, As Desired
- Cherry Tomatoes, As Desired
- Tempura Batter
- ½ teaspoon Paprika
- ½ teaspoon Ground Ginger
- ½ teaspoon Poultry Seasoning
- ¼ teaspoon Black Pepper
- ¼ teaspoon Salt
- ¼ teaspoon Crushed Red Pepper
- 2 ½ cups Flour
- 3 cups Ice Water

UTENSILS/COOKWARE NEEDED:

- Frying Pan or Deep Fryer
- 2 Mixing Bowls
- Sauté Pan
- Total Time:

SERVES: 6

- Note: If you have cold seltzer water on hand, use that in place of the ice water for the tempura batter.

STEP 1. Preheat frying oil to 350 degrees.

STEP 2. Wash and break up the head of cauliflower into bite sized pieces then place in a mixing bowl and set aside.

STEP 3. FOR BREADING THE CAULIFLOWER: Pour the panko breadcrumbs into a mixing bowl or bag and set aside. Mix together all the ingredients FOR THE TEMPURA BATTER in a large bowl, then begin dipping the pieces of cauliflower into the batter. Toss the dipped cauliflower in the panko breadcrumbs and place the breaded pieces on a wire rack. Repeat until all the cauliflower is breaded.

STEP 4. Place the cauliflower in the frying oil for 5-8 mins, or until the cauliflower is golden-brown. Drain the fried cauliflower on a wire rack or paper towels and set aside.

STEP 5. Pour the buffalo sauce into a sauté pan and toss the fried cauliflower in the sauce, then place it back onto the wire rack or paper towels the cauliflower was draining on.

STEP 6. FOR ASSEMBLY: Warm a flour tortilla and place the vegan blue cheese, shredded lettuce, cherry tomatoes and buffalo cauliflower inside. Wrap the tortilla around the filling and sear in a pan or on a griddle for 2 mins on each side.

STEP 7. Cut, plate and serve hot.

VEGAN VIBES

BBQ OYSTER MUSHROOM SLIDERS

STEP 1. Warm a sauté pan over medium heat then drizzle in the vegetable oil and add in the mushrooms and bell peppers. Season with garlic powder, soy sauce and liquid smoke then sauté together for 3-5 mins. Pour in the BBQ sauce and mix well, then remove the mixture from the pan and set aside.

STEP 2. FOR THE SLAW: In a mixing bowl combine the veganaise, vinegar, salt, black pepper and sugar. Whisk well! (The sauce should be thin so if it feels too thick, add more vinegar). Toss in the shredded red and green cabbage and make sure the cabbage is well-coated in the sauce.

STEP 3. FOR ASSEMBLY: Toast the Hawaiian buns then place a scoop of the BBQ mushroom mixture onto the bottom buns and top with some of the cabbage slaw. Place the top bun over the slaw and serve with your favorite chips or BBQ sides!

- 1 teaspoon Vegetable Oil
- 2 cups Oyster Mushrooms, Sliced
- ¼ Green Bell Pepper, Sliced
- ¼ Red Bell Pepper, Sliced
- ½ teaspoon Garlic Powder
- 1 tablespoon Soy Sauce
- ½ teaspoon Liquid Smoke
- ¼ cup of Your Favorite BBQ Sauce
- 2 Red Sweet Peppers, Sliced
- 2 Yellow Sweet Peppers, Sliced
- 4 King's Hawaiian Rolls

SLAW

- ¼ cup Veganaise
- ¼ cup Vinegar
- ⅛ teaspoon Salt
- ¼ teaspoon Black Pepper
- ½ teaspoon Sugar
- ½ cup Shredded Red Cabbage
- ½ cup Shredded Green Cabbage

UTENSILS/COOKWARE NEEDED:

- Sauté pan
- Spatula
- Mixing bowl

TOTAL TIME: 30 MINS
SERVES: 4

VEGAN VIBES

CALLALOO WRAP

- Oil for Frying
- 1 Ripe Plantain
- 2 teaspoons Vegetable Oil
- 1 Red Bell Pepper, Small Diced
- ½ Yellow Bell Pepper, Small Diced
- ½ White Onion, Small Diced
- 2 cloves Garlic, Chopped
- ¼ teaspoon Salt
- ¼ teaspoon Black Pepper
- ¼ teaspoon Crushed Red Pepper
- 1 can Callaloo, Drained
- 4-6 Large Flour Tortillas

UTENSILS/COOKWARE NEEDED:

- Frying Pan or Deep Fryer
- Sauté Pan
- Small Rubber Spatula

TOTAL TIME: 20 MINS
SERVES: 4

STEP 1. Heat frying oil to 350 degrees. Slice the plantain into rounds and fry for 5-8 mins, or until they're golden brown and have softened. Drain the fried plantains on paper towels or a wire rack, then set aside.

STEP 2. Warm a sauté pan over medium heat then drizzle in the oil and sauté the red bell peppers, yellow bell peppers, onions and garlic together for 3-5 mins, or until the veggies begin to soften. Season with salt, pepper and crushed red pepper then stir in the callaloo and cook for another 5 mins.

STEP 3. FOR ASSEMBLY: Warm a flour tortilla and place 4-5 slices of the friend plantain inside then add the callaloo mixture on top of the plantains. Wrap the tortilla around the filling and sear in a pan or griddle for 2 mins on each side.

STEP 4. Cut, plate and serve hot.

VEGAN VIBES

GENERAL TSO'S CAULIFLOWER

STEP 1. Preheat frying oil to 350 degrees.

STEP 2. Wash and break up the head of cauliflower into bite sized pieces then place in a mixing bowl and set aside.

STEP 3. FOR BREADING THE CAULIFLOWER: Pour the panko breadcrumbs into a mixing bowl or bag and set aside. Mix together all the ingredients for the tempura batter in a large bowl, then begin dipping the pieces of cauliflower into the batter. Toss the dipped cauliflower in the panko breadcrumbs and place the breaded pieces on a wire rack. Repeat until all the cauliflower is breaded.

STEP 4. Place the cauliflower in the frying oil for 5-8 mins, or until the cauliflower is golden-brown. Drain the fried cauliflower on a wire rack or paper towels and set aside.

STEP 5. Pour the General Tso's sauce into a sauté pan and toss the fried cauliflower in the sauce until it is well-coated.

STEP 6. Plate the cauliflower over white rice and serve.

- Oil for Frying
- 1 head Cauliflower
- 2 cups Panko Breadcrumbs
- 1 cup General Tso's Sauce
- Cooked White Rice
- Tempura Batter
- ½ teaspoon Paprika
- ½ teaspoon Ground Ginger
- ½ teaspoon Poultry Seasoning
- ¼ teaspoon Black Pepper
- ¼ teaspoon Salt
- ¼ teaspoon Crushed Red Pepper
- 2 ½ cups Flour
- 3 cups Ice Water

UTENSILS/COOKWARE NEEDED:

- Frying Pan or Deep Fryer
- 2 Mixing Bowls
- Sauté Pan

TOTAL TIME: 20 MINS
SERVES: 6

NOTE: If you have cold seltzer water on hand, use that in place of the ice water for the tempura batter.

VEGAN VIBES

BUTTER BEAN STEW/PUMPKIN STEW

- 1 tablespoon Olive Oil
- 1 Medium Onion, Medium Diced
- 1 Bell Pepper, Medium Diced
- 2 Roma Tomatoes, Medium Diced
- 1 Scotch Bonnet, Minced
- 3-4 cloves Garlic, Chopped
- 3 sprigs Fresh Thyme
- 4 Green Onions, Chopped
- 2 cans Butter Beans or Lima Beans
- ½ tablespoon Garlic Powder
- ½ tablespoon Onion Powder
- 1 teaspoon Garlic Salt
- 1 teaspoon Crushed Red Pepper
- ½ tablespoon Black Pepper
- 1 tablespoon Blackened Seasoning
- 1 package Pumpkin Soup Mix
- 1 ½ cups Water
- 2 tablespoon Unsalted Butter

UTENSILS/COOKWARE NEEDED:

- Large Pan or Pot
- Wooden Spoon

TOTAL TIME: 45 MINS
SERVES: 6

STEP 1. Warm a large pan or pot over medium heat, drizzle in the olive oil and sauté the onions, bell pepper, Roma tomatoes, scotch bonnet, garlic, thyme and green onions for 5-8 mins, stirring occasionally.

STEP 2. Drain and rinse the butter beans and add them to the pan with the veggies, then season the beans with garlic powder, onion powder, garlic salt, crushed red pepper, black pepper, blackened seasoning. Stir, then pour in the pumpkin soup mix and water. Add in the butter then cover the pan and simmer for 30-35 mins, stirring occasionally.

STEP 3. Allow the soup to cool at least 5 mins before plating. Serve over jasmine rice (see pg. 176).

VEGAN VIBES

EGGPLANT PARMESAN

STEP 1. Preheat the oven to 400 degrees.

STEP 2. Wash and cut the tops off the eggplants, then slice them lengthwise about ½ inch thick and lay them on a flat surface. Salt the eggplant on both sides and let it sit for at least 10 mins, this will allow moisture to come out of the eggplant and make it crispier when it bakes. After the 10 mins, pat the eggplant slices dry and set aside.

STEP 3. Pour the flour and milk in a mixing bowl and whisk together until smooth, set aside.

STEP 4. Pour the panko breadcrumbs in a mixing bowl or baking dish and season with the nutritional yeast, Italian seasoning and oregano.

STEP 5. FOR BREADING: Dip the sliced eggplant in the flour/milk mixture then coat with the panko, making sure to coat both sides of the eggplant. Place the breaded eggplant on a parchment-lined baking sheet in one flat layer and bake for 10-15 mins, or until the eggplant starts to brown.

STEP 6. FOR ASSEMBLY: Remove the breaded eggplant from the oven and pour ¼ cup of spaghetti sauce onto each piece, then sprinkle the sauce with parmesan and place a slice of mozzarella on top of the parmesan. Bake the eggplant for 10 more mins, or until the cheese melts and begins to brown.

STEP 7. Plate family-style over spaghetti noodles and serve with more spaghetti sauce.

- 2 Eggplants
- ¼ teaspoon Salt
- ¼ cup Flour
- ⅔ cup Non-Dairy Milk
- 2 cups Panko Breadcrumbs
- ¼ cup Nutritional Yeast
- 1 tablespoon Italian Seasoning
- 1 teaspoon Dried Oregano
- 1 cup of Your Favorite Spaghetti Sauce
- 6 slices Vegan Mozzarella Cheese
- ½ cup Vegan Parmesan Cheese
- Cooked Spaghetti Noodles (optional)

UTENSILS/COOKWARE NEEDED:

- 2 Mixing Bowls
- Whisk
- Baking Sheet
- Parchment Paper

TOTAL TIME: 40 MINS
SERVES: 4

VEGAN VIBES

VEGAN LASAGNA ROLLS

- 1 teaspoon Olive Oil
- ½ Whole Shallot, Sliced
- ½ cup Bell Peppers, Sliced Thin
- 1 cup Vegan Sausage Crumbles
- 2 cups of Your Favorite Spaghetti Sauce
- ½ cup Vegan Parmesan Cheese
- Ricotta Mixture
- 1 pack Firm Tofu, Patted Dry
- 2 teaspoons Nutritional Yeast
- ½ teaspoon Lemon Juice
- ½ teaspoon Garlic Powder
- ½ teaspoon Onion Powder
- ½ teaspoon Black Pepper
- ½ teaspoon Dried Basil or Oregano
- 1-2 teaspoons Olive Oil

PASTA

- Pinch Salt
- 1 tablespoon Olive Oil
- 6-8 Lasagna Noodles

UTENSILS/COOKWARE NEEDED:

- Sauté Pan
- Food Processor
- Small Rubber Spatula
- Large Pot
- Casserole Dish
- Aluminium Foil

TOTAL TIME: 1 HR
SERVES: 6

STEP 1. Preheat the oven to 400 degrees.

STEP 2. Warm a sauté pan over medium heat, drizzle in the olive oil then add the shallot and bell peppers. Sauté the veggies for 3-5 mins, stirring occasionally, then sprinkle in the sausage crumbles. Cook for another 5 mins, then add the spaghetti sauce and stir until everything is well-combined. Reduce the heat to low and let the sauce simmer.

STEP 3. FOR THE RICOTTA: Remove the tofu from its packaging, then squeeze the remaining liquid from the tofu. Place the drained tofu into a food processor with the nutritional yeast, lemon juice, garlic powder, onion powder, black pepper, basil and olive oil. Blend until smooth then set aside.

STEP 4. FOR THE PASTA: Boil a pot of water with a pinch of salt and add a tablespoon of olive oil to keep the pasta from sticking. Toss in the lasagna noodles and boil for roughly 8 mins, or until the noodles are al dente then drain the pasta water.

STEP 5. FOR ASSEMBLY: Lay out the lasagna noodles on a cutting board then on each individual noodle, spread a layer of the ricotta mixture then a layer of the sauce, then sprinkle with some parmesan cheese. Roll the noodles into pinwheel shapes, you should have enough for about 12 lasagna rolls. Spread a layer of the sauce at the bottom of a casserole dish, then place the lasagna rolls side by side in the pan. Add another layer of cheese then sauce, then more cheese on top of the rolls. Cover with foil and bake for 30 mins.

STEP 6. Remove the lasagna rolls from the oven and let them cool for at least 10 mins before serving.

VEGAN VIBES

VEGGIE FRIED RICE

STEP 1. Warm a wok over medium-high heat, drizzle in the oil and sauté the onions, bell peppers, garlic paste and ginger paste for 3-5 mins, stirring often. Add in the chopped broccoli and sauté another 5 mins, then remove the veggies from the wok and set aside.

STEP 2. FOR THE TOFU SCRAMBLE (optional): Remove the tofu from its packaging, then squeeze the remaining liquid from the tofu. Crumble the drained tofu into a mixing bowl and season with salt, pepper, turmeric, paprika and cumin. In the same pan the veggies were cooked in, drizzle with more oil and add the seasoned tofu. Sauté everything together over medium heat for 5 mins, or until the tofu changes color.

STEP 3. Clean the wok then place it over medium heat and pour in another teaspoon of oil. Pour the Just Egg (optional) into the wok and scramble until the egg is cooked through. Remove the eggs from the pan and place them in the same bowl as the sautéed veggies.

STEP 4. Add the last of the oil to the wok and warm it over medium-high heat. Place the precooked white rice into the wok then season with soy sauce and stir until the rice is completely coated. Continue stir-frying the rice for 3-4 mins then add in the veggies and eggs.

STEP 5. Plate in a bowl and serve hot.

- 3 teaspoons Vegetable Oil
- 1 cup White Onions, Small Diced
- 1 cup Bell Peppers, Small Diced
- ½ teaspoon Garlic Paste
- ½ teaspoon Ginger Paste
- ½ cup Broccoli, Chopped
- 1 cup Tofu Scramble* or Just Egg
- 2 cups Cooked White Rice, Chilled 12-24 hrs
- ¼ cup Soy Sauce
- Tofu Scramble (optional)*
- ½ cup Firm Tofu, Patted Dry
- ½ teaspoon Salt
- ½ teaspoon Black Pepper
- ¼ teaspoon Turmeric
- ¼ teaspoon Paprika
- ¼ teaspoon Cumin

UTENSILS/COOKWARE NEEDED:

- KitchenEnvy Wok
- Rubber Spatula
- 2 Mixing Bowls

TOTAL TIME: 30 MINS

SERVES: 6

CHILI MARINATED TOFU PLATE

- 1 pack Firm Tofu, Patted Dry
- ¼ cup Corn Flour
- ¼ teaspoon Vegetable Oil
- 1 teaspoon Corn Starch
- Tofu Marinade
- ½ cup Veggie Stock
- 1 teaspoon Maple Syrup
- 3 cloves Minced Garlic
- 2 tablespoons Soy Sauce
- 2 tablespoons Lime Juice
- ⅛ teaspoon Salt
- ⅛ teaspoon Crushed Red Pepper
- Garlic Mashed Potatoes
- 4 Red Potatoes, Quartered
- 6 tablespoons Vegan Butter
- 2 tablespoons Garlic Paste
- ½ cup Coconut Milk
- 2 teaspoons Salt
- Black Pepper, to taste
- Broccoli Rabe
- 1 bundle Fresh Broccoli Rabe or Broccolini
- 1 teaspoon Grapeseed Oil
- 2 teaspoons Soy Sauce
- 1 teaspoon Garlic Chili Sauce
- ¼ cup Water

UTENSILS/COOKWARE NEEDED:

- Mixing Bowl
- Whisk
- Baking Sheet
- Parchment Paper
- Large Pot

TOTAL TIME: 1 HR
SERVES: 4

STEP 1. Preheat the oven to 350 degrees.

STEP 2. FOR THE MARINADE: In a mixing bowl whisk together veggie stock, maple syrup, minced garlic, soy sauce, lime juice, salt and crushed red pepper.

STEP 3. Drain the water from the tofu then slice a criss-cross pattern on one side, this will allow the marinade to flavor the tofu even more. Marinate the tofu for at least 15-20 mins. Once the tofu is done marinating, reserve the marinade and set aside.

STEP 4. Roll both sides of the marinated tofu in vegetable oil then the corn starch and place the tofu on a parchment-lined baking sheet. Bake for 15 mins, then remove from the oven and set aside.

STEP 5. FOR THE POTATOES: Boil the quartered potatoes in a large pot of water until they are tender then drain the water. Pour the potatoes back into the pot and mash them with the butter, garlic paste, coconut milk, salt and black pepper until smooth. Set aside.

STEP 6. FOR THE BROCCOLI: Warm a sauté pan over medium-high heat, drizzle in the grapeseed oil and add the broccoli rabe to the pan. Sauté for 3-5 mins, then pour in the soy sauce, garlic chili sauce and water. Stir then cover the pan for another 5 mins, or until the broccoli is fork tender.

STEP 7. Add the corn starch to the reserved marinade and whisk together. Toss the baked tofu in the sauce then plate alongside the mashed potatoes and broccoli rabe. Serve hot.

VEGAN VIBES

THE LOVE BOWL

STEP 1. Heat frying oil to 350 degrees. Slice the plantains into rounds and fry for 5-8 mins, or until they're golden brown and have softened. Drain the fried plantains on paper towels or a wire rack, then set aside.

STEP 2. Warm a sauté pan over medium heat, drizzle with oil and sauté the shredded green and red cabbage together for 3-5 mins. Season with salt and pepper to taste and stir, then remove the cabbage from the pan and set aside.

STEP 3. Drain and rinse the black beans then pour them into the same sauté pan the cabbage was cooked in. Season with garlic powder, onion powder and garlic chili paste then stir until well combined. Remove the beans from the heat and set aside.

STEP 4. FOR ASSEMBLY: Plate the cooked rice at the bottom of a serving bowl then place some of the fried plantains, cooked shredded cabbage, seasoned black beans, sliced carrot, sliced bell peppers and sliced avocado over the rice.

STEP 5. Garnish with sesame seeds and serve!

- Oil for Frying
- 2 Plantains
- 1 cup Shredded Green Cabbage
- 1 cup Shredded Red Cabbage
- ½ teaspoon Vegetable Oil
- ⅛ teaspoon Salt
- ¼ teaspoon Black Pepper
- 1 can Black Beans
- ½ teaspoon Garlic Powder
- ½ teaspoon Onion Powder
- ½ teaspoon Garlic Chili Paste
- 2 cups Cooked White Rice
- ½ Carrot, Sliced
- 1 Bell Pepper, Sliced Thin
- 1 Avocado, Sliced

UTENSILS/COOKWARE NEEDED:

- Frying Pan or Deep Fryer
- Sauté Pan

TOTAL TIME: 30 MINS
SERVES: 6

NOTE: Every part of this bowl is beautiful yet simple, so don't be afraid to get creative with your plating!

VEGAN BISCOFF BROWNIES

- 1 cup Rolled Oats
- 1 Mashed Banana
- ½ cup Sugar
- 2 tablespoons Oat Milk or Almond Milk
- 2 tablespoons Vanilla Extract
- 2 tablespoons Biscoff Cookie Butter
- 1 tablespoon Cocoa Powder
- ½ cup Vegan White Chocolate Chips
- ½ cup Vegan Milk Chocolate Chips
- Non-stick Cooking Spray

UTENSILS/COOKWARE NEEDED:

- Blender
- Mixing Bowl
- Hand Mixer
- Baking Dish

SERVES: 4
TOTAL TIME: 40 MINS

STEP 1. Preheat the oven to 300 degrees.

STEP 2. Pour the oats in a blender and mix until they become a fine powder.

STEP 3. Mash the banana in a mixing bowl and add the sugar, ground oats, oat milk, vanilla extract, Biscoff butter and cocoa powder. Mix until everything is well-combined, then fold the chocolate chips into the batter.

STEP 4. Coat a baking dish with non-stick cooking spray and pour the batter into the pan. Bake the brownies for 20 mins.

STEP 5. Remove the brownies from the oven and let cool for at least 10 mins before cutting and serving.

VEGAN VIBES

BLUEBERRY BANANA NUT LOAF

STEP 1. Preheat the oven to 350 degrees.

STEP 2. Combine all the ingredients in a mixing bowl, then pour the mixture into a loaf pan that's been coated with non-stick cooking spray. Bake for 30-45 mins, or until you can stick a toothpick in the center of the loaf and it comes out clean.

STEP 3. Remove the loaf from the oven and let cool for at least 10 mins before flipping it out of the pan and slicing it. Serve with dairy-free ice cream.

- 3 Mashed Bananas
- 1 cup Applesauce
- 1 cup Vegan Greek Yogurt
- ½ cup Honey
- 2 tablespoons Vanilla Extract
- 1 teaspoon Baking Soda
- ½ cup Flour
- 1 cup Blueberries
- 1 cup Chopped Nuts of Your Choice

UTENSILS/COOKWARE NEEDED:

- Mixing bowl
- Small Rubber Spatula
- Loaf Pan

TOTAL TIME: 1 HR

SERVES: 6

ZUCCHINI BREAD

- 2 cups Flour
- 1 teaspoon Salt
- 1 teaspoon Baking Powder
- 1 teaspoon Baking Soda
- ½ cup Vegetable Oil
- 2 cups Brown Sugar
- 1 cup White Sugar
- 1 cup of Applesauce
- 2 teaspoons Vanilla Extract
- 2 cups Grated Zucchini
- 1 ½ cups Chopped Nuts
- Non-stick Cooking Spray

UTENSILS/COOKWARE NEEDED:

- Mixing bowl
- Loaf Pan
- Rubber Spatula

TOTAL TIME: 45 MINS

SERVES: 4

NOTE: if you're making this recipe non-vegan, you can use 2 eggs in place of the applesauce.

STEP 1. Preheat the oven to 350 degrees.

STEP 2. In a mixing bowl, combine all the dry ingredients (flour, salt, baking powder, baking soda) and set aside.

STEP 3. In a separate bowl, combine the vegetable oil, brown sugar, white sugar, applesauce and vanilla extract. Mix well, then fold in the zucchini and chopped nuts. DO NOT over-mix your batter!

STEP 4. Coat a loaf pan with non-stick cooking spray, then pour the batter into the pan. Place the loaf pan in the oven and bake for 45 mins, or until you can stick a toothpick in the center of the bread and it comes out clean.

STEP 5. Remove the bread from the oven and let cool at least 10 mins before flipping it out of the pan and slicing it. Plate and serve!

VEGAN VIBES

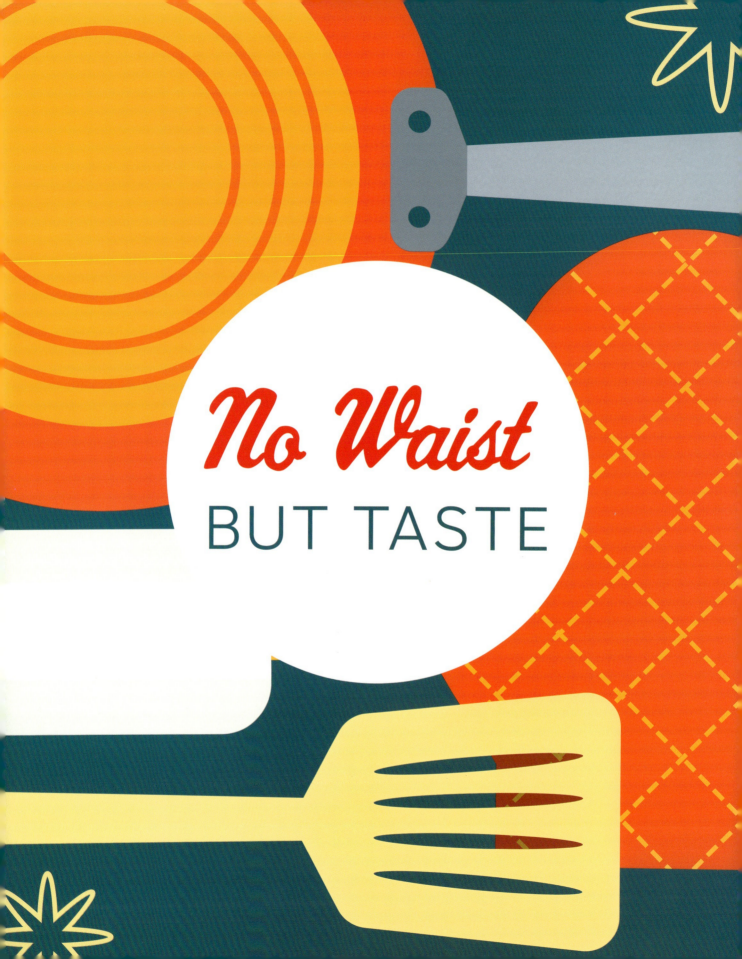

ZUCCHINI FRIES 334

CAULIFLOWER PIZZA CRUST 337

CAULIFLOWER CHEESY BREAD 338

TERIYAKI ZUCCHINI NOODLES 341

ZUCCHINI ENCHILADAS 342

BACON WRAPPED ASPARAGUS 345

AVOCADO TUNA SALAD 346

HONEY GARLIC CHICKEN & GREEN BEANS 349

LEMON GARLIC SHRIMP WRAP 350

LEMON GARLIC SHRIMP 353

SUNDRIED TOMATO & SPINACH CHICKEN 354

CILANTRO LIME LETTUCE TACOS 357

CINNAMON CRUNCH BANANA BREAD 358

BLUEBERRY MUFFINS 361

OATMEAL BARS 362

BANANA CHOCOLATE CHIP PANCAKES 365

ALMOND BUTTER CHOCOLATE CHIP COOKIES 366

SALAD 369

CHICKEN STIR FRY 370

YOGURT BITES 373

CHIPOTLE CHICKEN AVO BOWL 374

ZUCCHINI FRIES

- 2 Zucchini
- 1 tablespoon Olive Oil
- 1 tablespoon Paprika
- 1 tablespoon Onion Powder
- 1 tablespoon Garlic Powder
- ⅓ cup Panko Breadcrumbs
- ½ tablespoon Parsley, Chopped
- Non-stick Cooking Spray

UTENSILS/COOKWARE NEEDED:

- Mixing Bowl
- Baking Sheet
- Parchment Paper

TOTAL TIME: 30 MINS
SERVES: 4

STEP 1. Preheat the oven to 400 degrees.

STEP 2. Rinse the zucchini and slice them into the shape of fries then place them in a mixing bowl. Drizzle the zucchini fries with olive oil then season them with the paprika, onion powder and garlic powder. Add the panko breadcrumbs to the bowl and mix well.

STEP 3. Line a baking sheet with parchment paper and spray with non-stick cooking spray. Place the zucchini fries onto the baking sheet in a flat layer and bake for 15 mins, or until the fries are golden brown and crispy.

STEP 4. Remove the fries from the oven, garnish with more parsley and serve immediately.

> MY PLEASURE COMES FROM GIVING. I LOVE TO COOK FOR OTHERS AND SEE THE SATISFACTION ON THEIR FACES WHEN THEY TAKE A BITE OF MY FOOD.

NO WAIST BUT TASTE

CAULIFLOWER PIZZA CRUST

STEP 1. Preheat the oven to 400 degrees.

STEP 2. Break apart the head of cauliflower and place it into a blender or food processor, then blend the cauliflower in batches until it's broken down to the size of rice. Pour the blended cauliflower into a microwave-safe mixing bowl and microwave for 4 mins, then pour the cauliflower into a towel and wring it dry.

STEP 3. Pour the dried, blended cauliflower into a large mixing bowl and season it with the oregano, basil, garlic powder and onion powder. Mix well then add in the parmesan and pour the seasoned cauliflower mixture onto a parchment paper-lined baking sheet. Flatten it into the shape of a pizza crust then bake for 25-30 mins, or until the crust is golden-brown and firm.

STEP 4. Remove the crust from the oven then top with pizza sauce, arugula and the shredded and sliced mozzarella. Bake for another 10 mins, or until the cheese is browned and bubbly.

STEP 5. Cut, plate and serve hot!

- 1 head Fresh Cauliflower
- 1 teaspoon Dried Oregano
- 1 teaspoon Dried Basil
- 1 teaspoon Garlic Powder
- 1 teaspoon Onion Powder
- 1 cup Shredded Parmesan Cheese
- 1-2 cups Pizza Sauce
- 1 cup Arugula
- 1 ball Fresh Mozzarella Cheese, Sliced
- Shredded Mozzarella Cheese, As Desired

UTENSILS/COOKWARE NEEDED:

- Blender or Food Processor
- Mixing Bowl
- Baking Sheet
- Parchment Paper

TOTAL TIME: 1 HR
SERVES: 6

NOTE: If you have kids, this is a great way to sneak some veggies into their diet by disguising them in one of kids' favorite treats – PIZZA!

CAULIFLOWE CHEESY BREAD

- 1 head Fresh Cauliflower or 1 Bag Cauliflower
- 1 teaspoon Dried Oregano
- 1 teaspoon Dried Basil
- 1 teaspoon Garlic Powder
- 1 teaspoon Onion Powder
- 1 cup Shredded Parmesan Cheese
- Shredded Mozzarella Cheese, as desired

UTENSILS/COOKWARE NEEDED:

- Blender
- Mixing Bowl
- Baking Sheet
- Parchment Paper

TOTAL TIME: 45 MINS
SERVES: 6

STEP 1. Preheat the oven to 400 degrees.

STEP 2. Break apart the head of cauliflower and place it into a blender or food processor. Blend the cauliflower in batches until it's broken down to the size of rice, then pour the blended cauliflower into microwave-safe mixing bowl. Microwave for 4 mins then pour the cauliflower into a towel and wring it dry, all the water should come out.

STEP 3. Pour the dried, blended cauliflower into a large mixing bowl and season it with the oregano, basil, garlic powder and onion powder. Mix well then add in the parmesan and pour the seasoned cauliflower mixture onto a parchment paper-lined baking sheet. Shape the mixture into a circle or square and bake for 25-30 mins, or until the bread is golden-brown and firm.

STEP 4. Sprinkle the top of the cheesy bread with more shredded cheese then cut, plate and serve hot.

NO WAIST BUT TASTE

TERIYAKI ZUCCHINI NOODLES

STEP 1. Wash the salmon using vinegar and water then pat dry and season with Old Bay, blackened seasoning, black pepper and garlic powder. Warm a sauté pan or griddle over medium-high heat, add the oil then sear the seasoned salmon for 5-8 mins, skin-side down first to get it crispy then flipping it over halfway through the cooking time. Remove the salmon from the pan and set aside.

STEP 2. FOR THE SAUCE: Warm a saucepan over medium heat and pour in all the ingredients for the sauce, simmer for 3-5 mins then add in the zucchini noodles. Sauté for 5 mins and make sure to use tongs to toss the noodles so they don't break apart in the pan.

STEP 3. Plate the teriyaki zucchini noodles then place the salmon filets on top of the noodles and serve.

- 2-3 Salmon Filets
- ½ tablespoon Old Bay Seasoning
- ½ tablespoon Blackened Seasoning
- ½ tablespoon Black Pepper
- ½ tablespoon Garlic Powder
- 1 teaspoon Vegetable Oil
- 1 bag Pre-Made Zucchini Noodles
- Sauce
- 1 cup Brown Sugar
- ¼ cup Hoisin Sauce
- 1 tablespoon Sriracha Sauce
- 4 Whole Chiles de Arbol
- 1 tablespoon Soy Sauce
- ¼ teaspoon Ground Ginger
- 1 tablespoon Sweet Chili Crisp

UTENSILS/COOKWARE NEEDED:

- Sauté Pan or Griddle
- Saucepan
- Spatula

TOTAL TIME: 30 MINS
SERVES: 6

NOTE: You can make your own zucchini noodles if you have fresh zucchini and a mandolin – just set it to the julienne-blade option and watch your fingers!

NO WAIST BUT TASTE

ZUCCHINI ENCHILADAS

- 1 teaspoon Olive Oil
- ½ White Onion, Small Diced
- 1lb Ground Turkey
- 1 teaspoon Garlic and Herb Seasoning
- 1 teaspoon Black Pepper
- 1 teaspoon Garlic Powder
- 1 teaspoon Onion Powder
- 1 can Red Enchilada Sauce
- 4 Zucchinis, Thinly Sliced
- Shredded Colby Jack Cheese, As Desired

UTENSILS/COOKWARE NEEDED:

- Sauté pan
- Spatula
- Mandolin or potato peeler
- Casserole Dish

TOTAL TIME: 1 HR
SERVES: 6

STEP 1. Preheat the oven to 400 degrees.

STEP 2. Warm a large sauté pan over medium heat, then add oil and the diced onions. Sauté for 3 mins then add in the ground turkey and season with garlic and herb seasoning, black pepper, garlic powder and onion powder. Mix well and cook the ground turkey for 10-12 mins, or until the meat is cooked through and there's no more pink. Pour in 1/3 cup of the enchilada sauce and stir. Remove the pan from the heat and set aside.

STEP 3. Use a mandolin or potato peeler to slice the zucchini into thin strips, set aside.

STEP 4. FOR ASSEMBLY: Layer 4 strips of zucchini side-by-side and slightly overlapping, then place ¼ cup of the ground turkey at the center of the strips. Top the turkey with cheese and roll the strips of zucchini over the filling to create the shape of an enchilada. Repeat until you've used all the filling. Pour some enchilada sauce at the bottom of a casserole dish and place the rolled zucchini enchiladas in the dish in one flat layer. Pour more enchilada sauce over the top of the enchiladas then sprinkle with shredded cheese and bake for 30 mins.

STEP 5. Remove the enchiladas from the oven and let cool at least 10 mins before serving. Plate and serve with your favorite enchilada toppings.

NO WAIST BUT TASTE

BACON WRAPPED ASPARAGUS

STEP 1. Wrap one slice of bacon around 3 pieces of asparagus then stick toothpicks throughout, so the bacon is secured then repeat until all the asparagus is wrapped.

STEP 2. Warm a sauté pan or griddle over medium-high heat and sear the bacon wrapped asparagus until the bacon is crispy and cooked through and the asparagus is tender.

STEP 3. Plate and serve hot!

- 1 pack Sliced Bacon
- 1 bunch Asparagus

UTENSILS/COOKWARE NEEDED:

- Sauté Pan or Griddle
- Tongs

TOTAL TIME: 30 MINS
SERVES: 4

NOTE: This is a great appetizer for parties!

NO WAIST BUT TASTE

AVOCADO TUNA SALAD

- 2 cans Tuna
- 2 Avocados, Small Diced
- ⅓ cup Green Bell Peppers, Small Diced
- ⅓ cup Cucumbers, Small Diced
- 5 Strawberries, Small Diced
- 2 tablespoons Mayonnaise
- ½ tablespoon Dijon Mustard
- ½ teaspoon Garlic Salt
- ½ teaspoon Black Pepper
- 1 tablespoon Parsley, Chopped
- Spring Mix

UTENSILS/COOKWARE NEEDED:

- Mixing Bowl
- Spatula

TOTAL TIME: 10 MINS

SERVES: 4

STEP 1. Open the cans of tuna and pour the fish into a mixing bowl, then add all the ingredients except the spring mix and stir.

STEP 2. FOR ASSEMBLY: Place a couple handfuls of spring mix at the bottom of a serving bowl then place the tuna salad on top and serve!

NO WAIST BUT TASTE

HONEY GARLIC CHICKEN & GREEN BEANS

STEP 1. Clean the chicken in a mixture of vinegar and water.

STEP 2. Warm a sauté pan over medium heat then add the olive oil and chicken breast. Season the chicken with 3 tablespoons of the minced garlic and all the garlic and herb seasoning, pollo seasoning and black pepper. Mix well and cook for 10-12 mins, or until the chicken is cooked through and there is no more pink.

STEP 3. Pour in the green beans and sauté for 3-5 mins then add the honey, soy sauce and cornstarch slurry. Cook another 5 mins or until the sauce thickens.

STEP 4. Plate and serve with brown rice.

- 1 Chicken Breast, Sliced
- 1 teaspoon Olive Oil
- 4 tablespoons Minced Garlic
- ½ teaspoon Garlic and Herb Seasoning
- ½ teaspoon Pollo Seasoning
- 1 teaspoon Black Pepper
- 1 cup Fresh Green Beans
- ⅓ cup Honey
- ⅓ cup Soy Sauce
- 3 tablespoons Cornstarch + Water (Slurry)
- 2 cups Cooked Brown Rice

UTENSILS/COOKWARE NEEDED:

- Sauté Pan
- Spatula
- Mixing Bowl

TOTAL TIME: 30 MINS
SERVES: 4

NO WAIST BUT TASTE

LEMON GARLIC SHRIMP WRAP

- ½ lb Shrimp, Peeled and Deveined
- 2 tablespoons Unsalted Butter
- 2 teaspoons Lemon Juice
- ½ teaspoon Adobo Seasoning
- ½ teaspoon Parsley, Chopped
- 1 bag Shredded Lettuce
- 1 pack Flour Tortillas

UTENSILS/COOKWARE NEEDED:

- Sauté Pan or Grill Pan
- Spatula

TOTAL TIME: 15 MINS
SERVES: 3

STEP 1. Wash the shrimp using vinegar and water then warm a sauté pan over medium heat and add the shrimp to the pan. Add the butter, lemon juice, adobo and parsley to the pan and cook for 3-5 mins. Remove the shrimp from the pan and set aside.

STEP 2. FOR ASSEMBLY: Warm the tortillas then lay them out, add the shrimp and lettuce to the center and roll the wrap like a burrito. Repeat until all the shrimp has been used. Warm a clean sauté pan or grill pan over medium heat and sear the wraps for 3-5 mins, making sure to turn them to sear each side.

STEP 3. Plate and serve hot!

NO WAIST BUT TASTE

LEMON GARLIC SHRIMP

STEP 1. Wash the shrimp using vinegar and water then warm a sauté pan over medium heat and add the shrimp to the pan. Add the butter, lemon juice, adobo and parsley to the pan and cook for 3-5 mins.

STEP 2. Remove the shrimp from the pan, plate and serve.

- ½ lb Shrimp, Peeled and Deveined
- 2 tablespoons Unsalted Butter
- 2 teaspoons Lemon Juice
- ½ teaspoon Adobo Seasoning
- ½ teaspoon Parsley, Chopped

UTENSILS/COOKWARE NEEDED:
- Sauté Pan

TOTAL TIME: 10 MINS
SERVES: 2

> WHENEVER SOMEONE ASKS WHAT MY PASSION IS, I SAY FASHION IS MY FIRST LOVE, BUT COOKING IS WHERE MY HEART IS.

NO WAIST BUT TASTE

SUNDRIED TOMATO & SPINACH CHICKEN

- ½ lb Chicken Breast, Sliced
- 1 teaspoon Olive Oil
- ½ tablespoon Garlic Powder
- ½ tablespoon Adobo Seasoning
- ½ tablespoon Black Pepper
- ½ tablespoon Italian Seasoning
- ½ tablespoon Cilantro, Chopped
- 3 cups Spinach
- 1 cup Sundried Tomatoes
- 2 cups Cooked Brown Rice

UTENSILS/COOKWARE NEEDED:

- Large Pan

TOTAL TIME: 20 MINS
SERVES: 6

STEP 1. Wash the chicken using vinegar and water, then slice the chicken into strips.

STEP 2. Warm a large pan over medium heat and drizzle with olive oil, then add in the sliced chicken. Season the chicken with all the seasonings listed (garlic powder, adobo, black pepper, Italian seasoning, cilantro) and mix well. Cook for 10-12 mins or until the chicken is cooked through and there is no more pink.

STEP 3. Toss the spinach and sundried tomatoes into the pan with the cooked chicken and stir all the ingredients together, then continue cooking until the spinach is wilted (about 2-3 mins).

STEP 4. Remove from the pan, plate and serve over brown rice.

NO WAIST BUT TASTE

CILANTRO LIME LETTUCE TACOS

STEP 1. Wash the chicken breasts using vinegar and water, then small dice them and place the chicken in a mixing bowl. Season the chicken with all the seasonings listed (garlic powder, Mrs. Dash, onion powder, Italian seasoning, pollo seasoning, cilantro) and mix well.

STEP 2. Warm a sauté pan over medium heat, drizzle oil in the pan then add in the seasoned chicken. Sauté for 3-5 mins, then add the minced garlic and lemon juice and cook 5-8 more mins, or until the chicken is cooked through and there is no more pink. Remove the cooked chicken from the pan and set aside.

STEP 3. FOR ASSEMBLY: Cut the end off the romaine lettuce and separate the leaves. Place ¼ cup of the cooked chicken in the center of each leaf, then top the chicken with the diced avocado and tomato.

STEP 4. Plate and serve with your favorite taco toppings!

- 2 Chicken Breasts, Small Diced
- ¼ teaspoon Garlic Powder
- ¼ teaspoon Mrs. Dash Seasoning
- ¼ teaspoon Onion Powder
- ¼ teaspoon Italian Seasoning
- ¼ teaspoon Pollo Seasoning
- ¼ teaspoon Cilantro, Chopped
- 1 teaspoon Olive Oil
- ½ teaspoon Minced Garlic
- ½ tablespoon Lemon Juice
- 1 head Romaine Lettuce
- 1 Avocado, Small Diced
- 1 Roma Tomato, Small Diced

UTENSILS/COOKWARE NEEDED:

- Mixing Bowl
- Sauté Pan

TOTAL TIME: 25 MINS
SERVES: 4

CINNAMON CRUNCH BANANA BREAD

- 1 ½ cups Almond Milk
- ½ cup Maple Syrup
- 1 teaspoon Ground Cinnamon
- 1 teaspoon Ground Nutmeg
- 1 teaspoon Vanilla Extract
- 1 teaspoon Baking Powder
- ⅓ cup Melted Unsalted Butter
- ½ cup Brown Sugar
- 2 Eggs
- 3 cups Rolled Oats
- Non-stick Cooking Spray

UTENSILS/COOKWARE NEEDED:

- Mixing Bowl
- Small Rubber Spatula
- Loaf Pan

TOTAL TIME: 1 HR
SERVES: 4

STEP 1. Preheat the oven to 350 degrees.

STEP 2. In a mixing bowl combine the almond milk, maple syrup, cinnamon, nutmeg, vanilla, baking powder, melted butter and brown sugar. Stir then add the eggs and oats and mix well.

STEP 3. Coat the loaf pan with non-stick cooking spray and pour in the batter, then bake for 45 mins.

STEP 4. Take the bread out of the oven and let it cool at least 10 mins before removing it from the loaf pan. Slice, plate and serve!

NO WAIST BUT TASTE

BLUEBERRY MUFFINS

STEP 1. Preheat the oven to 350 degrees.

STEP 2. In a mixing bowl, combine all the ingredients (remembering to sift the flour over the bowl!) and mix well.

STEP 3. Spray a muffin pan with non-stick cooking spray and fill each space with ¼ cup of the muffin mixture, then bake for 30 mins or until the muffins have risen and they're golden-brown.

STEP 4. Remove the muffins from the oven and let cool for at least 5 mins before serving.

- 1 cup Almond Milk
- ½ cup Lemon Juice
- ¼ cup Melted Unsalted Butter
- 1 tablespoon Vanilla Extract
- 1 ½ teaspoons Baking Powder
- 1 ½ cups White Sugar
- 1 cup Fresh Blueberries
- 2 ½ cups Flour, Sifted

UTENSILS/COOKWARE NEEDED:

- Mixing Bowls
- Sifter
- Small Rubber Spatula
- Muffin Pan

TOTAL TIME: 45 MINS

SERVES: 4

OATMEAL BARS

- 2 cups Frozen Strawberries
- ¼ cup Honey
- 8 tablespoons Melted Unsalted Butter
- 2 cups Light Brown Sugar
- ½ cup Honey
- 3 cups Rolled Oats
- ⅓ cup Flour
- 1 bag White Chocolate Wafers, Melted
- 1 bag Dark Chocolate Wafers, Melted
- Non-stick Cooking Spray

UTENSILS/COOKWARE NEEDED:

- Saucepans
- Masher
- Whisk
- Rubber Spatula
- Baking Dish
- Parchment Paper

TOTAL TIME: 30 MINS
SERVES: 4

NOTE: If you don't want to use strawberries for the topping, try making it with your favorite fruit instead!

STEP 1. Preheat the oven to 350 degrees.

STEP 2. Warm a saucepan over medium heat and pour in the frozen strawberries and ¼ cup of honey. Simmer 10-12 mins or until the strawberries are soft enough to mash. Remove them from the heat and continue mashing until the berries look like a puree. Set aside.

STEP 3. In a separate pan melt together the butter, brown sugar and honey over medium heat. Cook for 3-5 mins, whisking often, then add the rolled oats. Fold the rolled oats into the brown sugar mixture until it is well-combined, then add the flour and stir more.

STEP 4. FOR ASSEMBLY: Line a baking dish with parchment paper and coat it with non-stick cooking spray. Pour half of the oat mixture at the bottom of the dish then place a thin layer of the strawberry puree on top. Repeat the step for one more layer (remainder of the oat mixture and another thin layer of strawberry puree) then place the pan in the oven for 20-25 mins. Make sure to set aside the remaining puree to use as a topping!

STEP 5. Remove the pan from the oven and let it cool at least 15 mins. Drizzle the top with some of the remaining puree and the melted white and dark chocolate. Place the pan in the fridge for 1-2 hrs to allow the toppings to harden.

STEP 6. Once the mixture for the oatmeal bars has cooled completely and the toppings have set, remove the parchment from the pan and cut the mixture into squares. Plate and serve.

NO WAIST BUT TASTE

BANANA CHOCOLATE CHIP PANCAKES

STEP 1. Mash the bananas in a mixing bowl then add all the other ingredients and stir until well-combined.

STEP 2. Warm a large pan or griddle pan over medium heat then coat with non-stick cooking spray and pour a ½ cup of batter onto the pan. Cook the pancakes until bubbles form on the top then flip the pancakes and brown them on the other side. Remove the pancakes from the pan then repeat until all the batter is used.

STEP 3. Plate and serve with your favorite syrup and breakfast sides!

- 6 Bananas, Mashed
- 1 cup Oats
- 2 Eggs
- 1 tablespoon Vanilla Extract
- 1 cup Chocolate Chips
- ½ cup Brown Sugar
- 2 tablespoons Maple Syrup
- 1 teaspoon Ground cinnamon
- ½ teaspoon Ground nutmeg
- Non-stick Cooking Spray

UTENSILS/COOKWARE NEEDED:

- Mixing Bowl
- Large Pan or Griddle

TOTAL TIME: 20 MINS
SERVES: 4

ALMOND BUTTER CHOCOLATE CHIP COOKIES

- 1 cup Almond Butter
- ½ cup Brown Sugar
- 1 teaspoon Vanilla Extract
- 1 Egg
- ½ cup Chocolate Chips
- Non-stick Cooking Spray

UTENSILS/COOKWARE NEEDED:

- Mixing Bowl
- Hand Mixer
- Baking Sheet
- Parchment Paper

TOTAL TIME: 40 MINS
SERVES: 4

STEP 1. Preheat the oven to 300 degrees.

STEP 2. In a mixing bowl pour the almond butter, brown sugar, vanilla extract and egg. Blend with a hand mixer until well-combined, then fold in the chocolate chips.

STEP 3. Line a baking sheet with parchment paper and coat it with non-stick cooking spray. Roll ½ tablespoon of the cookie dough in your hands to form a ball then place the cookies on the baking sheet, making sure to keep them at least 2 inches apart. Use a fork to press into the cookies horizontally and vertically, creating a cross shape.

STEP 4. Place the cookies in the oven and bake for 15-20 mins, then remove them the oven and serve hot.

NO WAIST BUT TASTE

SALAD

STEP 1. Plate the spring mix in a large bowl, then top with the apples, strawberries, avocado, cucumber, bell pepper, onion and cherry tomatoes. Drizzle with the balsamic dressing and sprinkle on the garlic salt and black pepper. Garnish with the cranberries and walnuts and serve!

- Spring mix
- 2 Red Apples, Small Diced
- 4-8 Strawberries, Small Diced
- 1 Avocado, Small Diced
- ½ Cucumber, Small Diced
- 1 Bell pepper, Small Diced
- ½ White Onion, Small Diced
- 1 cup Cherry Tomatoes, sliced
- Balsamic Dressing, as Desired
- ⅛ teaspoon Garlic Salt
- ½ teaspoon Black Pepper
- Handful of Cranberries
- Handful of Walnuts

UTENSILS/COOKWARE NEEDED:
- Large Bowl

TOTAL TIME: 10 MINS
SERVES: 6

I LOVE COOKING FOR THE SAME REASON THAT I LOVE FASHION — THE THRILL OF CREATING SOMETHING NEW.

NO WAIST BUT TASTE

CHICKEN STIR FRY

- 1 pack Chicken Breast, Sliced
- 1 tablespoon Pollo Seasoning
- ½ tablespoon Garlic Powder
- 1 tablespoon Olive Oil
- 1 cup Snap Peas
- 1 cup Carrots
- 1 cup Broccoli
- ⅓ cup Hoisin Sauce
- ⅓ cup Soy Sauce
- 2 tablespoons Garlic Chili Paste
- 2 tablespoons Minced Garlic
- 3 tablespoons Cornstarch + Water (Slurry)

UTENSILS/COOKWARE NEEDED:

- Mixing Bowl
- KitchenEnvy Wok
- Spatula

SERVES: 4

TOTAL TIME: 20 MINS

STEP 1. Wash the chicken breast using vinegar and water, then slice it into strips then place the chicken in a mixing bowl. Season the sliced chicken with pollo seasoning and garlic powder and mix well.

STEP 2. Warm a wok over medium-high heat then pour in olive oil and sear the chicken for 5-8 mins or until it is cooked through (no more pink). Add in the snap peas, carrots and broccoli then pour in the hoisin sauce, soy sauce, chili paste and minced garlic. Mix well, then add in the cornstarch slurry to thicken the sauce and simmer for 5 more mins.

STEP 3. Remove from the pan, plate and serve with jasmine rice (see pg. 176).

NO WAIST BUT TASTE

YOGURT BITES

STEP 1. Have a muffin pan lined with cupcake liners ready and set aside.

STEP 2. FOR THE CRUST: Pour the granola, coconut, dried strawberries, dried mangos, dried cranberries and sliced almonds into a food processor and pulse. Slowly pour in the almond butter and continue mixing, then place 2 tablespoons of the mixture at the bottom of each cupcake liner.

STEP 3. FOR THE FILLING: Whisk together ¼ cup of honey and the vanilla Greek yogurt in a mixing bowl, then whisk the remaining honey together with the strawberry Greek yogurt in a separate mixing bowl.

STEP 4. FOR ASSEMBLY: Pour ¼ cup of the vanilla yogurt filling into half of the crusts, then repeat with the strawberry yogurt filling for the remaining crusts. Top the yogurt bites with the frozen berries and fresh kiwi, then cover the pan and let them freeze for 2-3 hours or until the yogurt is firm.

STEP 5. Plate and serve!

- 1 cup Granola
- 1 cup Shaved Coconut
- ½ cup Dried Strawberries
- ½ cup Dried Mangos
- ½ cup Dried Cranberries
- ¼ cup Sliced Almonds
- ½ cup Almond Butter

FILLING

- ½ cup Honey
- 2 cups Vanilla Greek Yogurt
- 2 cups Strawberry Greek Yogurt
- 1 cup Frozen Blueberries
- 1cup Frozen Strawberries
- 1cup Frozen Raspberries
- 1 cup Fresh Kiwi, Small Diced

UTENSILS/COOKWARE NEEDED:

- Muffin Pan
- Cupcake Liners
- Blender or Food Processor
- Mixing Bowl

TOTAL TIME: 15 MINS
SERVES: 4

CHIPOTLE CHICKEN AVO BOWL

- 1 Chicken Breast, Sliced
- 1 teaspoon Adobo Seasoning
- 1 teaspoon Chipotle Powder
- 1 teaspoon Garlic Powder
- 1 teaspoon Lemon Juice
- 1 teaspoon Olive Oil
- Spring Mix
- ¼ cup Cooked Brown Rice
- 1 can Corn
- 1 Avocado, Diced
- 1 tablespoon Sour Cream

BEANS

- 1 can Pinto Beans
- 1 can Black Beans
- ¼ teaspoon Black Pepper
- ¼ teaspoon Garlic Powder
- ¼ teaspoon Garlic Salt

UTENSILS/COOKWARE NEEDED:

- Mixing Bowl
- Medium-Sized Pan
- Colander

SERVES: 6
TOTAL TIME: 30 MINS

STEP 1. Wash the chicken using vinegar and water then slice it into strips and place the chicken in a mixing bowl. Season with the adobo, chipotle powder, garlic powder and lemon juice.

STEP 2. Warm a medium-sized pan over medium heat then pour in the olive oil and sear the chicken for 10-12 mins, or until it is cooked through and there is no more pink. Remove the chicken from the pan and set aside.

STEP 3. FOR THE BEANS: Drain and rinse all the beans and pour them into the same pan the chicken was cooked in. Simmer for 3-5 mins, then season the beans with black pepper, garlic powder and garlic salt and stir. Remove the beans from the pan and set aside.

STEP 4. FOR ASSEMBLY: place a handful of spring mix in a serving bowl then arrange the brown rice, chicken, beans, corn and avocado on the bed of lettuce. Garnish with the sour cream and serve.

NO WAIST BUT TASTE

MONKEY BREAD 378

CINNAMON ROLL APPLE PIES 381

MINI CHEESECAKE BITES 382

WHITE CHOCOLATE CHIP BROWNIES 385

OREO & VANILLA CAKE POPS 386

MANGO PEACH PIES 389

CARAMEL PECAN STICKY BUNS 390

STRAWBERRY LEMON POKE CAKE 393

APPLE CRUMB MUFFINS 394

OREO CHEESECAKE COOKIES 397

SNICKERDOODLE COOKIES 398

2-LAYER PEACH COBBLER 401

LEMON LOAF CAKE 402

CRÈME BRULÉ 405

HOT CHOCOLATE BOMBS 406

RED VELVET BROWNIES 409

LAVA CAKE 410

STRAWBERRY CRUMB CAKE 413

FRIED CHEESECAKE BARS 414

FUNNEL CAKES 415

CANDY & CARAMEL APPLES 417

MONKEY BREAD

- 4-5 rolls of Ready-Made Cinnamon Roll Dough or Regular Biscuit Dough
- 1 cup White Sugar
- ⅓ cup Ground Cinnamon
- Non-stick Cooking Spray

SAUCE

- 6 tablespoons Unsalted Butter
- 1 cup Brown Sugar
- ¼ teaspoon Ground Nutmeg
- 1 tablespoon Vanilla Extract

GLAZE

- 1 cup Powdered Sugar
- ⅔ cup Heavy Cream
- ⅛ cup Cream Cheese, Softened
- 2 teaspoons Vanilla Extract
- 1 teaspoon Lemon Zest (optional)

UTENSILS/COOKWARE NEEDED:

- Mixing Bowls
- Saucepan
- Whisk
- Bundt Pan

TOTAL TIME: 2 HRS

SERVES: 6

STEP 1. Preheat the oven to 350 degrees.

STEP 2. Open the packs of cinnamon rolls, then cut each roll into 4 pieces and place the pieces in a mixing bowl. Set aside.

STEP 3. In a separate mixing bowl, mix the white sugar and cinnamon then toss the cut cinnamon roll pieces in the cinnamon sugar, coat well and set aside.

STEP 4. FOR THE SAUCE: Warm a saucepan over medium heat and melt the butter in the pan, then add all the other ingredients listed for the sauce. Whisk until the mixture is smooth. If the sauce gets too thick, add more melted butter, 1 tablespoon at a time.

STEP 5. Spray a Bundt pan with non-stick cooking spray, then pour a layer of sauce at the bottom of the pan. Place a layer of the tossed cinnamon roll pieces on top of the sauce and repeat until all the sauce and cinnamon roll pieces are used. Bake for 30 to 45 mins, or until the monkey bread has cooked through.

STEP 6. FOR THE GLAZE: In a clean mixing bowl, combine all the ingredients listed for the glaze and whisk until the glaze is smooth. If the glaze feels too thick, add more heavy cream, ¼ cup at a time, until it gets to the consistency you like.

STEP 7. Remove the monkey bread from the oven and allow to cool for at least 10 mins, then place a plate over the top of the Bundt pan and flip the monkey bread onto the plate. Pour the glaze onto the monkey bread, then cut and serve hot.

GETTIN' SUM'N SWEET

CINNAMON ROLL APPLE PIES

STEP 1. Preheat the oven to 350 degrees.

STEP 2. Peel and dice the apples then place them in a cold saucepan with the butter, white sugar, brown sugar, nutmeg, cinnamon, vanilla extract and orange zest. Place the pan onto the stove and cook over medium heat for 5-8 mins. In a small mixing bowl, combine cornstarch with water to create a slurry then pour the slurry into the pan, 1 tablespoon at a time, until the filling thickens. Remove the filling from the pan and set aside, allowing it to cool at least 10 mins before pouring it into the cinnamon rolls.

STEP 3. Spray a muffin pan with non-stick cooking spray and place one cinnamon roll into each space, stretching the dough to make it go up the sides of the muffin pan. Pour 1 tablespoon of the cooked apple filling into each space, then bake for 30-45 mins or until the cinnamon roll dough is cooked through. Remove from the oven and set aside.

STEP 4. FOR GLAZE: In a clean mixing bowl, combine all the ingredients listed for the glaze and whisk until the glaze is smooth. If the glaze feels too thick, add more heavy cream, 1 teaspoon at a time, until it gets to the consistency you like.

STEP 5. Plate the pies and glaze before serving.

- 4 Green Apples, Peeled and Small Diced
- 5 tablespoons Unsalted Butter
- ½ cup White Sugar
- ½ cup Brown Sugar
- ¼ teaspoon Ground Nutmeg
- 1 teaspoon Ground Cinnamon
- 1 teaspoon Vanilla Extract
- 1 teaspoon Orange Zest
- 2 tablespoons Cornstarch
- 4 tablespoons Water
- Non-stick Cooking Spray
- 2 rolls Ready-Made Cinnamon Roll Dough

GLAZE:

- 1 cup Powdered Sugar
- ⅔ cup Heavy Cream
- ⅛ cup Cream Cheese, Softened
- 2 teaspoons Vanilla Extract
- 1 teaspoon Lemon Zest (optional)

UTENSILS/COOKWARE NEEDED:

- Saucepan
- Mixing Bowls
- Small Rubber Spatula
- Muffin Pan
- Whisk

TOTAL TIME: 45 MINS
SERVES: 6

MINI CHEESECAKE BITES

- 8 oz Cream Cheese, Softened
- ⅓ cup Sweetened Condensed Milk
- 1 teaspoon Vanilla Extract
- ½ cup Heavy Whipping Cream
- ½ cup Powdered Sugar

CRUSTS:
- 2 cups Graham Cracker Crumbs
- 2 cups Oreo Cookie Crumbs
- 2 cups Biscoff Cookie Crumbs
- 12 tablespoons Melted Unsalted Butter

BISCOFF CHEESECAKE FILLING
- 8 oz Cream Cheese, Softened
- ⅓ cup Biscoff Butter
- 1 teaspoon Vanilla Extract
- ½ cup Heavy Whipping Cream
- ½ cup Powdered Sugar

OREO CHEESECAKE FILLING
- 8 oz Cream Cheese, Softened
- ⅓ cup Sweetened Condensed Milk
- 1 teaspoon Vanilla Extract
- ½ cup Heavy Whipping Cream
- ½ cup Powdered Sugar
- ½ cup Oreo Cookies, Crushed

GARNISH (OPTIONAL):
- Canned Fruit Topping of Your Choice
- Melted Biscoff Butter
- Graham Cracker Crumbs
- Oreo Cookie Crumbs
- Biscoff Cookie Crumbs

UTENSILS/COOKWARE NEEDED:
- Muffin Pan
- Cupcake Liners
- Blender
- Mixing Bowls
- Hand Mixer

TOTAL TIME: 30 MINS
SERVES: 6

STEP 1. Have a muffin pan filled with cupcake liners ready.

STEP 2. FOR THE CRUSTS: Crush the graham crackers by blending them in a blender until they're crumbs, then pour the graham cracker crumbs in a mixing bowl. Mix in 4 tablespoons of melted butter into the crumbs, then place 1 ½ tablespoons of the mixture at the bottom of half of the cupcake liners. Repeat the same process with the Oreos and Biscotti cookies, filling the remaining cupcake liners with Oreo and Biscotti crusts. Press the crumbs down to form one flat layer of crust and set aside. You should have about 1 cup of crust left from each crumb mixture, so set that aside for garnish (optional).

STEP 3. FOR THE ORIGINAL CHEESECAKE FILLING: Place 8 oz of cream cheese in a large mixing bowl with the sweetened condensed milk and 1 teaspoon of vanilla extract. Combine the ingredients using a hand mixer until everything is smooth. In a separate bowl, whip ½ cup of the heavy whipping cream with the powdered sugar until it thickens then fold it into the cream cheese mixture. Pour some of the filling into the graham cracker crusts.

STEP 4. FOR THE BISCOFF CHEESECAKE FILLING: Place 8 oz of cream cheese in a large mixing bowl with the Biscoff butter and 1 teaspoon of vanilla extract. Combine the ingredients using a hand mixer until everything is smooth. In a separate bowl, whip ½ cup of the heavy whipping cream with the powdered sugar until it thickens then fold it into the cream cheese mixture. Pour some of the filling into the Biscoff cookie crusts.

STEP 5. FOR THE OREO CHEESECAKE FILLING: Place 8 oz of cream cheese in a large mixing bowl with the sweetened condensed milk and 1 teaspoon of vanilla extract. Combine the ingredients using a hand mixer until everything is smooth. In a separate bowl, whip ½ cup of the heavy whipping cream with the powdered sugar until it thickens then fold it into the cream cheese mixture. Crush ½ cup of Oreos and fold them into the mixture as well, then pour some of the filling into the Oreo cookie crusts. Cut a few Oreos in half and place the halves on top of the cheesecakes.

STEP 6. Place the assembled cheesecake bites in the freezer for 1-2 hours or until the filling is firm. Garnish them with your favorite toppings and serve.

GETTIN' SUM'N SWEET

WHITE CHOCOLATE CHIP BROWNIES

STEP 1. Preheat the oven to 350 degrees.

STEP 2. Pour the chocolate wafers and melted butter in a microwave-safe bowl or in a bowl over a double boiler and melt the chocolate. Set aside.

STEP 3. In a mixing bowl, combine the white sugar, brown sugar and 1 egg. Whisk the mixture, then gradually add 1 egg at a time, whisking often. Add in the vanilla extract and salt, then pour in the melted chocolate. Stir until everything is combined.

STEP 4. Place a sifter over the bowl and add in the flour and cocoa powder, sifting it into the wet mixture. Fold the dry into the wet (the batter should become thick), then fold in the white and regular chocolate chips.

STEP 5. Pour the batter into a parchment-lined baking dish that's been coated with non-stick cooking spray. Bake the brownies for 30-40 mins or until you can stick a toothpick in the center of the brownies and it comes out clean.

STEP 6. Cut, plate and serve with your favorite toppings.

- 1 bag Chocolate Wafers
- ½ stick Unsalted Butter
- 1 cup White Sugar
- ½ cup Brown Sugar
- 3 Eggs
- 1 teaspoon Vanilla Extract
- ¼ teaspoon Salt
- 1 cup Flour
- 3 tablespoons Cocoa Powder
- ½ cup Chocolate Chips
- ½ cup White Chocolate Chips
- Non-stick Cooking Spray

UTENSILS/COOKWARE NEEDED:

- Microwave Safe Dish
- Mixing Bowls
- Whisk
- Small Rubber Spatula
- Sifter
- Baking Dish
- Parchment Paper

TOTAL TIME: 1 HR
SERVES: 6

GETTIN' SUM'N SWEET

OREO & VANILLA CAKE POPS

- 1 box of Vanilla Cake Mix
- 2 tablespoons Vanilla Cake Frosting
- ½ pack Oreos
- 8 oz Cream Cheese, Softened

TOPPINGS (OPTIONAL):

- 1 bag Milk Chocolate Wafers, Melted
- 1 bag White Chocolate Wafers, Melted
- Food Coloring
- Multicolored Sprinkles

UTENSILS/COOKWARE NEEDED:

- Mixing Bowls
- Baking Dish
- Small Rubber Spatula
- Ice Cream Scoop
- Baking Sheets
- Parchment Paper
- Blender
- Wooden Sticks

TOTAL TIME: 30 MINS
SERVES: 6

STEP 1. Preheat the oven to 350 degrees.

STEP 2. FOR THE VANILLA CAKE POPS: Pour the vanilla cake mix into a mixing bowl and follow the package instructions for baking. Once the cake is done baking, remove it from the oven and allow it to cool for at least 15 mins. When the cake is cool, flip it out of the baking dish onto a cutting board and cut off the browned edges, top and bottom of the cake (this will help your cake pops to stay moist). Crumble the cake into a large mixing bowl, then add the vanilla frosting and mix well. Form the cake pops using a small ice cream scoop then roll them in your hands to create perfect rounds. Place the rounds on a parchment-lined baking sheet then put them in the freezer for 1-2 hours or until the rounds are solid.

STEP 3. FOR THE OREO CAKE POPS: In a blender, add the Oreos and cream cheese and blend. Transfer the mixture to a bowl and mix well, then form the cake pops using a small ice cream scoop. Roll them in your hands to create perfect rounds, then place the rounds on a parchment-lined baking sheet. Place them in the freezer for 1-2 hours or until the rounds are solid.

STEP 4. Melt the white and milk chocolate wafers in 2 separate bowls, then set aside someplace you can keep the melted chocolate warm.

STEP 5. After removing all the cake pops from the freezer, dip a wooden stick into the melted chocolate then insert the stick into the center of one of the rounds, repeat until all the rounds have become cake pops. Dip the cake pops in the melted chocolate & add your favorite decorations, then place them back in the freezer for another 1-2 hrs before serving.

GETTIN' SUM'N SWEET

MANGO PEACH TURN OVERS

STEP 1. Preheat the oven to 425 degrees.

STEP 2. Peel and dice the mango and place it in a mixing bowl. Dice the canned peach slices and place them in the same bowl as the mango, then pour the fruit into a saucepan with the lemon juice, sugar and slurry. Warm the pan over medium heat and cook the mixture for 5-8 mins or until the mangoes are soft and the sauce thickens. Remove the pie filling from the pan and set aside, allow the mixture to cool at least 10 mins before assembling the pies.

STEP 3. FOR ASSEMBLY: Roll out a sheet of puff pastry with a rolling pin then cut it into 4ths then brush the edges of each one with egg wash. On one half of the pastry, place a tablespoon of filling about 1 ½ inches from the edge. Fold the other half of the pastry over the filling and seal the sides using a fork, then brush the tops with egg wash and place the pies on a parchment lined baking sheet. Repeat the steps above until all the filling is used.

STEP 4. Bake the pies for 15 mins or until they're golden brown, then plate and serve.

- 1 Fresh Mango
- 1 can of Sliced Peaches, Drained
- Juice of ½ a Lemon
- ⅓ cup White Sugar
- 2 tablespoons Cornstarch + Water (Slurry)
- Ready-Made Puff Pastry
- 1 Egg + Water (Eggwash)

UTENSILS/COOKWARE NEEDED:

- Mixing Bowls
- Saucepan
- Rolling Pin
- Pastry Brush
- Baking Sheet
- Parchment Paper

TOTAL TIME: 35 MINS

SERVES: 4

GETTIN' SUM'N SWEET

CARAMEL PECAN STICKY BUNS

- 5 tablespoons Unsalted Butter
- 1 ½ cups Brown Sugar
- ¼ teaspoon Nutmeg
- ½ tablespoon Vanilla Extract
- ½ cup Heavy Whipping Cream
- 1 cup Chopped Pecans (optional)
- 1 roll Ready-Made Cinnamon Roll Dough

GLAZE

- 1 cup Powdered Sugar
- ¼ cup Heavy Whipping Cream

UTENSILS/COOKWARE NEEDED:

- Saucepan
- Whisk
- Long Baking Dish
- Mixing Bowls
- Small Rubber Spatula
- Platter

TOTAL TIME: 1 HR
SERVES: 6

STEP 1. Preheat the oven to 350 degrees.

STEP 2. Warm a saucepan over medium heat then melt the butter and add the brown sugar, nutmeg, vanilla extract and heavy cream. Whisk the ingredients together and bring to a simmer, then pour the sauce into the bottom of a baking dish and sprinkle in the chopped pecans. Place the ready-made cinnamon roll dough on top of the pecans and sauce, then bake for 25-30 mins or until cinnamon rolls are golden-brown.

STEP 3. FOR THE GLAZE: in a mixing bowl, combine the powdered sugar and heavy cream. Mix well and set aside.

STEP 4. When the cinnamon rolls are done, let them cool for 5 mins then place a platter over the baking dish and flip the baking dish over onto the platter so the nuts and caramel sauce are on top of the cinnamon rolls. Drizzle the buns with the glaze and serve hot.

GETTIN' SUM'N SWEET

STRAWBERRY LEMON POKE CAKE

STEP 1. Preheat the oven to 350 degrees.

STEP 2. Bake the white cake mix per the package instructions. Once the cake has baked, use a straw or stick to poke holes all over the cake. Set aside.

STEP 3. Mix together the strawberry Jell-O, then pour it all over the poked cake. Place the cake in the fridge to cool for at least 30 mins, this is so your frosting doesn't melt once you put it on the cake.

STEP 4. FOR THE FROSTING: In a mixing bowl, combine the cream cheese, lemon juice and powdered sugar. Slowly pour in the heavy cream, ¼ cup at a time, until the frosting is smooth but not runny.

STEP 5. FOR ASSEMBLY: Remove the cake from the fridge and pour on the frosting, making sure to spread it out in an even layer over the top of the cake. Place the sliced strawberries on top of the frosting, then zest the lemons over the strawberries.

STEP 6. Cut, plate and serve!

- 1 box White Cake Mix
- 1 box Strawberry Jell-O
- 6-10 Fresh Strawberries, Sliced
- Zest of 2 Lemons

FROSTING

- 8 oz Cream Cheese, softened
- 2 tablespoons Lemon Juice
- 1 cup Powdered Sugar
- ¼ cup Heavy Whipping Cream

UTENSILS/COOKWARE NEEDED:

- Long Cake Pan
- Straw of Stick
- Mixing Bowls
- Small Rubber Spatula

TOTAL TIME: 1 HR

SERVES: 6

GETTIN' SUM'N SWEET

APPLE CRUMB MUFFINS

- 3-4 Green Apples
- 1 Lime, Juiced
- 2 cups Flour, Sifted
- 4 tablespoons Baking Powder
- ¼ teaspoon Salt
- ½ cup Brown Sugar
- 1 cup White Sugar
- 1 tablespoon Ground Cinnamon
- ½ cup Unsalted Butter, Melted
- 2 tablespoons Vanilla Extract
- 2 Eggs
- ½ cup Milk

CRUMB TOPPING

- 2 cups Brown Sugar
- ¼ cup White Sugar
- 1 tablespoon Ground Cinnamon
- ¼ teaspoon Ground Nutmeg
- ½ cup Unsalted Butter, Melted
- ¾ cup Flour

UTENSILS/COOKWARE NEEDED:

- Mixing Bowls
- Sifter
- Hand Mixer
- Small Rubber Spatula
- Muffin Pan
- Cupcake Liners

TOTAL TIME: 45 MINS

SERVES: 8-12

NOTE: if you don't like apples, feel free to leave them out of the recipe – the crumb muffins alone are just as good!

STEP 1. Preheat the oven to 350 degrees.

STEP 2. Wash, peel and small dice the apples then place them in a mixing bowl filled with water and lime juice and set aside (the lime water will keep the apples from turning brown).

STEP 3. FOR THE CRUMB TOPPING: Pour the brown sugar, white sugar, cinnamon, nutmeg, melted butter and flour into a clean mixing bowl and mix well using your hands or a large spoon. Set aside.

STEP 4. In a clean mixing bowl sift the flour, baking powder and salt then combine with brown sugar, white sugar and cinnamon. In a separate mixing bowl, combine the wet ingredients (melted butter, vanilla extract, eggs and milk) using a hand mixer then pour the dry into the wet. Stir until well combined then fold in 1 ½ cups of the diced apples.

STEP 5. Line a muffin pan with cupcake liners and scoop 1 tablespoon of the batter into each section of the pan. Next sprinkle a thin layer of the crumb mixture on top of the batter, then place another tablespoon of batter on top of that, and finish with one more layer of the crumb mixture.

STEP 6. Bake for 25-30 mins, or until the muffins have risen and turned golden-brown. Serve hot!

GETTIN' SUM'N SWEET

OREO CHEESECAKE COOKIES

STEP 1. Preheat the oven to 300 degrees.

STEP 2. Crush the Oreos in a blender or food processor until they're smooth, then pour the crushed Oreos into a mixing bowl and set aside.

STEP 3. In a separate mixing bowl use a hand mixer to cream the sugar, vanilla, butter, shortening and cream cheese together. Scrape down the sides of the bowl then place a sifter over the bowl and sift in the flour and baking powder. Pour in the crushed Oreos and mix well, the mixture should become like a dough. Cover the bowl and set aside on the counter for 10 mins.

STEP 4. FOR THE ICING: Place the cream cheese, powdered sugar and heavy cream in a mixing bowl and blend together using a clean hand mixer or whisk. Fold in the crushed Oreos and set aside.

STEP 5. Scoop a ½ tablespoon of the cookie dough into your hands then roll the dough into balls and place them onto a parchment-lined baking sheet that's been coated with non-stick cooking spray. Press down on the dough balls to flatten them into the shape of the cookies, then bake for 15-20 mins.

STEP 6. Remove the cookies from the oven and allow them to cool on a wire rack for at least 10 mins before icing them. Plate and serve!

- 1 ½ cups Oreos
- ½ cup White Sugar
- 1 teaspoon Vanilla Extract
- 12 tablespoons Unsalted Butter, Softened
- 4 tablespoons Shortening, Softened
- 8 oz Cream Cheese, Softened
- 1 ½ cup Flour, Sifted
- 1 tablespoon Baking Powder
- Non-stick Cooking Spray

ICING

- 4 oz Cream Cheese, Softened
- 1 cup Powdered Sugar
- ½ cup Heavy Whipping Cream
- 1 teaspoon Oreos, Crushed

UTENSILS/COOKWARE NEEDED:

- Blender
- Mixing Bowls
- Hand Mixer
- Sifter
- Baking Sheet
- Parchment Paper

TOTAL TIME: 35 MINS

SERVES: 4

SNICKERDOODLE COOKIES

- 3 cups Flour
- 1 tablespoon Ground Cinnamon
- ¼ teaspoon Ground Nutmeg
- 1 teaspoon Cream of Tartar
- ¼ teaspoon Salt
- ½ cup Brown Sugar
- 1 cup White Sugar
- 2 Eggs
- 1 cup Unsalted Butter, Melted
- 1 tablespoon Shortening, Softened
- 3 tablespoons Vanilla Extract
- Non-stick Cooking Spray

CINNAMON SUGAR

- 1 ½ teaspoon Ground Cinnamon
- ½ cup White Sugar

UTENSILS/COOKWARE NEEDED:

- Mixing Bowls
- Sifter
- Hand Mixer
- Small Rubber Spatula
- Baking Sheet
- Parchment Paper

TOTAL TIME: 15-20 MINS
SERVES: 6

STEP 1. Preheat the oven to 350 degrees.

STEP 2. In a mixing bowl sift the flour, cinnamon, nutmeg, cream of tartar and salt. Pour in the brown sugar and white sugar then mix everything together.

STEP 3. In a separate mixing bowl use a hand mixer to combine the eggs, butter, shortening and vanilla extract. Slowly pour the dry ingredients into the wet and mix well, the mixture should form a dough.

STEP 4. FOR THE CINNAMON SUGAR: In another mixing bowl, mix together the white sugar and cinnamon and set aside.

STEP 5. Scoop 1 tablespoon of the cookie dough into your hands then roll the dough into balls and roll them in the cinnamon sugar. Place the dough onto a parchment-lined baking sheet that's been coated with non-stick cooking spray, then press down on the dough balls to flatten them into the shape of the cookies.

STEP 6. Bake for 15-20 mins, then remove the cookies from the oven and allow them to cool on a wire rack for at least 10 mins before serving.

GETTIN' SUM'N SWEET

2-LAYER PEACH COBBLER

STEP 1. Preheat the oven to 350 degrees.

STEP 2. FOR THE CINNAMON SUGAR: In a mixing bowl, combine the white sugar and cinnamon and set aside.

STEP 3. Warm a large pot over low heat and add the peaches, 4 tablespoons of butter, white sugar, brown sugar, cinnamon, nutmeg and vanilla extract. Simmer for 5-8 mins or until the peaches are softer, then mix in the slurry and continue to cook until the sauce thickens. Remove the peaches from the pan and set aside.

STEP 4. Spray a casserole dish with non-stick cooking spray, then place the first layer of pie crust at the bottom of the dish. Brush it with melted butter and sprinkle with the cinnamon sugar, then place the crust in the oven for 15 mins.

STEP 5. FOR ASSEMBLY: Layer half of the peach filling over the cooked crust, then place another pie crust over the filling. Brush the raw crust with butter and sprinkle on some of the cinnamon sugar, then pour on the other half of the peaches. Slice the last raw pie crust into strips and place them in a criss-cross pattern on top of the peaches. Top with more butter and cinnamon sugar then cover the dish with foil. Bake the peach cobbler for 45 mins, then uncover the dish and bake for another 20 mins.

STEP 6. Remove the peach cobbler from the oven and let cool at least 10 mins before cutting. Plate and serve hot!

- 4 cans of Sliced Peaches
- 6 tablespoons Melted Unsalted Butter
- 1 cup White Sugar
- ½ cup Brown Sugar
- 1 tablespoon Ground Cinnamon
- 1 teaspoon Ground Nutmeg
- 2 tablespoons Vanilla Extract
- ¼ cup Cornstarch + Water (Slurry)
- Ready-Made Pie Crusts, As Needed
- Non-stick Cooking Spray

CINNAMON SUGAR

- ½ cup White Sugar
- 1 ½ teaspoon Ground Cinnamon

UTENSILS/COOKWARE NEEDED:

- Mixing Bowls
- Large Pot
- Casserole Dish
- Aluminum Foil

TOTAL TIME: 2 HRS
SERVES: 6

GETTIN' SUM'N SWEET

LEMON LOAF CAKE

- 1 ½ cups Flour, Sifted
- 2 tablespoons Baking Powder
- ¼ teaspoon Salt
- 3 Eggs
- ½ cup Unsalted Butter, Softened
- ½ tablespoon Shortening, Softened
- Zest of 3 Lemons
- 2 cups White Sugar
- 4 tablespoons Lemon Juice
- 3 tablespoons Lemon Extract
- 2 tablespoons Vanilla Extract
- ½ cup Greek Yogurt
- ⅔ cup Milk
- 2 drops Yellow Food Coloring (optional)
- Non-stick Cooking Spray

SYRUP
- ½ cup White Sugar
- ⅛ cup Lemon Juice

GLAZE
- 1 cup Powdered Sugar
- ½ cup White Sugar
- ⅓ cup Lemon Juice

UTENSILS/COOKWARE NEEDED:
- Mixing Bowls
- Sifter
- Hand Mixer
- Loaf Pan

TOTAL TIME: 1 HR
SERVES: 6

STEP 1. Preheat the oven to 310 degrees.

STEP 2. In a mixing bowl sift the flour, baking powder and salt. Set aside.

STEP 3. In a separate mixing bowl use a hand mixer to combine the eggs, butter, shortening, lemon zest, white sugar, lemon juice, lemon extract, vanilla extract, Greek yogurt, milk, and yellow food coloring (optional). Slowly pour the dry ingredients into the wet and mix well.

STEP 4. Spray a loaf pan with non-stick cooking spray and pour the batter into the pan, then bake for 45 mins or until you can stick a toothpick in the center of the cake and it comes out clean.

STEP 5. FOR THE SYRUP: Whisk together the white sugar and lemon juice in a mixing bowl then set aside.

STEP 6. FOR THE GLAZE: Whisk together the powdered sugar, white sugar and lemon juice in a mixing bowl then set aside.

STEP 7. Remove the cake from the oven and let cool at least 10 mins before adding the syrup. Let the syrup soak into the cake for 5 mins then drizzle with the glaze. Slice and serve!

GETTIN' SUM'N SWEET

CREME BRULEE

STEP 1. Preheat the oven to 325 degrees.

STEP 2. Pour the heavy cream into a saucepan and warm it over medium heat for 5 mins, then set aside.

STEP 3. In a mixing bowl, separate the egg yolks from the whites (you will only need the yolks for this recipe). Whisk together the egg yolks, vanilla extract, sugar and salt then gradually add the warm cream, whisking continuously.

STEP 4. Sit the ramekins in a deep baking dish, then pour the crème mixture into the ramekins and fill the baking dish with water, making sure the water only goes halfway up the outside of the ramekins and does not get in the crème mixture. Bake for 45 mins-1 hr, then place the ramekins in the fridge for at least 3-6 hrs (this is a crucial step, if the crème mixture is not chilled enough, the brulée will not work properly!)

STEP 5. FOR THE BRULEE: sprinkle a layer of sugar over the tops of each crème brulée, then use a hand-held torch to brown the sugar to create the brulée over the crème. Be careful not to brulée the sugar too much because it burns very easily. Plate and serve immediately!

- 2 cups Heavy Whipping Cream or Half & Half
- 5 Egg Yolks
- 1 Vanilla Bean or 1 teaspoon Vanilla Extract
- ¼ cup White Sugar
- ⅛ teaspoon Salt
- Boiling Water

BRULÉE:
- White Sugar, as needed

UTENSILS/COOKWARE NEEDED:
- Saucepan
- Mixing Bowls
- Whisk
- Small Baking Dishes or Ramekins
- Deep Baking Dish
- Hand-Held Torch

TOTAL TIME: 4-7 HRS
SERVES: 6

NOTE: If you do not have a hand-held torch, turn your broiler up all the way and brulée your desserts under the broiler instead – just keep an eye on them so they don't burn!

GETTIN' SUM'N SWEET

HOT CHOCOLATE BOMBS

- 1 bag Milk Chocolate Wafers
- 3 packets Hot Chocolate Mix
- 1 bag Mini Marshmallows

DECORATION (OPTIONAL)

- Dark Chocolate Wafers, Melted
- White Chocolate Wafers, Melted
- Food Coloring
- Multicolored Sprinkles

UTENSILS/COOKWARE NEEDED:

- Microwave Safe Bowl
- Silicone Molds
- Small Rubber Spatula

TOTAL TIME: 40 MINS

SERVES: 6

NOTE: You can do the same recipe with white chocolate wafers to make white chocolate bombs! And for adult hot chocolate bombs, you can add a splash of Bailey's Irish Cream to the inside of the chocolate bomb.

STEP 1. Melt the milk chocolate wafers in a microwave-safe bowl or over a double boiler.

STEP 2. Add 1 tablespoon of the melted chocolate to the silicone molds, then scrape off the excess chocolate and place the molds in the fridge or freezer for 5-10 mins. After the first layer of chocolate is solid, add a second coat to the molds, making sure to scrape off the excess chocolate again. Place the molds back in the fridge or freezer for another 5-10 mins (this will help so the chocolate won't crack while being removed from the molds).

STEP 3. FOR ASSEMBLY: Carefully remove the chilled chocolate from the molds. Add ½ teaspoon of hot chocolate mix and 8-10 mini marshmallows to one half of the molds. Heat a glass plate in the microwave for 2-3 mins then use the plate to melt the open end of the other chocolate molds that haven't been filled with hot chocolate mix, making sure to only leave them on the plate for 2-4 seconds. Place them over the molds that have the hot chocolate mix and marshmallows in them (this is how you seal the bombs together). Use some of the melted chocolate from the heated plate to go around the edges and make sure the bombs are sealed, then decorate them with melted white or dark chocolate.

STEP 4. Place the bombs back in the fridge to let the melted chocolate decorations harden, this should take about 5-10 mins.

STEP 5. FOR USE: Drop one of the bombs into a mug, then pour hot milk into the mug and stir. Enjoy!

GETTIN' SUM'N SWEET

RED VELVET BROWNIES

STEP 1. Preheat the oven to 300 degrees.

STEP 2. In a mixing bowl combine the melted butter, white sugar, eggs, vanilla extract and red food coloring. Add in the cocoa powder, flour and salt and use a rubber spatula to fold the ingredients together (the batter should be thick!) then fold in the white chocolate chips.

STEP 3. Pour the batter in a baking pan that's been coated with non-stick cooking spray. Bake the brownies for 15 mins or until you can stick a toothpick in the center of the brownies and it comes out clean.

STEP 4. FOR THE ICING: In a mixing bowl, whisk together the powdered sugar and heavy cream and set aside.

STEP 5. Once the brownies are done, remove them from the pan and cut them then glaze with the icing before serving.

- ⅔ cup Melted Unsalted Butter
- 1 ½ cup White Sugar
- 2 Eggs
- 2 tablespoons Vanilla Extract
- ¼ teaspoon Red Food Coloring
- 2 tablespoons Cocoa Powder
- 2 cups Flour
- ¼ teaspoon Salt
- 1 ½ cup White Chocolate Chips
- Non-stick Cooking Spray

ICING

- 1 cup Powdered Sugar
- ⅓ cup Heaving Whipping Cream

UTENSILS/COOKWARE NEEDED:

- Mixing Bowls
- Small Rubber Spatula
- Baking Pan
- Whisk

TOTAL TIME: 35 MINS
SERVES: 6

CHOCOLATE LAVA CAKE

- 1 bar Semi-Sweet Baking Chocolate (should be 1/2 cup once melted)
- ½ cup Flour, Sifted
- 1 cup White Sugar
- 2 tablespoons Vanilla Extract
- ½ cup Melted Unsalted Butter
- 3 Eggs
- Cocoa Powder, As Needed

UTENSILS/COOKWARE NEEDED:

- Microwave Safe Bowl
- Sifter
- Mixing Bowls
- Whisk
- Small Baking Dishes or Ramekins

TOTAL TIME: 30 MINS
SERVES: 3

STEP 1. Preheat the oven to 400 degrees.

STEP 2. Melt the chocolate in a microwave-safe bowl or over a double boiler and set aside.

STEP 3. Sift the flour and sugar into a large mixing bowl, then whisk in the vanilla extract, melted butter, melted chocolate and eggs.

STEP 4. Butter the baking dish and dust with cocoa powder, then bake the cakes for 12-15 mins. The inside should still be runny, this is how you get the lava for your lava cakes.

STEP 5. Let the cakes cool at least 5 mins before flipping them onto a plate. Serve with vanilla ice cream!

GETTIN' SUM'N SWEET

STRAWBERRY CRUMB CAKE

STEP 1. Preheat the oven to 350 degrees.

STEP 2. Combine the yogurt, milk, eggs, vanilla extract, baking powder, butter, salt, sugar and flour in a mixing bowl and use a hand mixer to blend until smooth, then fold in the freeze-dried strawberries.

STEP 3. Coat a Bundt pan with non-stick cooking spray and pour the cake batter into the pan. Make sure it's an even layer of batter, then place the cake in the oven for 30 mins.

STEP 4. FOR THE CRUMB TOPPING: Toss the Oreos and freeze-dried strawberries into a blender or food processor, blend until smooth. Pour the crumb topping into a bowl and set aside.

STEP 5. FOR THE ICING: Use a clean hand mixer to combine all the ingredients listed for the icing, blend until smooth then set aside.

STEP 6. Allow the cake to cool at least 10 mins before flipping the cake onto a plate. Once the cake is cooled and plated, top with the crumb topping and icing. Cut and serve hot!

- ½ cup Greek Yogurt
- ½ cup Milk
- 4 Eggs
- 2 tablespoons Vanilla Extract
- 2 tablespoons Baking Powder
- ½ cup Melted Unsalted Butter
- ¼ teaspoon Salt
- 2 cups White Sugar
- 2 ½ cups Flour
- 2 cups Freeze-Dried Strawberries
- Non-stick Cooking Spray

CRUMB TOPPING:
- ½ pack Golden Oreos
- 2 cups Freeze-Dried Strawberries

ICING
- 4 cups Powdered Sugar
- 4 oz Cream Cheese, Room Temp
- ⅓ cup Heavy Whipping Cream

UTENSILS/COOKWARE NEEDED:
- Mixing Bowls
- Hand mixer
- Bundt Pan
- Blender

TOTAL TIME: 50 MINS
SERVES: 6

FRIED CHEESECAKE BARS

- 16 oz Cream cheese, Softened
- 3 tablespoons Vanilla extract
- 1 tablespoon Lemon Extract
- 2 tablespoons Lemon Juice
- 1½ cups White Sugar
- ½ cup Powdered Sugar
- 1½ cups Heavy Whipping Cream
- Oil for Frying
- Non-stick Cooking Spray

BREADING

- 2-3 packs Graham Crackers, Blended
- 4 cups Flour
- 6 Eggs

UTENSILS/COOKWARE NEEDED:

- Mixing Bowls
- Hand Mixer
- Long Baking Dish
- Parchment Paper
- Large Frying Pan or Deep Fryer
- Blender
- Ziplock Bags (Optional)

TOTAL TIME: 5 HRS

SERVES: 6

STEP 1. In a mixing bowl combine the cream cheese, vanilla extract, lemon extract, lemon juice, white sugar powdered sugar and heavy cream. Mix until everything is smooth.

STEP 2. Line a long baking dish with parchment paper then coat the parchment with non-stick cooking spray. Pour the cream cheese mixture into the pan and place it in the freezer for at least 4-6 hrs. Once the cheesecake is chilled, remove it from the pan and cut it into bars.

STEP 3. Heat frying oil to 350 degrees.

STEP 4. FOR THE BREADING: Place the graham crackers in a blender or food processor and blend until smooth. Pour the graham cracker crumbs into a Ziplock bag or onto a plate. Pour the flour into a separate Ziplock bag or onto a plate. Scramble the eggs and pour them into a dish. Dip the cheesecake bars in the flour, then egg, then graham cracker crumbs and fry for 3-5 mins, or until golden-brown. Drain the cheesecake bars on paper towels or a wire rack.

STEP 5. Plate and serve hot!

FUNNEL CAKES

STEP 1. Preheat frying oil to 350 degrees.

STEP 2. Pour the pancake mix into a mixing bowl and prepare them per the package instructions, then transfer the mixture into a funnel pitcher or a large Ziplock bag. If you use a Ziplock bag, snip the tip off of one corner to create a pastry bag.

STEP 3. Starting at the center of the oil, pour the batter in a spiral motion and cook for 2-3 mins or until golden brown. Flip the cake over and fry for another 2-3 mins, then drain it on paper towels or a wire rack and set aside. Repeat until all the batter is used.

STEP 4. Plate and serve with your favorite toppings.

- 2 cups Pancake Mix
- Oil for Frying

TOPPINGS (OPTIONAL):
- Powered Sugar
- Whipped cream
- Sliced strawberries
- Crushed Oreo cookies

UTENSILS/COOKWARE NEEDED:
- Large Frying Pan or Deep Fryer
- Mixing Bowl
- Funnel Pitcher
- Tongs
- Whisk

TOTAL TIME: 20 MINS

SERVES: 4

> THE KITCHEN IS A PLACE TO EXPERIENCE HAPPY VIBES, MAKE GREAT MEMORIES AND BOND WITH LOVED ONES.

GETTIN' SUM'N SWEET

CANDY & CARAMEL APPLES

STEP 1. Dip the apples in boiling water for 5 seconds then wipe them off. This step removes the waxy outside layer from the apples and helps the candy stick to the apples better. Don't leave them in the pot too long or they'll start to cook. Place a wooden stick in the center of the top of each apple, set aside.

STEP 2. FOR THE CANDY APPLES: Add the sugar, food coloring, corn syrup and water into a cold saucepan before placing it over medium heat. Simmer for 30 mins, then place the candy thermometer in the pot to make sure the temperature reaches 300 degrees. Once the sauce is hot enough, remove the pan from the heat and allow to cool for 5 mins (any longer and the candy will cool too much and start to crack!) Dip the apples and place them on a non-stick surface. If you want to add sprinkles to the apples, add them quickly after dipping the apples.

STEP 3. FOR THE CARAMEL APPLES: Add all the ingredients listed for the caramel into a cold saucepan before placing it over medium-high heat. Once the caramel starts to thicken, use the candy thermometer to make sure it's reached 300 degrees. Once the sauce is hot enough, remove the pan from the heat and let the caramel sit for 7-10 mins. After the caramel has cooled down, start dipping the apples. If you want to add nuts to the apples, add them quickly after dipping the apples then place the apples on a non-stick surface.

STEP 4. Decorate the apples, plate and serve!

- 6-8 Green Apples
- Boiling Water
- 2 cups Sugar
- 1 tablespoon Red Food Coloring
- 1 ½ cups Corn Syrup
- 1 ½ cups Water

CARAMEL:
- 2 cups Brown Sugar
- 1 cup Heavy Cream
- 1 cup Corn Syrup
- ½ stick Butter
- 1 teaspoon Vanilla Extract

TOPPINGS (OPTIONAL):
- Nuts
- Sprinkles
- White chocolate wafers, melted

UTENSILS/COOKWARE NEEDED:
- Large Pot
- Thick Wooden Sticks
- Saucepans
- Candy Thermometer

TOTAL TIME: 2 HRS
SERVES: 6

Juices & Smoothies

C3 421

O'BERRY JUICE 422

GREEN WITH ENVY 425

MOVE ME 426

YELLOW GAL 429

JUICY FRUIT 430

THE BEET DOWN 432

REFRESH ME 434

MAKE IT HOT 437

EVERYTHING'S PEACHY 438

WE CANT-ALOPE 441

WATERMELON ME DOWN 442

TROPICAL BREEZE/APPLE APPLE 445

THE O'RELL SPECIAL 446

MANGO-SICKLE 449

AVOCADO MADNESS 450

SUPER GREEN 453

BAY BREEZE 454

VERY BERRY 457

RASPBERRY DREAM 458

GREEN TEA MATCHA LATTE 461

BISCOFF ICED COFFEE 462

C3

STEP 1. Juice the cucumbers, apple and celery then mix in the ginger powder and turmeric powder.

STEP 2. Stir well, then pour and serve over ice!

- 3 Whole Cucumbers
- 1 Red Apple
- 1 Full Bunch Celery
- 1 teaspoon Ginger Powder
- ½ teaspoon Turmeric Powder

SERVES: 3

NOTE: Use 2-3 dashes of cayenne pepper on top to add some heat!

JUICES AND SMOOTHIES

O'BERRY JUICE

- 2 medium Oranges
- 2 cups Spinach
- 1 tablespoon Fresh Ginger Root, Peeled
- 1 cup Berries

SERVES: 3

- Benefits: Vitamin C

STEP 1. Wash and peel the oranges and chop the spinach, then place them in a juicer with the ginger and berries. Mix well, then pour and serve over ice.

JUICES AND SMOOTHIES

GREEN WITH ENVY

STEP 1. Wash and cut the collard greens, kale and spinach then place them in the juicer along with the basil, celery, lime and green apple. Stir and serve over ice

- 1 cup Collard Greens
- 1 cup Kale
- 1 cup Spinach
- ¼ cup Basil
- 4 Stalks of Celery
- ½ Lime, Peeled
- 2 Green Apples.

SERVES: 6

BENEFITS: Vitamin C, E, A, K and B

JUICES AND SMOOTHIES

MOVE ME

- 4 Carrots
- 2 Green Apples
- 2 tablespoons Ginger Powder
- 8 Radishes
- 2 Beets

SERVES: 6

BENEFITS: Improves digestive function.

STEP 1. Wash all the veggies, then peel the carrots. Remove the seeds from the apples then juice everything together. Pour and serve over ice.

JUICES AND SMOOTHIES

YELLOW GAL

STEP 1. Wash, peel and cut the produce and remove all the seeds. Juice everything together, then pour and serve over ice.

- 2 cups Pineapple
- 1 Yellow Bell Pepper
- 1 Lemon
- 3 Apples
- 1 tablespoon Fresh Ginger

SERVES: 6

BENEFITS: Improves digestive function.

JUICES AND SMOOTHIES

JUICY FRUIT

- 2 Green Apples
- 3 Grapefruits
- 3 Oranges
- 2 Lemons

SERVES: 6

BENEFITS: Vitamin C

STEP 1. Wash, peel and cut the produce and remove all the seeds. Juice everything together, then pour and serve over ice.

JUICES AND SMOOTHIES

THE BEET DOWN

STEP 1. Wash, peel and cut the produce and remove all the seeds. Juice everything together, making sure to take your time with the beets because they are tough.

STEP 2. Serve over ice and enjoy!

- 4 Beets
- 1 ½ Red Apple
- 1 Lime
- 1 cup Cilantro

SERVES: 6

BENEFITS: Vitamin A and C

JUICES AND SMOOTHIES

REFRESH ME

- 8 cups Watermelon Cubes
- 1 ½ Cucumber
- ½ Pineapple
- ½ Lime
- ½ cup Mint Leaves

SERVES: 6

BENEFITS: A great source of hydration for the thirsty.

STEP 1. Wash, peel and cut the produce and remove all the seeds. Juice everything together, then pour and serve over ice.

JUICES AND SMOOTHIES

MAKE IT HOT

STEP 1. Wash, peel and chop the produce and remove all the seeds. Juice everything together then pour and serve on ice!

- 1 Big Piece of Ginger
- 1 Lemon
- 1 Lime
- 1 Orange
- 1 Apple
- 4 Dashes of Turmeric

SERVES: 6

BENEFITS: Improves immunity.

JUICES AND SMOOTHIES

EVERYTHING'S PEACHY

- 2 tablespoons Agave
- 1 cup Peaches
- ½ cup Blueberries
- ½ cup Cherries
- ½ cup Strawberries
- ½ cup Raspberries
- 1 tablespoon Hemp Seeds
- 1 cup Coconut Water
- 1 scoop Peach Sorbet

SERVES: 2

NOTE: For quicker preparation, use frozen fruit!

STEP 1. Throw all the ingredients into a blender and mix until smooth and creamy. Pour and serve!

JUICES AND SMOOTHIES

WE CANT-ALOPE

STEP 1. Throw all the ingredients into a blender and mix until smooth and creamy. Pour and serve!

- 3 cups Cantaloupe Chunks
- ½ cup Blueberries
- ½ cup Blackberries
- 1 Banana
- 1 ½ cups Yogurt
- 1 tablespoon Honey

SERVES: 2

JUICES AND SMOOTHIES

WATERMELON ME DOWN

- 1 cup Lemon or Lime Sparkling Water
- 6 cups Watermelon Cubes
- 6 Fresh Basil Leaves
- 12 Ice Cubes
- 1 tablespoon Honey
- 1 cup Strawberries, Stems Removed

STEP 1. Throw all the ingredients into a blender and mix until smooth. Pour and serve!

SERVES: 2

NOTE: This one is a great summer drink, sip this by the pool!

JUICES AND SMOOTHIES

TROPICAL BREEZE/ APPLE APPLE

STEP 1. Add all the ingredients except the ice into a blender, blend until well combined then pour in the ice and mix until the drink reaches your desired consistency.

STEP 2. Pour and serve!

- 2 cups Diced Mango
- 2 cups Diced Pineapple
- 2 cups Diced Apple
- 5 cups Spinach
- 2 cups Water
- 2 cups Ice
- 2 tablespoons Honey

SERVES: 2

NOTE: If you want to use frozen fruit instead of fresh fruit, you may not need to add ice or as much honey so taste as you go!

JUICES AND SMOOTHIES

THE O'RELL SPECIAL

- 1 ½ cup Almond Milk
- ⅔ cup Almonds
- 2 Bananas
- ⅓ cup Granola
- 2 tablespoons Honey
- 1 cup Ice
- 3 Fresh Strawberries (Optional)
- 1 oz Bailey's Irish Cream (Optional)

SERVES: 2

NOTE: To give this drink a fun brunch twist, pour in some Bailey's and/or fresh strawberries after adding in the ice. The strawberries will give it a bright taste and a cute pop of pink!

STEP 1. Blend the almond milk, almonds, bananas, granola and honey until well combined.

STEP 2. Add in the ice gradually until the mixture reaches a smooth consistency, then pour and serve!

JUICES AND SMOOTHIES

MANGO-SICKLE

STEP 1. Wash, peel and dice all the produce then place in a blender with all the other ingredients.

STEP 2. Blend until creamy and frothy then pour and serve!

- 4 Bananas
- 3 Fresh Mangoes, Diced
- 2 cups Frozen Mango
- Juice of ½ a Lime
- 1 cup Almond Milk
- 1 scoop Mango Sorbet

SERVES: 6

JUICES AND SMOOTHIES

AVOCADO MADNESS

- 1 cup Apple, Peeled and Cored
- 1 cup Pears, Peeled and Cored
- 1 Avocado
- 2 Dates
- 1 cup Non-Dairy Milk
- 1 tablespoon Hemp Seeds
- 1 tablespoons Agave
- 1 Handful of Spinach Or Kale
- ½ cup Water
- 1 cup Ice

SERVES: 1

STEP 1. Wash, peel and dice the apple and pear.

STEP 2. Add all the ingredients except the ice into a blender, blend until well combined then pour in the ice and mix well. Pour and serve!

JUICES AND SMOOTHIES

SUPER GREEN

STEP 1. Add all the ingredients except the ice into a blender, blend until well combined then pour in the ice and mix well. The drink should be smooth and frothy.

STEP 2. Pour and serve!

- 1 diced Green Apple
- 1 cup Diced Cucumber
- 2 Handfuls of Kale
- ¼ cup Lime Juice
- 2 Slices of Fresh Ginger
- 2 cups Water or Coconut Water
- 1 cup Ice
- 3 scoops Passion Fruit Puree
- 2 tablespoons Honey
- 1 tablespoon Sea Moss (Optional)

SERVES: 2

JUICES AND SMOOTHIES

BAY BREEZE

- ¼ cup Yogurt
- ¼ cup Orange Juice
- ¼ cup Non-Dairy Milk
- 1 cup Pineapple Chunks
- 1 ½ cups Banana
- 1 scoop Mango Sorbet
- 1 cup Ice

SERVES: 3

STEP 1. Add all the ingredients except the ice into a blender, blend until well combined then pour in the ice and mix until the drink is smooth.

STEP 2. Pour and serve!

JUICES AND SMOOTHIES

VERY BERRY

STEP 1. Throw all the ingredients into a blender and mix until smooth and creamy. Pour and serve!

- 2 cups Strawberries
- ½ cup Blueberries
- 2 Bananas
- ½ cup Rolled Oats
- 1 cup Orange Juice
- 1 cup Yogurt
- 1 tablespoon Agave
- ½ cup Blackberries

SERVES: 2

JUICES AND SMOOTHIES

RASPBERRY DREAM

- 1-6 oz container Fresh Raspberries
- 1 cup Cold Aloe Water
- 1 scoop Raspberry Sorbet
- ½ tablespoon Lime Juice
- 1 tablespoon Honey
- 1 tablespoon Ginger Powder (Optional)
- 1 cup Ice

SERVES: 2

STEP 1. Add all the ingredients except the ice into a blender, blend until well combined then pour in the ice and mix until the drink reaches your desired consistency.

STEP 2. Pour and serve!

JUICES AND SMOOTHIES

GREEN TEA MATCHA LATTE

STEP 1. Mix the matcha powder with boiling hot water and froth together. Set aside and let cool at least 5 mins.

STEP 2. Mix the milk and vanilla sweetener and froth together.

STEP 3. FOR ASSEMBLY: Pour some ice into a cup, then pour the frothed milk over the ice and top with the frothed matcha mixture. Drink and enjoy!

- 2 tablespoons Matcha Powder
- 1 cup Hot Water
- 1 cup Your Choice of Non-Dairy Milk
- 1 tablespoon Vanilla Sweetener
- Ice

SERVES: 1

JUICES AND SMOOTHIES

BISCOFF ICED COFFEE

- 1 tablespoon Caramel or Vanilla Sweetener
- 1 cup Ice
- 1 cup Cold Brew Iced Coffee
- ¼ cup French Vanilla Coffee Creamer
- ⅓ cup Caramel Creamer
- Biscoff Cookies

SERVES: 1

NOTE: I use my favorite flavors of coffee creamer and sweetener, but if you don't like these, feel free to substitute for your favorite!

STEP 1. In a chilled glass, drizzle the caramel sauce around the glass. Add the ice, coffee and vanilla sweetener, coffee creamer.

STEP 2. In a separate cup, froth the caramel creamer and pour on top of the coffee and garnish with Biscoff cookies. Serve and enjoy!

JUICES AND SMOOTHIES

EASY LIKE SUNDAY MORNING 467

GRAPE GODDESS 468

WAKE ME UP 471

GOLD RUSH 472

LEMON-LIME TWIST 475

RANDOM LINK-UPS 476

BERY SPECIAL 479

LA VIDA ES UN BRISA (LIFE'S A BREEZE) 480

KIWI MOJITO 483

DON'T BE SHADY 484

JAMANGO TANGO 487

EASY LIKE SUNDAY MORNING

STEP 1. PART 1: Wash, peel and dice the banana, mango and watermelon then set aside the watermelon. Place the mango and banana in a blender with the lime juice, pineapple juice, vodka, ice and honey and mix until the drink is smooth and frothy. Pour the mixture into serving cups and place them in the freezer for at least 10 mins.

STEP 2. PART 2: in a clean blender mix together the watermelon, simple syrup, vodka, lime juice and ice. Pull the mango drinks from the freezer and top them with a layer of the watermelon mixture.

STEP 3. Serve!

PART 1
- ½ Banana
- 1 ½ cup Mango Chunks
- 2 cups Fresh Watermelon Chunks
- ½ cup Fresh Lime Juice
- 1 cup Mango Pineapple Juice
- 1 oz Vodka
- 1 cup Ice
- 1 teaspoon honey

PART 2
- 1 teaspoon Simple Syrup
- 1 oz Vodka
- 1 tablespoon Lime Juice
- 1 cup Ice

SERVES: 2

SIP AFTER DARK

GRAPE GODDESS

- 2 cups Frozen Red Seedless Grapes
- 2 cups Red Grape Juice
- 1 scoop Lime Sorbet
- 1 oz Malibu Coconut Rum

SERVES: 4

STEP 1. Toss all the ingredients into a blender and mix until smooth and creamy. Pour and serve!

SIP AFTER DARK

WAKE ME UP

STEP 1. Toss all the ingredients into a blender and mix until smooth and creamy.

STEP 2. Drizzle caramel around a glass, then pour your drink over the caramel and serve!

- 4 oz Bailey's Irish Cream
- 1 tablespoon Cocoa Powder
- 3 tablespoons Almond Milk
- 2 tablespoons Almond Milk Coffee Creamer
- 1 cup Cold Brew
- 1½ cups Frozen Bananas
- 1 cup Ice
- 1 scoop Vanilla Ice Cream
- Caramel Drizzle (optional)

SERVES: 4

GOLD RUSH

- 2 oz Bourbon
- 4 oz Pineapple Juice
- 1 cup Ice

SERVES: 1

STEP 1. Pour the ingredients into a cocktail shaker, then strain the drink into a chilled cocktail glass and serve!

SIP AFTER DARK

LEMON-LIME TWIST

STEP 1. Pour all the ingredients except the soda into a cocktail shaker and shake vigorously.

STEP 2. Strain the drink over ice and fill the rest of the glass with soda.

- 3 oz Jack Daniels
- 1 oz Triple Sec
- 2 oz Sour Mix
- 1 can Lemon-Lime Soda

SERVES: 1

RANDOM LINK-UPS

- 1 oz Southern Comfort
- 1 oz Vodka
- 1 oz Amaretto
- 1 oz Triple Sec
- 1 oz Gin
- 2 oz Orange Juice
- 1 oz Lime Juice
- 1 oz Sweet Lemon Lime Juice
- 1 oz Simple Syrup

SERVES: 2

STEP 1. Pour the ingredients into a cocktail shaker, then strain the drink into a chilled cocktail glass and serve!

SIP AFTER DARK

BERRY SPECIAL

STEP 1. Pour all the ingredients except the soda and into a cocktail shaker and shake vigorously.

STEP 2. Strain the drink into a glass and fill the rest of the glass with soda, garnish with lemon.

- 1 oz Chambord
- 1 oz Crown Royal
- 1 splash of Sour Mix
- 1 oz Captain Morgan
- 1 oz Apple Pucker
- Ice
- 1 splash of Lemon Lime Soda

SERVES: 6

LA VIDA ES UN BRISA (LIFE'S A BREEZE)

- 1 Fresh Cucumber
- 3 oz Tequila Silver
- 4 oz Margarita Mix
- Tamarindo Rim Dip
- Tajin Powder
- Ice

SERVES: 6

STEP 1. Cut the cucumber into round slices and set aside.

STEP 2. Fill a cocktail shaker halfway with ice, then add the tequila, ½ of the cucumber slices and margarita mix. Shake vigorously.

STEP 3. Prep the cup by dipping it into the Tamarindo rim dip then dipping it into the tajin powder. Use a fork to drizzle some of the Tamarindo onto the inside of the cup, then pour the drink.

STEP 4. Garnish with the remaining cucumbers slices and 3 pinches of tajin.

SIP AFTER DARK

KIWI MOJITO

STEP 1. Muddle the mint in a cocktail shaker, then set aside.

STEP 2. Rub lime around the rim of a glass and dip the glass into the raw sugar, then add ice to the glass.

STEP 3. Blend the kiwi in a small blender along with the agave and ½ tablespoon lime juice, then pour the mixture into a cocktail shaker.

STEP 4. Add the remaining lime juice and rum, then shake vigorously and strain the drink into the dressed glass.

STEP 5. Top the drink off with club soda, garnish and serve!

- 4 Mint Leaves
- 2 tablespoons Raw Sugar
- 2 Kiwis, Peeled and Sliced
- 1 tablespoon Agave
- ½ tablespoon Lime Juice
- 2 oz Malibu Rum
- 1 oz Captain Morgan Spiced Rum
- 4 oz Club Soda

GARNISH:

- Sliced Kiwi
- Fresh Mint
- Raw Sugar
- Lime

SERVES: 2

SIP AFTER DARK

DON'T BE SHADY

- 2 oz Vodka
- 2 oz Malibu Rum
- 1 oz Peach Juice
- 1 oz Pineapple Juice
- 1 oz Cranberry Juice
- 1 tablespoon Lime Juice
- ½ cup Frozen Cherries
- ½ cup Strawberries, Diced
- ½ cup Dragonfruit, Diced
- ½ cup Pineapple, Diced
- ½ cup Mango, Diced
- ½ cup Peach, Diced
- 1 scoop of Mango Sorbet
- 1 scoop Strawberry or Lime Sorbet

SERVES: 2

NOTE: Alcohol is optional for this one!

STEP 1. Toss all the ingredients into a blender and mix until smooth. Pour and serve!

SIP AFTER DARK

JAMANGO TANGO

STEP 1. Toss all the ingredients into a blender and mix until smooth.

STEP 2. Dip a glass into the chamoy rim dip then the tajin powder, then pour your drinks and serve!

- 4 oz Tequila Silver
- ¼ oz Lime Juice
- 1 ½ cups Water
- 2 cups Frozen Mango
- 1 scoop Mango Sorbet
- 1 scoop Passionfruit Sorbet
- 1 scoop Lime Sorbet
- 2 tablespoons Chamoy
- 1 cup Ice

GARNISH:

- Dried Mango
- Chamoy Rim Dip
- Tajin Powder

SERVES: 2

NOTE: Alcohol is optional for this one!

SIP AFTER DARK

Index

A

Ackee and Salt Fish, 51
Air Fried Salmon Bites, 259
Air Fryer Cornish Hens, 264
Alfredo, Chicken Lasagna, 146
Alfredo, Crab Fettuccini, 124
Alfredo, Shrimp & Broccoli, 72
Almond Butter Chocolate Chip Cookies, 366
Apple Apple, Tropical Breeze, 445
Apples, Candy & Caramel, 417
Apple Crumb Muffins, 394
Apple Pies, Cinnamon Roll, 381
Avocado Madness, 450
Avocado Toast, 202
Avocado Tuna Salad, 346

B

Bacon Wrapped Asparagus, 345
Bacon Wrapped Jalapeno Poppers, 244
Bacon Wrapped Shrimp, 260
Bacon Wrapped Stuffed Burger, 84
Baked Beans, 163
Baked Spaghetti, 277
Banana, Blueberry Nut Loaf, 329
Banana Chocolate Chip Pancakes, 365
Banana, Cinnamon Crunch Bread, 358
Banana Foster Stuffed French Toast, 18
Bay Breeze, 454
BBQ Oyster Mushroom Sliders, 309
Beef & Cheese Empanadas, 256
Beef Pot Roast, 236
Beet Down, The, 432
Bery Special, 479
Birria, Chicken Tacos, 201
Birria Tacos, 198
Biscoff Iced Coffee, 462
Biscoff, Vegan Brownies, 326
Black Eyed Peas, 175
Blueberry Banana Nut Loaf, 329

Blueberry Muffins, 361
Breakfast Bombs, 9
Breakfast Hot Pockets, 29
Breakfast, Loaded Potatoes, 13
Breakfast Plate, Vegan, 305
Breakfast Quesadillas, 25
Broccoli & Cheddar Bread Bowl, 128
Broccoli Cheddar Rice Casserole, 167
Brown Stew Chicken, 56
Brown Stew Fish, 52
Brownies, Red Velvet, 409
Brownies, Vegan Biscoff, 326
Brownies, White Chocolate Chip, 385
Buffalo Cauliflower Wrap, 306
Buffalo Chicken Dip, 189
Buffalo Chicken Fries, 190
Butter Bean Stew/Pumpkin Stew, 314

C

C3, 421
Cajun Spiced Whole Chicken, 104
Cake, Lava, 410
Cake, Lemon Loaf, 402
Cake, Strawberry Crumb, 413
Cake, Strawberry Lemon Poke, 393
Cake Pops, Oreo & Vanilla Pops, 386
Cakes, Crab, 209
Cakes, Funnel, 415
Cakes, Salmon, 255
Callaloo Wrap, 310
Candied Yams, 228
Candy & Caramel Apples, 417
Caramel Pecan Sticky Buns, 390
Cauliflower, Buffalo Wrap, 306
Cauliflower Cheesy Bread, 338
Cauliflower, General Tso's, 313
Cauliflower Pizza Crust, 337
Cheesecake Bars, Fried, 414
Cheesecake Bites, Mini, 382
Cheesecake Cookies, Oreo, 397

Chicken & Cheese Enchiladas, 185
Chicken & Cheese Taquitos, 186
Chicken & Dumplings, 108
Chicken Alfredo Lasagna, 146
Chicken Birria Tacos, 201
Chicken, Brown Stew, 56
Chicken, Buffalo Dip, 189
Chicken, Buffalo Fries, 190
Chicken, Cajun Spiced Whole, 104
Chicken, Chipotle Avo Bowl, 374
Chicken, Curry, 55
Chicken Fries, 281
Chicken, Granny's Fried, 239
Chicken, Honey Garlic & Green Beans, 349
Chicken, Jerk Flatbread Pizza, 193
Chicken, Jerk Stir Fry, 286
Chicken, Orange, 103
Chicken Parm, 115
Chicken, Southern Fried & Biscuits, 26
Chicken Stir Fry, 370
Chicken, Stuffed Breasts, 96
Chicken, Stuffed Mushroom, 271
Chicken, Sundried Tomato & Spinach, 354
Chicken, Sweet Chili Stir Fry, 107
Chicken, Sweet Chili Thai Thighs, 99
Chicken, Sweet Heat Tenders, 182
Chicken, Tandoori Skewers, 100
Chicken, Whiskey Glazed, 111
Chicken, Whole Spiced, 240
Chili Marinated Tofu Plate, 322
Chipotle Chicken Avo Bowl, 374
Chipotle Shrimp Fajitas, 251
Chopped Cheese Sandwich, 290
Cilantro Lime Lettuce Tacos, 357
Cinnamon Crunch Banana Bread, 358
Cinnamon Roll Apple Pies, 381
Cinnamon Roll, Mini Waffle Sandwiches, 22
Cinnamon Roll Pancakes, 2
Coconut Shrimp, 268
Collard Greens, 224

Cornbread Dressing, 219
Cornish Hens, Herb Roasted, 235
Cornish Hens, Air Fryer, 264
Crab Cakes, 209
Crab Fettuccini Alfredo, 124
Crab Garlic Bread, 127
Crab Legs, 91
Creamed Spinach, 168
Creamy Scalloped Potatoes, 155
Crème Brulé, 405
Curry Chicken, 55

D
Don't Be Shady, 484

E
Easy Like Sunday Morning, 467
Eggplant Parmesan, 317
Everything's Peachy, 438

F
Festival, 47
Flamin' Hot Wings, 292
French Toast, Banana Foster Stuffed, 18
French Toast Bites, 14
French Toast Rolls, 17
French Toast, Vegan, 298
Fried Cheesecake Bars, 414
Fried Chicken, Granny's, 239
Fried Corn, 171
Fried Dumpling, 48
Fried Rice, Veggie, 321
Fried Rice, Lamb, 83
Fries, Chicken, 281
Fries, Poutine, 160
Fries, Zucchini, 334
Funnel Cakes, 415
Fully Loaded Shrimp Potato, 68

G

Garlic & Herb Turkey, 220
Garlic Bread, Crab, 127
Garlic Bread Pizza, 282
Garlic Chili Green Beans, 156
Garlic Noodles, 138
Garlic Parm Brussel Sprouts, 248
Garlic Steak Bites, 247
General Tso's Cauliflower, 313
Gold Rush, 472
Granny's Fried Chicken, 239
Granny's Potato Salad, 179
Grape Goddess, 468
Green Tea Matcha Latte, 461
Green with Envy, 425
Grilled Cheese Sloppy Joe's, 274

H

Herb Roasted Cornish Hens, 235
Honey Butter Cornbread, 232
Honey Garlic Chicken & Green Beans, 349
Honey Garlic Jerk Lamb Chops, 43
Honey Pineapple Baked Ham, 223
Hot Chocolate Bombs, 406

I

Ital (Pumpkin Stew), 36

J

Jamaican Cabbage, 59
JaMango Tango, 487
Jasmine Rice, 176
Jerk Chicken Flatbread Pizza, 193
Jerk Chicken Stir Fry, 286
Jerk, Honey Garlic Lamb Chops, 43
Jerk, Mango Wings, 40
Jerk Marinade, 39
Jerk, Pineapple Shrimp Bowl, 44
Juicy Fruit, 430

K

Kiwi Mojito, 483

L

La Vida Es Un Brisa (Life's a Breeze), 480
Lamb Chops, Honey Garlic Jerk, 43
Lamb Fried Rice, 83
Lasagna, Chicken Alfredo, 146
Lasagna Rolls, 145
Lasagna, Vegan Rolls, 318
Lava Cake, 410
Lemon Garlic Shrimp, 353
Lemon Garlic Shrimp Wrap, 350
Lemon Loaf Cake, 402
Lemon-Lime Twist, 475
Loaded Breakfast Potatoes, 13
Loaded Crunch Wrap, 206
Loaded Lobster Tail, 64
Loaded Mashed Potatoes, 159
Loaded Nachos, 289
Loaded Potato Skin, 194
Loaded Potato Soup, 149
Lobster Rolls, 92
Lobster Spicy Noodles, 67
Lobster Tail, Loaded, 64
Love Bowl, The, 325

M

Mac & Cheese Balls, 285
Mac and Cheese, 227
Make It Hot, 437
Mango Jerk Wings, 40
Mango Peach Pies, 389
Mango-Sickle, 449
Mashed Potato & Chicken Bowl, 142
Mashed Potatoes, Loaded, 159
Meatballs, Stuffed, 252
Meatballs, Turkey Stuffed, 112
Mini Cheesecake Bites, 382

Index | 493

Mini Omelets, 10
Mini Pancake Sandwiches, 294
Mini Waffle Cinnamon Roll Sandwiches, 22
Mongolian Beef & Broccoli, 80
Monkey Bread, 378
Move Me, 426
Mozzarella Sticks, 205
Muffins, Apple Crumb, 394
Muffins, Blueberry, 361

O

Oatmeal Bars, 362
Orange Chicken, 103
Oreo & Vanilla Cake Pops, 386
Oreo Cheesecake Cookies, 397
Oxtails, 35
Oxtail, Stew, 32
O'Berry Juice, 422
O'Rell Special, The, 446

P

Pancake Fruit Tacos, 6
Pancake, Mini Sandwiches, 294
Pancakes, Banana Chocolate Chip, 365
Pancakes, Cinnamon Roll, 2
Pancakes, Strawberries & Cream, 4
Peach Cobbler, 2-Layer, 401
Peach, Mango Pies, 389
Peachy, Everything's, 438
Pigs In a Blanket, 263
Pin Wheels, 21
Pineapple Jerk Shrimp Bowl, 44
Pizza, Cauliflower Crust, 3337
Pizza, Garlic Bread, 282
Pizza, Jerk Chicken Flatbread, 193
Pizza, Salmon Flatbread, 197
Pork Chops with Roasted Potatoes, 267
Potato, Fully Loaded Shrimp, 68
Potato, Loaded Skins, 194
Potato, Loaded Soup, 149

Potatoes, Creamy Scalloped, 155
Potatoes, Loaded Breakfast, 13
Potato Salad, Granny's, 179
Poutine Fries, 160

R

Random Link-Ups, 476
Raspberry Dream, 458
Red Beans and Rice, 172
Red Velvet Brownies, 409
Refresh Me, 434
Rib Tips, 88
Rice, Broccoli Cheddar Casserole, 167
Rice, Jasmine, 176
Rice and Peas, 60
Rice, Red Beans, 172
Rice, Seafood, 134
Rice, Yellow, 164
Roasted Potatoes & Green Beans, 152
Roasted Potatoes, Pork Chops, 267

S

Salad, 369
Salmon, Air Fried Bites, 259
Salmon Bowl, 202
Salmon Cakes, 255
Salmon Flatbread Pizza, 197
Salmon Linguini, 120
Salmon Philly, 79
Seafood Rice, 134
Shrimp & Broccoli Alfredo, 72
Shrimp, Bacon Wrapped, 260
Shrimp, Coconut, 268
Shrimp, Spicy Dumplings, 75
Shrimp, Chipotle Fajitas, 251
Shrimp, Fully Loaded Potato, 68
Shrimp, Lemon Garlic, 353
Shrimp, Lemon Garlic Wrap, 350
Shrimp Lo Mein, 123
Shrimp Pho', 137

Shrimp, Pineapple Jerk Bowl, 44
Shrimp Scampi, 71
Sliders, 278
Sliders, BBQ Oyster Mushroom, 309
Smothered Turkey Wings, 116
Snickerdoodle Cookies, 398
Southern Fried Chicken & Biscuits, 26
Southern Gravy, 231
Spicy Rigatoni Florentine, 141
Spicy Shrimp Dumplings, 75
Spinach & Artichoke Dip, 213
Stir Fry, Chicken, 370
Stir Fry, Jerk Chicken, 286
Stir Fry, Sweet Chili Chicken, 107
Strawberries & Cream Pancakes, 5
Strawberry Crumb Cake, 413
Strawberry Lemon Poke Cake, 393
Stuffed Chicken Breasts, 96
Stuffed Meatballs, 252
Stuffed Meatballs, Turkey, 112
Stuffed Mushroom Chicken, 271
Stuffed Pasta Shells, 131
Sundried Tomato & Spinach Chicken, 354
Super Green, 453
Surf & Turf, 87
Sweet Chili Chicken Stir Fry, 107
Sweet Chili Thai Chicken Thighs, 99
Sweet Heat Chicken Tenders, 182
Sweet Potato Pie, 216

T

Taco Salad, 210
Tacos, Birria, 198
Tacos, Chicken Birria, 201
Tacos, Cilantro Lime Lettuce, 357
Tandoori Chicken Skewers, 100
The Beet Down, 432
The Love Bowl, 325
The O'Rell Special, 446
Tropical Breeze/Apple Apple, 445

Turkey Chili, 76
Turkey, Garlic & Herb, 220
Turkey Stuffed Meatballs, 112
Turkey Wings, Smothered, 116

V

Vegan Biscoff Brownies, 326
Vegan Breakfast Plate, 305
Vegan Burrito, 301
Vegan French Toast, 298
Vegan Lasagna Rolls, 318
Veggie Fried Rice, 321
Very Berry, 457

W

Wake Me Up, 471
Watermelon Me Down, 442
We Cant-alope, 441
Whiskey Glazed Chicken, 111
White Chocolate Chip Brownies, 385
Whole Spiced Chicken, 240

Y

Yellow Gal, 429
Yellow Rice, 164
Yogurt Bites, 373

Z

Zucchini Bread, 330
Zucchini Enchiladas, 342
Zucchini Fries, 334
Teriyaki Zucchini Noodles, 341

SHOP NOW!
KITCHEN ENVY
www.thekitchenenvy.com

WWW.THEKITCHENENVY.COM

GET THE KITCHEN ENVY COOKBOOK VOL. 1 KUISINE & TINGZ NOW AT

www.thekitchenenvy.com

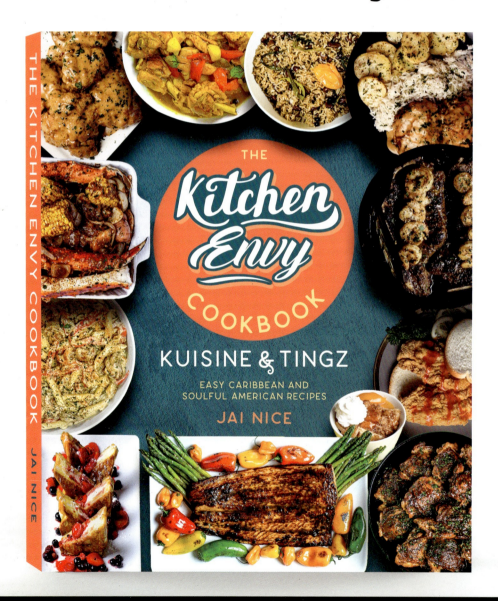